15

D0891959

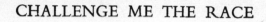

CHALLENGE ME THE RACE

# CHALLENGE ME THE RACE

by

MIKE HAWTHORN

WILLIAM KIMBER

LONDON

Published by
WILLIAM KIMBER AND CO. LIMITED
Godolphin House, 22a Queen Anne's Gate,
London SW1H 9AE

*First edition April 1958*
*Reprinted seven times*
*This edition 1973*

© Copyright William Kimber and Co. Limited, 1958

ISBN 07183 0003 3

*This book is copyright. No part of it may be reproduced in any form without
permission in writing from the publishers except by a reviewer who wishes to
quote brief passages in connection with a review written for inclusion in a
magazine or newspaper or a radio broadcast.*

Printed in Great Britain by
Redwood Press Limited
Trowbridge, Wiltshire

## DEDICATION

To the memory of my father but for
whose generosity and faith in me I
would not have had a story to tell.

M. H.

## PUBLISHERS' NOTE

In preparing most of the material for this book Mr. Hawthorn worked in collaboration with Mr. Gordon Wilkins, Motoring Correspondent of *The Observer*. For advice on the final form of the book the Publishers wish to thank Mr. Nevil Lloyd.

# CONTENTS

## PART I

## EARLY DAYS

## PART II

## THE PRANCING HORSE

## PART III

## ILL-FATED YEAR

CONTENTS

## PART IV

# TRIUMPH AND DISASTER

## PART V

# CHEQUERED

## PART VI

# FERRARI AGAIN

# ILLUSTRATIONS

PART 1

EARLY DAYS

# CHAPTER ONE

## LEARNER DRIVER

ONE afternoon before the war, an army officer went down to a garage in Farnham to collect an old Jowett car which he had left for repair, but before he turned in at the door something attracted his attention in a field at the rear. There was his car driving slowly round over the hummocky grass and, almost invisible behind the steering wheel, was a small boy with flaxen hair who had an expression of pure joy on his chubby, oil-smeared face. The engine was not running, but the car was in gear and a small fist pressed on the starter button kept it grinding slowly forward. The army man showed wonderful self-control; he was livid with rage, but when he caught up with the toiling car he just looked down at the small demon in the driving seat and demanded in icy tones: "Just what do you think you are doing, young man?"

I doubt if it would have comforted him to know that he was witnessing the first drive by a future Grand Prix driver, but the event sticks in my mind, not only for the thrill I felt at first having a moving car under my control, but also for the painful interview I had with my father afterwards.

I was eight years old at the time and during the school holidays Father found it practically impossible to keep me away from the family garage. I grew up in an atmosphere of enthusiasm for cars and motor-cycles and I am told that even as a tiny tot I used to cling to the steering wheel of the family Morris Cowley and cry like mad when I had to get out.

We lived originally in Yorkshire, at Mexborough, near Doncaster, where I was born on April 10, 1929. My father had served his apprenticeship as an engineer and at first worked in a power station, but he began racing motor-bikes and tuning them, and so moved into the motor trade, which eventually took us down to the south of England, Brooklands was becoming a great centre for speed on two wheels,

13

with giants like Worters, Le Vack, Baragwanath and Pope performing legendary feats on the Outer Circuit and when Father went into partnership with Paddy Johnstone, the T.T. rider, in 1931, we all moved down to Farnham in Surrey to be near the track. The original garage there was a wooden one, but a few years later they had some hop kilns converted to make another one, which formed the nucleus of the place which I now own.

The first motor races I ever saw were at Brooklands. I was only a very small boy, but to me it was heaven to watch the cars thundering round those towering cliffs of concrete where the banking curved under the Members' Bridge, to wander along the lines of brightly coloured cars in their stalls in the paddock, to jump as an exhaust snarled suddenly and to sniff the aroma of castor oil. As Father was a Riley enthusiast, I was introduced to Freddie Dixon, a craggy, courageous little man who could make a Riley go faster than anyone else, but whose colourful vocabulary caused a few raised eyebrows, for Brooklands had the atmosphere of a rather exclusive club and motor racing had nothing like the popular mass appeal it has today. There was John Cobb, fighting homeric battles in the Napier Railton on the Outer Circuit against Oliver Bertram in the Delage, and Sir Malcolm Campbell and Earl Howe immaculate in blue overalls. I used to go and watch Percy Maclure too, another great tuner and driver of Rileys. It all seemed wildly unattainable, but I knew it was the life for me. Father used to tune several of the cars that raced at the track and raced himself sometimes in an 1,100 c.c. Riley which had belonged to Freddie Dixon. One day he took me round the track in a 2-litre Riley and I shall never forget how bumpy it was; I thought I was going to be flung clean out of the car and clung grimly to any support I could find.

However, any hopes that we youngsters cherished of racing at Brooklands were finally extinguished by the war, when hangars were erected on the track, roads were cut through the banking, and the way was paved for the final sell-out to the aircraft industry. Probably the track had had its day, for racing was already governed by some irksome restrictions. Protests by people who had come and built houses nearby resulted in the rule that every car and motor-bike racing at the track had to carry a big cumbersome silencer and fishtail, which was one of the reasons why the Grand Prix Mercedes and Auto Unions of pre-war days never raced at Brooklands and the same residents had secured a ban on racing at night, so the track was rendered useless for 24-hour racing and long-distance-record attempts. But nothing has really taken the place of Brooklands and when you think of the problems involved in testing and tuning fast cars in England today, it is sad to reflect that you could run a car down to Brooklands and test it in complete safety for a mere ten shillings.

During the war there were not many opportunities for motoring; Father went off to serve as a ferry-pilot with the Air Transport Auxiliary, having learned to fly before the war at the Farnborough Flying Club, and I was at school at Ardingly. We played football, hockey and cricket, but my cricket career was soon cut short. One Saturday afternoon I went in as wicket-keeper and while the batsmen were putting their pads on the bowler sent down a practice ball which thumped me hard on the nose.

Shooting appealed to me much more, although I made rather a shaky start. When I was about thirteen I went off into the woods with another boy to shoot rabbits; he had an air rifle and I had an air pistol. He was leading the way, swinging the rifle backwards and forwards; as he swung it outwards I took aim at the butt to give him a bit of a surprise, but there must have been something wrong with the sights; the pellet went into his leg. We were not far from a church, so I whipped him into the churchyard and bathed his leg with the water from a flower vase. Eventually I managed to squeeze the pellet out and we both went home. Of course his leg turned septic, but he talked his way out of it and his family never really knew what happened.

I did better later and managed to get into the rifle team of the Junior Training Corps, successor to the school O.T.C. This had one big practical advantage—we were able to put on some comfortable clothes and go and blaze away on the shooting range while the other boys, with polished brass and shiny boots, went slogging on route marches and exercises. Being indolent by nature I took out a second insurance against route marches by joining the band. The band had to conserve its breath, so we stayed behind while the rest of them went off on long marches; later, we would go out to meet them and pep up the step by playing them in as they returned, footsore and weary.

This brief musical interlude was not entirely prompted by a desire to dodge hard work. I always had a feeling I would like to play the trumpet and, after breaking-in as a bugler, I have since bought a trumpet. I doubt if I shall cause Eddie Calvert any sleepless nights, unless he happens to be in the next room while I am practising, and I do not aspire to emulate Johnny Claes, who was popular both as a racing driver and a dance-band leader, but if both race-driving and the motor trade fail, I may still be able to make an honest coin.

My other recreation in those days was riding, but I never got into the class of Stirling Moss, who was quite famous as a horseman before he ever drove a car. I was never quite sure what the horse was going to do next and later experiences have only increased my doubts.

The first vehicle I ever owned was a 1927 Norton motor-bike which I bought for thirty shillings with the big-end bearing in ruins. As I was only fourteen I was still too young to hold a licence, but I tinkered with it for a time and eventually sold it for £10. I was already learning to drive, as Father used to let me take the wheel of his car occasionally off the public highway and when I was fifteen, he bought me a little 125 c.c. James motor-bike, with which I went putt-putting around the fields until my sixteenth birthday arrived and I took it out on the road for the first time. It only did about 35 m.p.h. flat-out, but it seemed a terrifying speed at the time.

A 1939 250 c.c. o.h.v. Triumph was the next acquisition. Father had bought it in a fairly decrepit condition, but he rebuilt it with his own special skill and know-how and as a result it would leave most of my friends' 350s behind. In the summer of 1946 I left school and, after the holidays, I started my apprenticeship at Dennis Bros. at Guildford, using the motor-cycle to go to work.

Then came the day when I got my first brand-new machine, a 1947 350 c.c. Competition B.S.A. with knobbly tyres and upswept exhaust pipe. It was on this machine that I made my entrée into motor sport by competing in trials and in my very first event won the Novice Cup. I also tried scrambles, which are rather like trials run at racing speeds. You go hurtling across country, standing on the footrests, and fighting with feet, wrists and knees to hold the machine as it bucks and slides over grass, gravel, mud and rocks. One moment you are hurtling for the sky; a second later you are over the hump, the wheels hit the ground, the suspension crashes onto the bump-stops and you fight to straighten it out for the next bend. It is a terrific sport but very hard work. Once again I won a Novice Cup, but I didn't do any more. I would have liked to keep my hand in at motor-cycling and in 1954 Jock West lent me a 350 c.c. Matchless on which I won a second-class award in the South Reading M.C.C. Three Musketeers

With my 1½-litre Riley T.T. Sprite at the Goodwood Members' Meeting, June 1951. *[Benjafield*

Unloading the Cooper-Bristol for my first race at Goodwood, 1952. *[Hulton Library*

Taking the hairpin in the French Grand Prix at Rouen [*Klemantaski*

Mudplugging with a 350 c.c. Matchless. [*Dunn*

Trial, but the next day I left for Modena en route for the Argentine, and that was the end of my motor-cycle career.

While I was still an apprentice my parents concluded that daily use of a motor-bike on the road would have to stop if I was to stay in this world, so I was allowed to borrow a Fiat 500. This was a grand little car, which held the road like a baby sports car, and with it I first learned how to take corners fast on four wheels. But the hard driving eventually wore it out. I broke the back axle and Father fixed it. Someone then challenged me to climb a rather rocky trials hill in it, which I did, but I broke the axle again. Father fixed it again. Then I got stuck in a sandy lane and broke the axle and—well, by this time Father was running out of temper and axle parts, so he bought me a 1930 Riley Nine. That car was eighteen years old, with a rather tattered saloon body, but it stood up to endless hard driving, and I soon began to share my father's enthusiasm for Rileys. Eventually I had to tie a piece of string across from one front door to the other to keep them shut, which meant that I had to enter by one of the rear doors and climb over the backs of the front seats. Another unusual feature was the "bonnet speedometer". This was no complicated scientific invention; it arose from the lack of clips to hold the bonnet down. When the car was on the move, wind pressure lifted the sides of the bonnet, which was one of the old style, hinged down the centre. At medium speeds it seemed to sprout a pair of graceful gull wings, but as I approached terminal velocity, the bonnet sides would lift right up and meet over the engine, where they hung uncertainly in the breeze. When that happened, things became rather precarious, and it was prudent to reduce speed, brakes permitting.

Eventually the Riley was sold to an army officer and I became the proud owner of a Lancia Aprilia. This was a real revelation. It did 70 m.p.h. and 30 m.p.g. and I doubt if it is possible to get from point to point on England's crowded roads much faster on any other car. It had a short V-4 engine unlike anything else and a squat angular body which stopped short at front and rear wheels. Standing alongside average modern cars with projecting snouts and long trailing tails, it looked like an Eton jacket among a lot of tail coats, but it had light, quick steering and was as sure-footed as a cat. There is not anything much better after twenty years of progress.

Part of my time as an apprentice was spent putting together lawn mowers with JAP engines. There were two of us apprentices working with a charge hand and when the mowers were completed we had to drive them down to the paint shop. We used to sit on a little seat on a roller which hitched on behind and there was some pretty hectic cornering on the way. The charge hand, a chap named Gill, was very efficient and really made us work hard; in fact he so got me into the habit of working that I overdid it. I was assembling gearboxes, and the clutch cross shaft had to have some metal ground off it before fitting. One day we ran rather short of gearbox castings and I was looking round for something else to do, so I took about fifty cross shafts and ground them down. Too late, I found these parts had already been modified so that it was no longer necessary to grind away that particular spot of metal and I had reduced the lot to scrap. The charge hand was very good about it; he managed to fix it so that they got thrown away in little batches and the disaster never came to light.

Working on lawn mowers seemed small stuff when there was a stream of big, powerful Dennis lorries leaving the works. These seemed much more interesting and presented a challenge which I finally could not resist.

One day I announced: "Today, I am going to drive a Dennis lorry."

I found one parked in the yard; it was a chassis, with cab, but no body, ready for delivery to the body-builder. Bonnet panels were stacked on the back and not fastened down, but I didn't notice that at the time. Delighted to be at the wheel of something bigger and more powerful than I had ever handled before, I went belting off down the yard, when who should come out but the apprentice supervisor. I slammed on the brakes and bits of bonnet slid off the back with a fearful clang and landed at his feet.

All this time I dreamed of getting into motor racing. I went to events like Goodwood and the Brighton Speed Trials, and read all the motoring magazines, but finance was the problem. For most competitors, motor racing was still highly expensive. In recent history Dick Seaman was the only Englishman to have broken into the charmed circle of professional Grand Prix drivers, and then only after years of effort backed by the expenditure of many thousands of pounds in running his own racing cars. There were only about twenty jobs going with the leading Continental teams and nobody bothered to advertise them in the Situations Vacant columns. For an unknown Englishman to break in seemed an impossible dream.

## CHAPTER TWO

## THE RILEYS

I HAD one priceless asset: my father, Leslie Hawthorn, knew the racing game, both as a driver and an engineer, and was keen to get me into it, but he also knew the difficulties from hard experience and was determined to make me learn a trade and earn my living. He wanted me to become an automobile engineer, so from Dennis Bros. I moved on to Kingston Technical College and finally to the College of Automobile Engineering at Chelsea, but I never shone very brightly at mathematics and engineering theory. The driving-seat, not the drawing-board, was the place where I wanted to be.

Father's own enthusiasm for the sport was so great that he took a tolerant view of my failure to make engineering history and one day, when we were down at a Goodwood race meeting together, he exclaimed: "Oh yes! I think we must get you into this!" He soon took some practical steps and one day I arrived home to find he had bought an 1100 c.c. ex-works Riley Ulster Imp. It had been used pretty hard, as cars of this kind usually are, and George Abecassis, who sold it, said it was not very fast, but it would go round a roundabout quicker than most cars. He was certainly right about the cornering and I was in raptures about it. The body was slim and low-slung, with a pointed tail; it had slim cycle-type wings and racing wheels with knock-on hub caps; as I ran my eyes over it from the quick-action radiator filler cap, along the plentifully louvred bonnet to the big racing fuel filler on the tail, I could already picture myself at the wheel, forcing it flat out round some complicated corner. But there was a lot to be done before that happened. That week-end when I went out in it to visit some friends the brakes began sticking, the engine started to boil and finally, after I had wound it up to full speed a few times, a most ominous noise started to come from the engine. It did not sound like a big-end or a main bearing—setbacks with which I was by now familiar— and I struggled slowly home it rapidly got worse. I was worried to death

19

but when my father heard of it he said brightly: "Oh, it's probably the crankshaft." My heart sank still further.

We stripped it down and found that the flywheel had come loose; having got so far we decided to overhaul it completely and bring the design up to date in various details, in particular by fitting hydraulic shock absorbers and converting the cable-operated brakes to hydraulic operation. Father took over the rebuilding of the engine. He was one of that select band of expert tuners who can go through an engine piece by piece, polishing, lightening, balancing and lining up every component, until it gives far more power than the makers ever planned and without making it too temperamental.

The conversion of the brakes was done by Joe Bickell, a mechanic who had just joined us. He was the brother of the late Ben Bickell, who used to race an immaculate copper JAP-engined bike at Brooklands, and later rode a blown Ariel Square Four, but was finally killed racing. The brakes nearly drove Joe to distraction, but he made a good job of them.

While this was going on, Father bought another Imp, a standard model, from Francis Beart, the famous motor-cycle tuner, who had been rebuilding it as a spare-time job during the war. He had really gone to town, making special parts and lightening existing ones. So we took the best parts from that and added them to mine and made a beautiful little job of it. I still had ideas about using it to go to work, but when it was finished Father said: "No, it's much too good to use on the road. We must keep it for racing." The die, as they say, was cast.

Meanwhile Father had bought himself a 1½-litre Riley T.T. Sprite with the idea of competing in 1500 c.c. events while I ran in the 1100 c.c. classes and we went off together to the 1950 Brighton Speed Trials, my first motoring competition. It was a lovely day, very hot, and my beginner's luck held good. A friend of mine, Michael Currie, also had a Riley and quite a rivalry had grown up between us. We were drawn to run off together and with this extra incentive I won my class. To make it a family affair, Father managed to get second place in the 1500 c.c. class. My second and last appearance that year was at the Gosport Speed Trials, where I came second in my class to Harry Lester, who in those days was having a lot of success with the light sports chassis he built with M.G. engines and front suspension. Those were in fact the only speed trials in which I ever drove.

That winter was the longest I can remember. I could think of little but the coming racing season as we stripped and rebuilt the two Rileys, lightening and modifying them in various ways. Eventually the great day arrived when we took the 1,100 c.c. car up for the opening meeting at Gamston. Father had strained his back and could not drive, so he came along to run the pit with a friend of mine, John Watling.

It was raining and the 1,100 was inclined to slide its tail rather sharply in the wet, but I managed to keep it pointing the right way and beat a couple of other Rileys to win the 20-mile race for 1,100 c.c. cars. I followed this up with second place in the 1,500 c.c. event. There was quite a difference between the two cars. The Imp had a preselector box, which I liked for racing, although once or twice I kicked the pedal with the wrong gear selected and the rev-counter needle hit the stop rather hard. It was a pity that the $1\frac{1}{2}$-litre was not ready, for it handled as near perfectly as one could hope for a car of pre-war design without independent suspension and, unlike the Imp, it could be cornered with incredible speed in the wet.

The brakes were enormous 16-inch Girlings, fitted by Neville Gee, the previous owner, and were better than those on any other sports car of this size which I have driven, but it suffered from bad wheel tramp when braking on bumpy roads. It caused mad excitement when I drove in the Leinster Trophy. There is one sharp corner under a railway bridge, approached by a fast bumpy run downhill, and every time I put the brakes on there the whole front end disappeared in a burl and officials dashed for cover, thinking I was out of control. We eventually cured it by fitting Woodhead-Monroe telescopic dampers instead of the old friction type; Girling piston-type dampers were added at the rear and the improvement was astonishing.

When my father bought the car from Gee, he got with it a set of four Amal carburetters which fitted on my Imp as though they had been made for it; in fact they had, for we found out later that both cars had been owned by Gee. This was just what I needed to give the Imp a little extra urge for the 1951 season. The Riley engine was a wonderful one for the tuner in search of high power, for it was one of the very few on which you could fit a separate carburetter and exhaust pipe to each cylinder and so get a smooth, unobstructed gas flow approaching that achieved on single-cylinder racing motor-cycle engines which were up to then the most efficient engines known in terms of power for a given size.

The Sprite did not exactly leave the line like a rocket, because it weighed 1850 lbs. fully equipped, but in second gear it really got going. Unlike the Imp, it had a four-speed crash box, which was one of the sweetest ever made. Crown wheel and pinion were straight cut, so there was a healthy howl from the rear end when it was travelling fast. The engine ran regularly up to 6000 r.p.m., but at Leinster I wound it round to 6400, which gave me a timed speed of 112 m.p.h. on the straight.

    •    •    •    •    •

At Castle Combe I repeated the Gamston result, with wins in the 1100 and 1500 c.c. cars, and I won a ten-lap sports-car race at Boreham after a fine scrap with Jim Mayers on a Lester-M.G. My first event outside England, and the first time I had run on a true road circuit made up of normal roads closed for the occasion, was at Dundrod where I entered in the ten-lap handicap race run on the same day as the Ulster Trophy for Grand Prix cars. The circuit, near Belfast, is 7.4 miles of narrow, winding, undulating road, often between high banks, with one very fast straight and, apart from the odd behaviour of the Riley's front end when I had to use the brakes hard on the bumpy bits, I really enjoyed it. During practice I began to catch up with an XK 120 Jaguar, and eventually I got past it. Suddenly something seemed to clutch me inside and I said to myself: "That was Louis Chiron—the great Louis Chiron—and I have passed him." It was a big moment for an unknown youngster of twenty-two, but fortunately the handicappers did not notice.

About forty cars started in the race, with Chiron's Jaguar and Sydney Allard's Cadillac Allard heavily handicapped at the rear, and the Riley, with a rather favourable handicap, romped home ahead of an 1100 Riley and an M.G. For anyone trying to foretell the future, all three races that morning might have provided some useful pointers; there was a Formula 3 event won by a certain P. J. Collins and a 1300 c c. scratch race won on a J.P. Vincent single-seater by a certain R. Flockhart.

    •    •    •    •    •

The next big event was the Leinster Trophy, another handicap event on the 8.3-miles Wicklow circuit. This looked a much tougher proposition and on the handicapping I did not think there was much chance of beating the Irish driver, J. A. Dickson, who was driving a single-seater 1250 c.c. TC M.G., but I was learning that there are few certainties in motor racing. When the cars lined up for the start they were a mixed assortment, including an H.W.M. driven by Oscar Moore, the ex-Parnell 4CLT Maserati driven by Bobbie Baird and a very fast Chrysler-engined Allard with Tom Cole at the wheel. Dickson took the lead with five of the sixteen laps still to go, and I could not see much hope of catching him, but on the last lap smoke was pouring from his engine and I caught him two miles from the finish. I did not know it at the time, but I should have won anyway, because the M.G. was later found to have been using methanol not specified beforehand and was dropped from the placings in the handicap event, giving second place to Bobbie Baird, who had broken the lap record with the Maserati in his efforts to catch me. The race was also treated as two scratch events, for racing and sports cars. Tom Cole was the winner of the sports category and I came second.

·　　·　　·　　·　　·

The last time I drove the 1100 Riley was at the second Gamston meeting, where I took both cars and won the 1100-event race.

When the cars were being checked before the meeting, one of the scrutineers pointed to the 1500 car and said: "One of your front wheels is loose."

I said: "Rubbish, there's nothing loose on that car."

But he insisted so we jacked it up—and one of the front wheels nearly fell off. The stub axle had fractured, but fortunately on the old Rileys there is a big nut which holds the hub on even if the axle breaks. That put me out of the 1500 race, but it taught me that scrutineers have an important job to do in motor racing.

Although I have experienced most of the hair-raising things that can happen to a racing driver, up to the time of writing I have been spared the sensation of losing a wheel during a race. Stirling Moss has had it happen to him several times, on an H.W.M. and on various Maseratis, and at one time it was almost a routine experience for drivers of Gordinis. It has always amazed me how many people get away with it and how few serious accidents it produces.

The only other trouble with the 1500 Riley during that season was at the Curragh races in Eire, when a big-end ran during practice, the day before the race. My father and a friend named Hugh Sewell, who was later to become my mechanic when I raced the Cooper-Bristol, worked all night to fit a new bearing, with Irish mechanics standing by on voluntary overtime to machine the white metal, but the bearing journal had been damaged and the big-end began to rattle again before we could get the car to the track.

The flimsiest of foreshadowings of the future was provided by a lap and a half in practice for the T.T. on Bobby Baird's 4.1-litre Ferrari.

That was my first full season, during which I drove at twelve meetings in England and Ireland. I had learned a lot, gained some confidence and had quite a few successes, which included winning the Motor Sport Brooklands Memorial Trophy for my aggregate performances in the three club meetings at Goodwood, but I had also had my moments. At one Goodwood meeting I was trying to catch Harry Lester's M.G. when I went into Lavant far too fast and spun off, eventually finishing third. Later I bagged a second place after spinning off again. After this I was called before the stewards to explain myself and Sammy Davis, looking at me very sternly from under his beetling brows, said: "I want you to tell me exactly what you did after you spun off."

Taking a deep breath, I said: "First I made sure to keep my engine running, then I drove to the edge of the circuit; I looked behind me to see that all was clear and then drove back onto the track."

I waited, expecting to get a real dressing down for making a fool of myself, but he simply said: "Excellent, my boy, that's exactly what I wanted to hear."

$$\cdot \qquad \cdot \qquad \cdot \qquad \cdot \qquad \cdot$$

When the last of the Goodwood meetings came round, Tony Crook and I had both accumulated the same number of points and we both won our scratch races, so the destiny of the Motor Sport Trophy was to be decided by the handicap, which we had both entered. Tony, who was well known as a tremendously hard trier, was driving a Frazer-Nash and I had a start over him. Working it out according to the best laps we had each done, I thought I could just about win, but I knew I was up against an experienced driver who would not miss a trick and on the last lap I had an anxious time as I saw him in my mirror streaking up behind me on the Lavant Straight. I flung the Riley into Woodcote corner right on the limit and then watched him coming up in the mirror as I hared for the finishing line. There was no chicane in those days, so it was flat out all the way, with the Riley giving all it had got; I just managed to reach the line first.

That was my first season and also my only one on pre-war cars with hard cart springs, but it made me realise why drivers of the previous generation wore wide, stiffened body belts like corsets. They just had to do it to keep their insides in place. I did not realise it at the time and I took an awful shaking at Dundrod. I did not feel too bad at the time, but the next evening I suddenly passed out and had to go to bed with whisky and hot milk. My interior organs were in revolt against being thrown about like a stone bouncing down a tin roof and this may have been the first sign of troubles for which I later had to have extensive repairs on the operating table.

## CHAPTER THREE

## FIRST BRUSH WITH FANGIO

W HEN we took stock of the season's results, we decided that the obvious next move was to try to get into Formula 2 racing on 2-litre single-seaters. My father had now given up racing and was putting everything into pushing forward my career, which meant not only using all his skill to give me cars that were fast and reliable, but also negotiating with people who might give me a drive while I was away continuing my engineering studies.

We had some talks with Rodney Clarke and I went down to Goodwood to try the 2-litre Connaught which was being prepared for the 1952 season. I was putting up some quite good lap times, but unfortunately I caught sight of Rodney and Mike Oliver, the Connaught development engineer, standing at Madgwick corner and I thought that on the next time round I would really show them what I could do. I did. When the car stopped spinning round and round, I realised that any hopes of driving a Connaught would have to be postponed for the time being.

We also talked to John Heath who let me try the H.W.M. They had done very well during 1951, winning three second and five third places, in spite of some unfortunate rear-axle trouble, and as Stirling Moss was leaving the team I hoped there might be room for me, but eventually Peter Collins was signed up.

Just as we were trying to decide on the next step, the telephone rang and it proved to be the decisive telephone call of my racing career. Bob Chase, an old friend of the family, was in bed with a cold and had been reading the motoring papers, where he saw the first photograph of the new Cooper-Bristol single-seater which was to be built for 1952 Formula 2 events.

He had a Bristol car of his own and was rather keen on motor racing. He had been watching my progress during the 1951 season and he simply said: "Leslie, if I buy one of these cars, will you look after it and let Michael race it?" The answer did not require any thought at all; this was the chance I had been praying for.

A few days later Bob Chase, my father and I went down to the little garage at Surbiton which has won world-wide fame by building more racing cars than any other factory, but we found they were not anxious to sell their new model to all and sundry. Alan Brown and Eric Brandon had ordered the first two and a third was being built, but they had not decided who was going to be the lucky owner. We saw John Cooper at the time and he told me afterwards that Bob Chase rang him up to try and fix the purchase of the car.

John asked: "Who's going to drive it?"

The answer was: "A chap called Mike Hawthorn."

"I've been watching him," said John. "He's all right. You can have it."

Nowadays, even more than in 1951, every new driver who begins to appear regularly in club events is watched, and people from far away, people he does not know, are forming opinions on whether he has what it takes to make a top-rank driver.

The deal was clinched when we all went down to Odiham aerodrome, where I tried the first prototype and thought it was a very snappy little motor-car.

Obviously we wanted to give it a first try-out at the Easter Goodwood meeting, but Coopers were very doubtful about whether they could have the car ready in time. The Brown and Brandon cars would probably be through on time, but Bristols did not think they could have a third racing engine ready to go into mine. So we went down to Filton to see the people at the Car Division of the Aeroplane Company, who promised to do their best and my mechanic, Hugh Sewell and I went over to Coopers at Surbiton and gave them a hand with the erection of the chassis. The engine arrived in the nick of time and we got it into the car on the Thursday before Easter. On the Good Friday we took all three cars down to Lasham aerodrome for their first trial runs. Both Brown's and Brandon's cars were going quite well, but mine started misfiring and, although we tried everything we could think of, it could not be cured, so we loaded it onto the lorry and took it back to our garage, where we found that it had very little compression. We took the head off—not a particularly easy job on the Bristol engine —and found that the valve seats had warped. As luck would have it we did not have any suitable valve-seat cutters, except a rather blunt one, so we worked right through the night until nine the next morning getting the engine right. I had a nap for half an hour and then set off for Goodwood, with the car in the van, to practise. Once in the car, I forgot I was tired, and I put up second fastest practice time, second only to the Thin Wall 4½-litre Ferrari, which pleased us no end. Then back home, to check the car over again completely before going back to Goodwood to race on Monday.

This last-minute work against the clock to get the car ready was becoming familiar, but I found eventually I could size up whether the car stood a chance of being ready or not and did not get worked up about it. Some delays can be avoided by proper forward planning, but sooner or later you are held up because components are late arriving, or something breaks in practice and then the best driver in the world is no use without mechanics who are prepared to work on until the job is done, without any thought of hours or overtime or food or sleep, working just as well and just as accurately in the middle of the night when they are dog-tired as when they are starting fresh during the day. I was lucky in having help of that calibre right from the beginning, with my father, backed up by Hugh Sewell, Joe Bickell and Brit Pearce. At first I used to stay up myself and lend a hand, but I soon found out I just had to get some sleep if I was going to drive well the next day.

I got a little rest before the Easter Monday meeting and, although I was keyed-up at the thought of racing the Cooper-Bristol for the first time, I did not rate my chances too high; I put in the second fastest practice time due to the fact that the big cars were probably not going very well at the time.

It was a fine day, there was a big crowd and there were big stars like Fangio and Gonzales appearing, so I did not expect anyone would be giving very much attention to me. The new Coopers certainly got a lot of publicity, but the big news was the fact that Fangio was going to drive one. As the cars were unloaded and clouds began to obscure the sun, I thought I would potter round as well as possible and snatch a place if I could. This was the first time I had raced a single-seater, and there was a lot to learn.

It was only when I was on the starting line that I realised that I had never practised a racing start with the car. I had no idea at what revs to let the clutch in or how much wheelspin to expect. On the line with me were experienced people like George Abecassis in an H.W.M.

and Alan Brown and Eric Brandon with the other two Cooper-Bristols; as they revved up their engines and fixed their eyes on the starter's flag, there was not much time to think it all out. Suddenly there flashed into my mind an article I had read in *Motor Sport*. It said how pleasant it was to watch somebody-or-other leave the line at the Brighton Speed Trials, as he took the revs up to a certain figure and then held them there instead of blipping the throttle as everyone else was doing. Down went my foot—I had no time to see what revs I was holding—the flag dropped, I let in the clutch and away I went. I twitched the car into a drift round the rising turn at Madgwick and pressed on as hard as I could through the nasty, fast and adversely cambered bends through Fordwater and down to the left-hander at St. Mary's. When I got a chance to size up what was going on behind, I simply could not believe it. I was well in the lead and gaining. For the whole five laps I had it all my own way and I won easily, with the other two Cooper-Bristols taking second and third places.

· · · · ·

The next event for which I had entered was the Formula Libre race for the Chichester Cup, which assembled some formidable competition, including Bob Gerard and Graham Whitehead with 1½-litre E.R.A.s, Ken Wharton with Peter Bell's two-stage supercharged E.R.A., Dennis Poore on his big 3.8-litre Alfa Romeo and Tony Rolt on a Delage with supercharged E.R.A. engine. Ken Richardson was driving the Thin Wall Special 4½-litre Ferrari, Fotheringham Parker had Duncan Hamilton's 4½-litre Lago Talbot and Fangio was driving one of the other Cooper-Bristols, lent to him by the Ecurie Richmond, which had been formed by Alan Brown and Eric Brandon. Once again I held the revs steady at the start, the car streaked into the lead as soon as the flag fell and it led all the way to the finish.

· · · · ·

Now I had to see what I could do in the big event, the 12-lap race for the Richmond Trophy, in which Gonzales, the stocky Argentino, was driving Tony Vandervell's Thin Wall Special, Duncan Hamilton was at the wheel of his own Lago Talbot and most other eligible cars up to 4½-litres unblown, or 1½-litres blown, were on the starting line. I could hardly hope to beat Gonzales on the big Ferrari, but I did get ahead for a short distance at the start before he pulled away with foot hard down to win at 88 m.p.h., setting up a new lap record at exactly 90 m.p.h. on the way. The Cooper-Bristol held second place and I finished 26 secs. behind Gonzales and 7 secs. ahead of Duncan Hamilton. The rain began to fall as the race ended, but we hardly noticed it. Luck was still on my side, for we had run into valve trouble before the race while there was time to cure it, while the other Cooper-Bristols, including the one Fangio drove, started having it during the race meeting. The new record lap by Gonzales was 1 min. 36 secs., and my best was only 3 secs. longer, with an engine less than half the size.

Next day, the newspapers really went to town and the motoring papers took up the story. I began to learn what it is to be in the spotlight and I cannot say that I did not enjoy it, but later I was to learn that there is another side to it which can be very unpleasant.

At least we no longer pretended that I was going to make my living in any way other than motor racing. I had left technical college and from then on I devoted all my time to driving, helping with the preparation of the car between races and looking after the steadily increasing business side involved in a full racing programme.

. . . . .

There was not much time to relax, for a week after Goodwood I was due to drive at Ibsley, in the meeting run by the West Hants and Dorset C.C. In the 31½-mile Formula 2 race the only serious opposition came from George Abecassis, who was getting a lot of wheelspin on the H.W.M., and I won fairly comfortably. I also won a 21-mile Formula Libre race from Graham Whitehead's E.R.A. Then came the handicap event, in which Duncan Hamilton was driving the H.W.M., and we found ourselves together on scratch. General Loughborough was starting the race and, as he went from car to car with his flag and his watches, Duncan and I with engines roaring were edging forward inch by inch. When it came to our turn, the General raised his flag and I edged forward a bit more, then Duncan got his nose in front again, the General dropped his arm slightly, Duncan let the clutch in and he was off. This was too much, so I let in the clutch and roared away after him and as we got to the first corner I looked back and there was the General still standing with his flag raised, and not a soul in sight.

I soon got past Duncan, but he was already an old hand with a load of experience and he kept right on my tail, worrying me and trying to pass at the slightest opportunity. It was the first time I had had this treatment and I started sliding all over the place, making a horrible mess of things. Duncan was roaring with laughter, and when he eventually got past me again I could picture him saying to himself: "That'll teach the young whippersnapper!" but his joy didn't last long, for his back axle broke, probably as a result of all the wheelspin that had been going on. I made the fastest lap, but I wasn't placed in the race.

· · · · ·

That taught me that I had to try somehow to keep calm when someone else was pressing me hard and the tuition continued during practice for the Daily Express Trophy race at Silverstone. It was a 2-litre event and on the first practice day I made fastest lap in 2 minutes dead, equal to 87.81 m.p.h., but the next day I got involved with Duncan again and I learned another lesson the hard way. I had overtaken him just before going into Abbey Curve and, just as I got into the corner, the flag marshal waved a blue flag at me, indicating that someone was trying to overtake. I knew Duncan was the only one behind me and I should have ignored it, but half-way round the corner I glanced in my mirror, and that started it. In a flash I had spun round and then went hurtling along the straw bales backwards, bouncing from one to the other. I was very frightened, as I thought it was going to turn over. I had a quick glimpse of Duncan taking avoiding action and when it was all over he just came up and said cheerfully: "That'll teach you, boy!"

He often helped me with advice on a circuit I did not know, saying: "Use third there, boy", or "Take that one in top".

I was in the first heat of the race and in the front row with me were Peter Collins (H.W.M.), Jean Behra (Gordini) and Lance Macklin (H.W.M.). Behind me were Downing (Connaught), Wharton (Frazer-Nash), Peter Whitehead (Ferrari), Harry Schell (Plate Maserati) and Johnny Claes (Gordini). By now I had mastered the art of starting and I got into the lead straight away, holding it to finish 2.4 seconds ahead of Behra. Both of us lapped in 2 minutes. The second heat was won by Manzon on a Gordini and about 25 cars lined up for the final. The start was terrific. I got away from the pack, with Behra breathing down my neck, but Manzon stripped the Gordini's axle on the line. Fischer, the Swiss Ferrari driver, was third, with Rolt, Brown and

Macklin in pursuit. Next lap Rolt and Macklin had passed Fischer and then, suddenly, I found my gear lever flapping uselessly with the connection broken off at the box. Behra then went into the lead, but soon the second Gordini stripped its transmission, and Lance Macklin on the H.W.M. moved into first place where he stayed to the end.

On my car the gearbox had an ordinary gear lever which had been cut off short and drilled to take a rod which was brought back to a remote control. It was this short stump which broke off, leaving nothing at all which I could use to change gear. When we took it out we found it was an experimental one which had already been cut and welded and there were several humorous stories about the way in which it was supposed to have found its way into our kit. It did not seem very humorous at the time, but I had the small satisfaction of tying for fastest lap with Peter Whitehead in 1 min. 59 secs.

. . . . . . .

Three weeks later I was in the Formula Libre race at the West Essex Car Club's meeting at Boreham. The main opposition was from Dennis Poore's 3.8 Alfa Romeo, Graham Whitehead's E.R.A. and Eric Thompson with the E.R.A.-Delage. Poore got into the lead, but he was having trouble with his oil pump and throwing oil back into my face, covering my visor. I had to keep wiping it and I could not get close enough to overtake him. Eventually he dropped back and I started to scrap with Whitehead, but I still could not see through the visor, so foolishly I threw it away and then I was in real trouble. The *Autocar* printed a picture of me gritting my teeth. In fact I was in shocking pain, because the wind was getting under my eyelids and lifting them up; when I finished, my eyes were as red as carrots, but I hung on and managed to win and make the fastest lap.

. . . . . . .

We were entered for the Ulster Trophy Race at Dundrod with Archie Bryde's Cooper-Bristol. I drove his car because my own was still being prepared for the Belgian Grand Prix the following week. In practice we had serious trouble with over-heating and in consequence the water pump completely packed up and was impossible to repair. There was no time to get spares from England, but, on enquiring in Belfast, we were given the address of a major who owned a standard

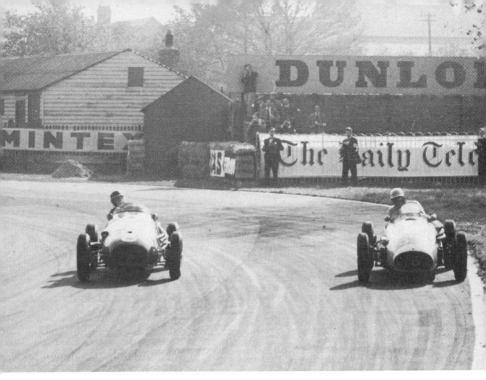

Forcing my Vanwall past on the inside of Harry Schell's Maserati on the last corner at [Dunn
Aintree, 1954, to beat him for second place.

Driving the Vanwall which won me a hundred bottles of champagne at Rheims, 1956. [Klemantaski

With my mother and father after winning the 2-litre class at Boreham with the Cooper-Bristol.

Smoke screen from the 2.4 Jaguar at Silverstone.

Bristol touring car, this having the same type of water pump. Jimmy Hall of Castrol and myself went along to see the Major to see if he would be kind enough to lend us the pump and it turned out that he was only too delighted to help on condition that we returned the pump in good order.

My father and Hugh Sewell worked all night on the car, but next morning when we drove to the circuit we discovered that the cylinder-head gasket was blowing into the water jacket pushing the water through the overflow pipe. We thought we would not be able to race the car but then somebody suggested that we try putting mustard into the radiator as that quite often will stop a water leak. We rushed around to various cottages near the circuit and came back loaded with tins of Colman's mustard. We put this in, started the car and the leak had stopped. There was very strong opposition in this race—Fangio and Stirling Moss driving the V-16 B.R.M.s, Taruffi in Tony Vandervell's Thin Wall, Joe Kelly with his 1½-litre supercharged Alta and Prince Bira in the 4½-litre O.S.C.A., on one of its rare appearances. When the flag dropped I made a perfect start and managed to get so far ahead in the first few miles that when I glanced round behind me there was nobody in sight and I began to wonder if there had been a false start. It turned out that the B.R.M.s did not make a very good get-away and Taruffi had forgotten to turn on his petrol and so was last away.

The early drizzle had cleared when Taruffi caught me up despite my prayers for rain. The B.R.M.s were not running well and were extremely difficult to handle on this narrow twisting circuit. In fact on the long run to the hairpin bend, Fangio, who was just in front of Moss, made 180° spin while braking and the two cars, instead of anticipating their future nose to tail work in the Mercedes team, careered down the circuit nose to nose. Kelly with the Alta had taken to the escape route once or twice and Bira's O.S.C.A. could be seen with its tail sticking out of a hedge where he had run out of brakes. Taruffi had built up a sizeable lead over me and there was nothing I could do about it as my water temperature was hovering very near the danger mark. But my hopes soared when passing the pits I saw Taruffi's car with mechanics swarming all over it. I now thought I had a fair chance of winning so long as the water temperature kept down, but it was not long before Taruffi again caught me up.

This time I noticed that he was only catching me on acceleration and not on maximum speed and he told me afterwards that he had lost top gear. Unfortunately, the water temperature went away past the danger mark and I had to call in for more water and oil. I made one further stop towards the end of the race and finished second to Taruffi. Unfortunately the Major's pump was of no further use to him or to anyone else, but Bristol's gave him a new one.

## CHAPTER FOUR

## CONTINENTAL DÉBUT

MY FIRST Continental race was the Belgian Grand Prix at Spa in which I drove the Cooper-Bristol. I went over to Belgium with my father and Hugh Sewell in our Bedford van with the racing car in the back. We had rather a job starting off because the van had only got about three miles up the road when it blew a top water hose. We managed to fix that, got it on to the ship at Dover and finally unloaded it at Ostend; then it started to boil in a big way. We could not find out what was wrong with it, but decided that the radiator must be blocked up. We stopped at a little garage; fortunately they had some special cleaner and we poured a few tins of that in which did the trick and we managed to press on.

It was my first race there—it proved to be a very fast circuit, long fast downhill stretches down to Stavelot corner, then uphill again with a lot of very fast corners. We got there in good time for practice and I managed to put up some quite good times, but we had some trouble with the clutch on the last night of practice. I thought it was beginning to slip a little so we took it back to the Hôtel Brittanique, where we put the car in one of the garages and started work on it, Hugh Sewell, my father and myself. Fortunately Peter Aston, the Mintex Competition Manager at the time, and his brother Bob came along and said: "Well, you go to bed, Mike, and we'll help your father to do this." So they very kindly got to work and finished the car off quite quickly. I had a good night's sleep.

It started to rain for the race—it quite often does over in Spa—and I was having a dice with Ken Wharton who was driving one of the Frazer Nash single-seaters with a Bristol engine in. It was an ungainly looking car, with rather a high chassis, and was not terribly quick, but Ken had more experience with this type of racing than I had and we kept changing backwards and forwards for several laps; then I got in front and I noticed he was missing. I did another lap and coming up the

35

back I noticed a crowd of people. I glanced over the side of the road—the ground fell away down a steep grassy hill with a wood at the bottom. Just sticking out of this wood was the tail of the Frazer Nash. Evidently Ken had spun on this corner and gone off the road. Fortunately he ducked his head, the barbed-wire fencing tore the shirt off his back and ripped along the top of the car. He went spinning down the field and crashed into the wood, but did not hurt himself very badly. If he had not ducked, the barbed wire would probably have had his head off as has happened to one or two other people in racing.

Ascari was leading the race and I was lying about fifth or sixth. Jean Behra passed me having a battle with Taruffi. But on a very fast downhill right-hand corner one of them spun and the other crashed into him. Fortunately neither car overturned and neither of the drivers was hurt, but I learnt this lesson—a valuable lesson in motor racing: always concentrate on what you are doing and do not look around you. As Taruffi was walking back, coming up the hill just as I was going down it in the opposite direction, I saw him stumping along, waved to him and then turned round to look at him. When I looked up, I was off the road on the grass and heading straight for a telegraph pole. I managed to get out of that one, but it frightened me very considerably; it was another lesson learnt.

A few laps from the end of the race the car started missing badly and I thought it must be fuel shortage. We had put in a long-range tank to cope with the distance, but something must have gone wrong and I only just managed to get it into the pit, spitting and banging, almost stopping. The pit topped me up with more fuel, but as they were not ready for me—they had not been expecting me to call in again—the fuel was not in the proper churns. It was all in jerry cans and we had to slop it in out of one of these. It took a long time.

At last I was pushed off down the hill; the clutch would not work. I got it out and it just would not come back. I thought I had broken it, but I suddenly realised that it had probably caught on the bulkhead and jammed. And so it had. I said to Hughie Sewell who was pushing it: "We've had it, Hugh. The clutch won't engage." Then I leant under the dash and groped for the pedal. I was right under the scuttle. I grabbed the clutch pedal and managed to pull it back; it engaged and I was off. But due to the long pit stop Paul Frere in the H.W.M. caught up considerably and he was only a few seconds behind me. I pressed on, but my father signalled me to come in again for some more fuel just in case we ran out, so I made a quick stop. This time they had the churns ready and we made a very quick getaway; I managed to beat Paul Frere and finish fourth.

· · · · ·

I went back to Boreham on August 2 for the International Meeting sponsored by the *Daily Mail* who were at that time spending a lot of money in an effort to build up the Boreham circuit as a rival to Silverstone. Unfortunately the weather at this meeting was one of the things which helped to defeat the project. The main event consisted of two races of 200 miles each run simultaneously for Formula 1 and Formula 2. There was an impressive line-up among the big cars, with Villoresi on a 4½-litre Ferrari—he had made fastest lap in practice at 103.45 m.p.h.—Gonzales and Wharton on the supercharged 16-cylinder B.R.M.s, two more 4½-litre Ferraris driven by Rosier and Landi and two 4½-litre Talbots driven by Etancelin and Giraud-Cabantous.

In the Formula 2 class there were Alan Brown, Eric Brandon, John Barber and André Loens besides myself on Cooper-Bristols, Moss on the experimental E.R.A., with several Ferraris, Maseratis and Connaughts. The rain was pelting down and once the race started I really did not know what was happening as we rushed around like speed-boats amid great waves of water and spray. I knew I was leading the 2-litre cars, Villoresi the big ones and I remember seeing a B.R.M. stuck among the straw bales at the end of the straight, with Gonzales walking back to the pits in a towering rage. Then I passed Landi's yellow Ferrari and began to close up on Rosier's big Ferrari; I tried to pass him, too, but I was a bit too enterprising and spun in the process. However, I kept going and soon got past the blue car and then to my astonishment I saw Villoresi's red Ferrari right ahead. Watching for my chance, to make sure there was no mistake this time, I got past him on a corner and pulled away.

I was making about five seconds a lap on the great driver, who was having a struggle to hold his big heavy car on the waterlogged track, and I built up my lead to 40 seconds at about 40 laps, but then the rain stopped and the track started to dry up. This robbed me of my advantage and the big cars began to speed up. Ten laps later Villoresi had me in sight again and eventually he caught me. I stayed with him for a while by going faster round the corners, but he drew away, to be followed later by Landi. Most people thought it was simply the change in the weather which had cancelled out my lead over the big cars, but what they did not know was that I was in trouble with the engine. There was a nasty little clank which rapidly got worse, and from 5,800 r.p.m. I cut down to 4,700 to try and keep going.

After the race we found that the flywheel had come loose and, if this had not happened, I believe I could have made it a fight to the finish for outright victory. However, I had not got much to complain about, with first place in the 2-litre event and third place overall. Villoresi came and congratulated me and the crowd obviously felt they had had their money's worth watching the David and Goliath act by the little Cooper against the big Ferraris.

* * * * *

My next Continental excursion with the Cooper-Bristol was to the Dutch Grand Prix on the tricky 2.6-mile Zandvoort circuit among the sand dunes on the coast, not far from Haarlem. It was the first official Grand Prix of Holland and the Ferrari works team was there in force with 2-litre cars driven by Ascari, Farina and Villoresi, backed up by de Tornaco's private entry. Behra, Trintignant and Manzon had 6-cylinder, twin-camshaft Gordinis and Paul Frere had a 4-cylinder 1½-litre. Hamilton, Macklin and the Dutch driver, Van der Lof, were driving H.W.M.s, Ken Wharton had the single-seater Frazer-Nash making one of its very few appearances, Bianco, Landi and Flinterman had 6-cylinder, Brazilian-entered Maseratis, Downing had his Connaught and Moss had the single-seater E.R.A. prototype. In practice I managed to get round fast enough to win a place in the front row at the start, alongside Ascari and Farina, while Villoresi on the other works' Ferrari was in the second row. At the start the Cooper's acceleration allowed me to stay with Ascari up to the first corner and I then stayed second for a lap until Farina came by. For four laps I was third, until Villoresi came past to put the works' Ferraris 1–2–3 and I then managed to stay in fourth position to the end of the race.

* * * * *

I was staying at the Funkler Hotel in Haarlem before the Dutch Grand Prix at Zandvoort; it is a pleasant old-fashioned hotel run by a very charming Dutchman and the food is extremely good. Ugolini, the Ferrari team manager, Lampredi, the chief designer, and Amorotti were also staying there.

After practice one day we came back to the hotel for dinner and afterwards we got chatting to Lampredi and Ugolini. The drink started flowing. I had a couple and then I said: "Right, I'm going to bed now and I'll leave you people to talk." Ugolini and Lampredi could speak French and my mechanic, Hughie Sewell, could speak a little French too, but my father could not speak anything but English. I think they began to understand each other better and better as they had more and more to drink. The outcome of it all was that they said that they might be interested in me and they would try and arrange a run for me in a Ferrari some time. They also said that they would have a word with Commendatore Ferrari when they got back to Italy. That was really when Ferrari's first looked on me as perhaps a possible driver in the future.

.    .    .    .    .

I had a telegram from Archie Bryde—it arrived on a Wednesday—asking me if I would drive the following Sunday in the race at Rheims in his Cooper-Bristol. I went up to see him that evening and he said he was sending the car over with Tony Hume; if I liked to fly across and make my way to Rheims it would be there for me. So I agreed to the plan. The next day I went to Rheims. I tried the car; we were obviously hopelessly outclassed though; long straight circuits did not suit the Cooper, as it was not fast enough. It was in this race that Jean Behra caused a big stir by beating the works Ferraris in his Gordini. He finished well ahead of them. At first the Cooper ran quite well during the race, but then it started to overheat and I guessed the cylinder head was lifting. I called in once or twice for oil and water and then on the last lap I saw Rosier ahead and I thought he was only just in front of me. I had been keeping the car down to low revs, but I thought: "Damn it, we're almost there; I'll really blind it till I get past him and put in for an extra place." So I hurtled past Rosier, but going round Thillois and down the long straight the engine gave up with a horrible clanking noise. I switched off quickly and ran it coasting over the line. Rosier passed me again in the meantime, but I later found out that he had been several laps behind so that it did not make any difference. I think a couple of pistons had got holes in the top of them, which had not done them any good, and the head was slightly warped. We whipped the car back to Cattaneo, who was in Paris, and he worked night and day on it for the next race at Rouen, which Archie had asked me to drive in as well. This was to be the French Grand Prix. They finished the car late in the afternoon and we had no lorry to get it to Rouen; I said: "Fair enough, I'll drive it there." So we started up the engine, it was getting on quite late by that time, I leapt into this single-seater racing car and drove off through Paris all the way to Rouen. It was a wonderful drive. Tony Hume, Archie and his wife drove in Archie's Bentley and I followed in the Cooper. Wherever we went the police held up the traffic immediately and waved us through and the people in the villages cheered us on. A wonderful sight. We eventually arrived in the dark, it was absolutely pitch black. We had no lights on the car, open exhausts, no mudguards, no lights, no insurance, no anything. Nobody seemed to give a damn over there.

Just before the race we found that our battery was flat. The Cooper ran on coil ignition so we had to have a battery and it was absolutely flat. We were desperately rushing round trying to find a spare battery and in the end we borrowed one off a police bike and put that in. We just managed to get to the starting line in time and off we went. We had quite a battle with Pete Collins and Lance Macklin in the H.W.M.s, but after a few laps they drew ahead and got in front. They fell out later, I believe, and I managed to work myself up to fifth place.

The car was going very well, but it was not particularly fast. It was the prototype Cooper, the very first one made, and it had had a pretty hard life. Suddenly the engine started missing rather badly and the water temperature shot up; I went into the pits. They topped it up with water and I went out again and the engine started missing again. I came in again and found the header tank had split and water was spraying on the plugs, shorting them out; it was useless going on—we were getting slower and slower—so we packed it in and that was the end of that. I went back to Paris with Tony Hume and spent a couple of days with him there and then went on down to the South of France for the Alpine Rally.

. . . . .

After gaining a *Coupe des Alpes* in the Alpine Trial as a member of Norman Garrad's Sunbeam team, I had to fly straight home the next day to Silverstone for the British Grand Prix. My father met me at the airport to drive me straight up to Silverstone. He said the engine had just been overhauled by Bristol's and was reputedly giving about 135 b.h.p. I think this was being very very optimistic. I tried the car and as far as I could see there was no difference. In fact, it did not seem very quick to me. I checked on this following Alan Brown's car, which had proved to be a slower car than mine, and I found I could not catch him even along the straight. I went back to my father and said: "Look, what fuel are we using in this thing, because it's just not going?"

He said, "We're using the fuel Bristol's recommended."

"Well, throw it away," I said, "and let's put our own fuel and jets and chokes back in, for goodness' sake."

So he did that. I took it out and the car was once more back on its form, going much better and quicker.

I made a bad start in the race and fell some way behind Dennis Poore who was fairly well up with the leaders. I was not too unhappy about this as I knew Poore would have to make a pit stop for fuel. Sure enough he did. Unfortunately, through some muddle, he had a drink out of a bottle of orange juice which must have had some methanol or something in it because it made him feel extremely ill and put him off for the rest of the race. I managed to finish in front of him and finished third behind Ascari and Farina. Villoresi, I believe, broke his gearbox at Copse Corner. I was quite pleased with the result.

· · · · ·

Just before the Monza race there was a race sponsored by the *Scottish Daily Express* at Turnberry, Scotland, which is a disused aerodrome. Raymond Mays rang me up and asked me if I would drive a B.R.M. up there. At the same time Tony Vandervell rang me up and asked me if I would drive his 4½-litre Thin Wall there. I was obviously very keen on doing this as my father did not want me to use my own car; he wanted to get it ready for the next race.

I went up to Bourne to try the B.R.M. first. I met Mays and Berthon and got into the car; they pushed me off. But it was no use—it was incredibly quick, the acceleration was fantastic, but every time I came to a corner and went below 8,000 revs the power went right off. You would come out of the corner with the revs down and as you accelerated it would just fluff and burble; then, suddenly, as you reached the 8,000 mark the full power would come in with a bang and you had a job to hold the car straight. At over 8,000 revs it really did motor, but the steering was nothing to write home about. I made the mistake of doing my first lap without ear plugs and that nearly shattered my eardrums—the noise was incredible. I told Mays that I had got to try the Thin Wall first and then I would let him know my decision as to which car I would like to drive later in the week.

I went to Silverstone and tried the Thin Wall. It was a beautiful car. I thoroughly enjoyed driving it and I believe I broke the Silverstone course record, which had been held by Farina in the same car. I was very pleased with it and I said that I would like to drive it at Turnberry. I told Mays that I had chosen the Thin Wall.

I went up to Turnberry. The Thin Wall was going like a rocket and we easily put up the fastest lap in practice. We had a little trouble, but the mechanics soon got it right. While I was up there, Rodney Clarke asked if I would like to drive one of the 2-litre Connaughts, as I had said that I had not brought up my own car. I said that I would like to and I won the race with it, although the car was only running on three cylinders. As I crossed the line the car was running very roughly so I stopped it immediately and pulled it to the side of the road.

Rodney Clarke ran out and said: "I'm awfully sorry, Mike, it's let you down like this."

I said: "Don't be a clot, we've won the race!"—he was delighted.

Then it came to the big race with the Thin Wall against the B.R.M.s, and we were on the starting line when something went wrong with the B.R.M. A big panic to get it going.

"Don't worry," I said. "Hang on, take your time, because we can sort of hold the race back a bit till you get it fixed. It would be a pity to start with one of them out—it'd spoil the race."

We all got in, they raised the flag. I tried to put the Thin Wall in gear —it would not go in. I was getting panicky and I tried all the gears; it would not go into any of them. They dropped the flag, I gave a terrific heave and it went into first. Everybody else got off nicely and I followed them. I found it terribly difficult to change gear. I got into second and then by heaving and waggling the gear lever I managed to get into third; I could not get into top at all. Third gear was pretty bad; I had to come out of second, almost put it into first and then whip it straight round into third.

I started to catch the B.R.M.s up quite rapidly. I was going down the straight flat out in second, did my usual stunt of putting it almost into first and then whipping it across into third, but this time I really did go into first. I let the clutch out and the revs went straight up to 9,000—the maximum's only seven. "God," I thought, "that's blown up the engine!" but it did not even falter and went on just as sweetly as ever.

I went on chasing the B.R.M.s. Suddenly there was the most horrible noise from the back axle, everything clanked and groaned. I thought it wiser to stop so I pulled the car up and looked underneath; there was a pool of oil and I thought: "Well, that's had it." I had to walk back to the pits.

The rev counter needle was stuck at 9,000—I thought: "If Tony Vandervell sees that, he'll throw a fit!" I dropped back to the pits and told them what had happened and said: "I think the back axle or the gearbox has packed up, I'm not sure which." Then I went over to see the mechanics and said: "Look, I've over-revved a little, it's stuck at 9,000. Can you nip over and put it back to 7,000?"

They were a very good bunch of boys and they nipped over and put it back for me—I think Lofty Wilson did it for me—so the old man never knew. It was only about last year, I think, that I told him about it. He laughed when I did tell him. So the B.R.M. won and the Thin Wall went out—actually it was a broken back-axle casing. The car was a very weak one and suffered badly from this. I believe Farina broke two or three on the Thin Wall when he raced it later on.

We had a jolly good party that night, a real binge, and that made up for the race—I sort of drowned my sorrows.

## Chapter Five

## I JOIN FERRARI

Our last Continental excursion was to Monza in September for the Italian Grand Prix. On this very fast circuit, we found the Cooper was undergeared and was easily reaching 6,000 r.p.m. in top gear. Unfortunately there was nothing we could do about it; there was no higher axle ratio, and we could not use any bigger tyres. I could not hope to keep up with the Ferraris and Maseratis on the straight, but I hoped to tuck into the slipstream behind one of them and let him pull me round. I managed to nip in behind Taruffi and it was working beautifully, but on the second lap the engine went dead and I pulled into the pits. I was there for $1\frac{1}{2}$ hours while we changed plugs, distributor, coil and checked everything imaginable without finding the cause of the trouble. As time went by some of the officials tried to persuade us to retire, but we were determined not to give up. One of them was very persistent and we all got so exasperated that we gave him Sir Winston Churchill's victory sign with some straightforward English vocal accompaniment and he left us alone. We were running out of ideas when Bernie Rodgers said: "Why not check the distributor drive shaft?" And that was it. There is a small pin which transmits the drive and that had sheared. We had no spare, so we rammed in a piece of welding wire which just fitted and off I went, miles behind.

That was my last race on the Cooper, which had given me such wonderful service. It handled well in the wet, steered well and drifted the corners with great ease, although wheel adhesion was not all it might have been. Perhaps the weakest point of the car was the braking system. The brake drums were integral with the wheels as on the 500 c.c. Coopers, and the liners sometimes distorted and cracked, so that the car pulled to one side or the other when the brakes were used. Spare wheels were almost unobtainable and we had to make do with two for the whole season.

We had no spare engine and so the one engine together with the rest of the car had to be checked over in detail after every race, which mean long hours of day-and-night work by my father and the mechanics. Contrary to popular belief, the engine was not extensively modified, but it was very carefully assembled and, as everyone in the business knows, you can set two people to assemble a given engine and one will always get more power and more reliability than the other. There had hardly been time to do anything before my first Goodwood meeting except cure the valve-seat trouble. We decreased the valve-seat angles, to improve the gas flow, and changed the ignition and carburetter settings. The compression ratio was not particularly high— about $9\frac{1}{2}$ to 1—but the choice of fuel was fairly critical. The mixture recommended by the makers didn't seem to us to be ideal, so we mixed our own.

Transmission ratios were another problem. There were only two combinations of crown wheel and pinion available and the ratios in the Frazer-Nash gearbox were too wide for use on a racing single-seater. We had only two available tyre sizes for the 15-inch wheels, so we often had to put up with gearing which was far from ideal for the particular circuit where we were racing. However, it was a wonderful year, and I shall be always grateful to those who made it possible.

· · · · ·

Whilst I was over at Monza with the Cooper, I was in the paddock one morning talking to Tony Vandervell and he said: "Come along and try a Ferrari—sit in one of them and see how it is for size, because I think Ferrari is going to offer you a drive next week."

Evidently Tony had been chatting with him and had said: "Why don't you give Hawthorn a trial and see how he gets on?"

The race following Monza was the Grand Prix of Modena and it was not a World Championship event: it would be a good place for me to try the Ferrari out and see if I would be any good in one. Tony had very kindly spoken up for me. Anyway I sat in the car and said that I would be very interested. Tony said: "Well, we will let you know later on if we'd like you to come down to Modena to try the car."

After the race at Monza I drove down to Modena with my father and Ferrari's asked if I would like to drive one of their cars. I said I would, but first of all I would like to try my Cooper-Bristol round; it was a twisty circuit and the Cooper had good acceleration and cornered quite well on that sort of track.

They said: "Yes, try it by all means, and if you think you can do better with the Cooper, drive that, but we would like you to try the Ferrari."

I said: "I don't think the Cooper will be quicker but I would like to try it." They took me out one day and we unloaded the Cooper, but it was not quite ready so they asked me to try the Ferrari.

I tried it and it certainly was a lovely motor car. The brakes were fantastic and the cornering wonderful. I said: "Well, I will definitely drive the Ferrari, there is no comparison with the Cooper." "Right," they said. "Come along tomorrow for your official practice. We'll paint the car green for you—as green is the British racing colour." They were extremely helpful. I went next day for practice and Ascari and Villoresi were there and there was only one car. Obviously, they had a practice first. While this was going on, my father said: "Why not take the Cooper round and just compare it—see how it goes?"

I asked Ugolini and he said: "Certainly, by all means, take it round and we'll let you know when the Ferrari is ready for you."

So I took the Cooper out and did a couple of warming-up laps. When I was going very quickly down the back straight—I thought I would try to put up a good time and see if I could get somewhere near the Ferrari time—I made the mistake of braking at the same point as I had been braking with the Ferrari. The result was that the brakes locked, and when I took them off and then put them on again, they locked on one wheel and the others would not go on at all. I arrived at the corner far too fast and I was obviously not going to get round; I put it into a broadside round the corner and got half-way round the corner before going off the road sideways and hitting the straw bales at the side of the road. These straw bales are backed by concrete posts and I hit them at about seventy or eighty.

From then on everything became a blur, I felt a terrific jar. I hit the bales and then I hit the ground with an almighty thump. I lay there and thought: "My God, I'm dead!"

I heard the car running and I opened my eyes and looked round. The Cooper was on its side, but the engine was still running; I thought: "I'd better switch it off!"—I have no idea why. I just crawled over to it on hands and knees, switched off and then sank back. The next moment a horde of Italian spectators descended on me, lifted me straight to my feet and whipped my helmet off; I felt pretty groggy. Lance Macklin had seen the crash from the pits—a lot of other people, including my father and Hughie, had missed it. Luckily Salvadori was there and he said: "Quick, into my car"—a little open Morris Minor—and he hurtled round to the corner in it bringing my father.

I said: "I think I'm all right, Pop, a bit shaken."

"We'd better take you to hospital," he said.

There were no ambulances or doctors there—nobody bothered with that sort of thing as this was only practice, not the race. Just as they were helping me into my car, I started to go blind—I think it was concussion actually. I was conscious, but everything just went sort of completely white. I thought: "My God, I'm going to go blind—damaged my eyesight in some way!" I just shut my eyes and sat in the car. Hughie Sewell held me in the back and there were a couple of motor-bike speed-cops there who set their sirens going and led me to hospital. I opened my eyes very gingerly when I got to the hospital and found I could see again. I was all right. They took me up into the operating theatre and the doctor had a look at me, felt me all over and said: "Well, I don't think anything's broken."

But I had only been wearing a jersey and where I had hit the deck it had been torn off; all one shoulder and my back had had the skin taken off and were covered in dirt and grit and so on. The doctor said: "I'll just clean this up for you."

He produced a bottle of alcohol and started to swab it off with that. I nearly went straight through the ceiling with alcohol on a sort of raw wound. "We'll leave it alone, shall we?" I said eventually. "I'm not having any more of that on it." "Well, if you like," he said, "I'll just put penicillin powder on and that won't hurt at all."

"Why on earth couldn't you have said that in the first place and just done it?"

He did that and actually the penicillin worked like a charm—in about four days the whole thing had healed up completely. They did not bother to take the dirt out or anything. It was wonderful. Then finally they looked me over and said: "Well, look, you're all right—but you'd better stay in bed for a couple of days just to make sure."

So I said: "All right, I will. . . . Is there any chance of racing?"

They said: "No."

"Well, do you think I'll be all right next week? I want to race in England."

"Yes," they said, "there is a strong possibility that that'll be all right."

So they put me to bed. After I had been in bed for a couple of days, everybody came to see me, Lance Macklin, John and Laurel Heath and a lot of Italians came to see me—one or two of them had been prisoners of war in England—and altogether everybody was very kind.

Ferrari had said he would like me to sign on for him next year after my first practice with the car but I had wanted time to think. Ugolini now came along to the hospital and said: "Look, Ferrari would still like you to drive for him. Will you sign on?"

"Well," I said, "just give me a week or two to think about it when I get back to England."

They agreed to that. I was hoping that there might be another British car which might give the Ferraris some competition, but there did not seem to be one.

After about a couple of days I began to find it difficult to breathe in deeply and I had a shocking pain in my chest. I told the doctor this and so they X-rayed me; they said that I had got some liquid on my lung— "there are two ways of getting rid of it: we can either leave it and let it go on its own accord; or we can stick a needle in you and drain it off."

I said: "Thanks very much, I'll just leave it and let it go away on its own."

So they said: "Fair enough."

I had gone to bed—I was feeling very unwell by this time—and one afternoon the doctor came in and said: "Well, we've decided that it's better to have it drained so we're going to drain it this afternoon."

I did not relish this very much, still less when they brought the male nurse in; he was a big strong husky character with black hair all over his arms—I had two male nurses, one was this big hulking bloke and the other was a much gentler type. I had to have a lot of penicillin injections, but the big one, the husky fellow, was always much the best; he would just get the needle and go bang, straight in and it was finished with. But the other chap tried to be kind and put it in gently; and that, of course, hurt much more.

They made me sit on the edge of the bed and arch my back; then the big chap grabbed me and said: "Right, now we're just going to give you a local anaesthetic on the skin, then we push this needle in and suck the liquid out."

I said: "Thanks very much."

They sprayed the skin with local anaesthetic—it was so local it was not true; I think it covered about a pinhead—and I could feel the great needle of the sucker going in and nearly passed out. Of course it did not hurt all that much, but it was a horrible sensation. When it got in a bit further it did begin to hurt, but eventually they said: "Right, that's got rid of it. You're fit now."

I felt much better after that, having had a rest, and after about ten days they said I could go home. An aeroplane was fixed up and I was put in an ambulance and driven up to Malhenza with my father and Hughie Sewell following in the Lancia. Inevitably the ambulance driver got lost in Milan and I thought: "God, we're going to miss the aeroplane." I was really longing to get back to England; I had had enough of Italy by this time—hard beds and dreadfully hot. My father suddenly spotted Ascari and Villoresi driving along together so he waved to them to stop and explained that I was flying back home. Ascari poked his head round the door and said: "Best of luck, Mike." He put the driver on the right road and we got there in time for the aeroplane. I was going straight home, originally, but Tony Vandervell would not hear of it. He fixed me up with a room in the London Clinic and had an ambulance to meet me at the airport and take me straight there.

The next day I was examined by the doctor and he said: "Well, I'm afraid you haven't got all the liquid out, we'll have to have another go at it." I was in there two or three weeks before they let me out and I felt terribly weak for a long time.

Ferrari sent me a letter asking me to come straight over and sign on for the next year. So I went over to Italy and signed on with Ferrari for the following year. Afterwards I had arranged to meet a great friend of mine, Mike Currie, in France, for some ski-ing in the Val d'Isére. I started off in my Lancia, but I got so snowed up I just could not make any headway at all; I dumped it in a garage and went on by train. I eventually found Mike and a friend of his and we had a fantastic party that night. I had been inoculated against smallpox for the first time only two or three days before. I woke up with the most monumental hangover I have ever had in all my life and it lasted for about four or five days. I felt really miserable and it was only on Christmas Day that I started to feel better. I tried some ski-ing, but found it—and I did not reckon this at all—most dangerous; I thought: "No, this isn't for you, Hawthorn; leave it alone." I kept on falling and I could feel the bones of my legs bending; I did not fancy it at all. I soon packed it up and then Mike Currie's friend, Richard, broke his leg while ski-ing and was put to bed. After a day or two Mike and he decided to go back to England. I thought that I would go back to Ferrari's to Modena. So they went to England and I spent New Year's Eve in Monte Carlo which was not very pleasant; I was by myself and I did not enjoy it very much. I was rather pleased to get back to Modena and I only had to wait a few days before we set off for the Argentine.

PART II

THE PRANCING HORSE

CHAPTER SIX

ARGENTINE TRIP

THE Argentine trip was a tremendous adventure for me; I was driving my first races as a member of the official Ferrari team and making my first visit to a new continent where everyone we met, from the head of the government down to the humblest peasant, seemed to be imbued with an ardent enthusiasm for motor racing. We moved among extremes of wealth and poverty such as I had not seen before. Invitations poured in from wealthy families who owned lovely villas with their own swimming-pools and who travelled about in fine cars and private aeroplanes; we danced with beautifully-dressed girls to South American rhythms under a velvet sky and we moved from one reception to another, surrounded by uniforms ablaze with decorations, while liveried flunkeys waited on the guests, but always round the corner there was the penniless multitude of the *descamisados*—the shirtless ones—whose living conditions were primitive despite all the regime was trying to do to improve their lot.

For those on the right side of the fence, life was good and we were given a wonderful reception, but over the centuries the Latin temperament, mingled with the native Indian blood, has produced an explosive brew and my memories are overshadowed by the nightmare scenes of panic and carnage when a wild-eyed screaming mob ran amok during our first race.

The Ferrari team, together with some members of the Maserati outfit, flew from Italy to Buenos Aires in a special plane chartered by the Argentine Government and although it was ten o'clock at night when we arrived, the plane was immediately surrounded by a seething mass of people. Fangio and Gonzales had come to meet us and we received the full V.I.P. treatment. It was the first time all the top European works teams had gone over for the South American season with their leading drivers and the whole population was infected by the motor-racing fever. The Ferrari team consisted of Ascari, the reigning World

Champion, Farina and Villoresi, with myself as the new boy. Maserati was relying largely on local talent, with Fangio and Gonzales, but Bonetto had come out from Europe. Gordini had brought Behra, Trintignant and Manzon from Europe and two more cars were entrusted to the Argentine drivers Menditeguy and Birger.

Charles Cooper and his son John had come out with three Cooper-Bristols, two for Alan Brown and John Barber and one which was eventually driven by the Argentine driver Schwelm, who once made a brief and meteoric appearance in the Mille Miglia. The Cooper outfit was being looked after by Eric Forrest Greene, a charming Englishman who was agent for Rolls Royce, Bentley and Jowett cars in the Argentine. He had a lovely house on a hillside overlooking the bay at San Isidro just outside Buenos Aires where he lived with his wife Dora; they also had with them John, his son by a previous marriage, and her daughter, also of a previous marriage. Eric was a most knowledgeable enthusiast who had done some racing in Bentleys before the war and longed to get back into the sport. He did get back later, but only to be burned to death in a particularly nasty accident.

Evita Peron had died some time before our visit to the Argentine and each of the racing teams made official visits to her tomb, where they laid wreaths. Because of the language problem with my new Italian colleagues, I spent a fair amount of time with the Cooper team and I joined them when they went to the ceremony, but the body of the general's wife was not there at the time as it was being embalmed.

On arrival in Buenos Aires we had been received by General Peron himself in his great pink palace in the centre of Buenos Aires. He was able to talk with the Italians; the rest of us talked to him about motor racing with the aid of interpreters, while we sat around and sipped coffee. After that came receptions by civic authorities and provincial governors and a host of private parties, so that I began to feel I should be completely worn out before the motor racing began.

•    •    •    •    •

Our first race was the *Gran Premio de la Republica Argentina*, run on January 18 at the Buenos Aires Autodrome under the current 2-litre capacity limit and over an extremely twisty 2.4-mile circuit. Fangio had not driven since his bad crash at Monza in June, 1952, when his Maserati somersaulted several times and he was thrown out, breaking one of the vertebrae in his neck, but in the first day's practice, driving one of the new season's 6-cylinder Maseratis with twin ignition, he easily made fastest lap in 1 min. 49.1 secs. Unfortunately for him, only the times recorded in practice on the day before the race counted for starting-grid positions and, on a wet track, Fangio's 1 min. 56.1 secs. was beaten by Ascari with 1 min. 55.4 secs. We were using 4-cylinder Ferraris very much like those of the previous season, but they had long twin external exhaust pipes merging into a single pipe running beside the cockpit, instead of the four short stubs which had been used previously.

Race day dawned fine and hot and the population, which had been harangued for days about the motor race from loudspeakers in the streets and squares of the city, trekked out en masse to the Autodrome. The race was not due to start until four in the afternoon, but the public enclosures were packed solid hours before and tempers rose as late-comers tried to force their way in. The police did their best to keep order, but some enterprising characters produced wire-cutters and started snipping holes in the boundary fences. When President Peron arrived there were several skirmishes going on as the police tried to keep order.

When he heard what was happening he simply said: "My children, my children! Let them in!"

With police resistance withdrawn, they simply flowed everywhere like a tidal wave, helped by a keen type who simply threw a hook over the wire, hitched it to a truck and drove away, tearing down hundreds of yards of the fence. They poured onto the circuit and as we lined up on the starting grid there was a solid wall of humanity eight and ten deep on each side of us. They invaded the grandstand, too, and drove out people who had paid for their seats by the simple trick of sticking lighted cigarettes into them.

In the first row at the start were Ascari, Fangio, Villoresi and Farina; in the second row were Gonzales, myself and Trintignant; and behind us were Manzon, Galvez, Menditeguy and Behra, then Brown, Schwelm and Birger, on a 1,500 c.c. Gordini, and finally Bonetto and Barber.

In spite of the chaos round the circuit, the start was only a few minutes late. My orders were to keep ahead of the Maseratis, but not to try and beat my more experienced team mates, Ascari, Farina and Villoresi. Ascari took the lead, pursued by Gonzales, Fangio, Bonetto, Farina and Villoresi. On the third lap Fangio moved into second place, but Ascari continued to draw away. Bonetto dropped back and before long Gonzales had stopped at the pits. It began to look as if the winter's work had still not given Maserati the answer to the Ferrari superiority of the previous season.

I moved up and passed Farina for a short spell, but the conditions round the circuit were fantastic. The crowd was edging further and further into the roadway, completely obscuring our view of the corners. They also stood in front of the warning signs before the corners and there was no hope of seeing any of the cut-off or braking points on which a driver normally relies. Time after time I waved to them to get out of the way, but this only made them worse. They began standing in the road holding shirts and pullovers, which they only snatched away at the last possible moment like a toreador playing a bull. It was an old-time Roman Holiday in modern dress. We were the gladiators and obviously none of the crowd who lined the track were the least bit worried by the prospect that their antics might kill us or themselves. I remembered how Jean-Pierre Wimille, champion of France, had been killed out there in 1948 when the crowd forced him off his line on a corner, and the thought was not encouraging. Then things really began to happen.

On the 21st lap, a broken axle stub on Schwelm's Cooper sent a wheel careering into the crowd, injuring several. Birger and Manzon retired with transmission failures and Bonetto arrived at the pits with the engine of his Maserati on fire. No sooner had the fire been quelled and Bonetto despatched on his way with new plugs than a small boy ran across the track right in front of Farina. Automatically Farina swerved to avoid him, got into a long high-speed slide and slammed broadside into the close-packed ranks of the crowd lining the track. Dead and dying were scattered all around and, in the ensuing panic, another child dashed into the roadway to be killed on the spot by Brown's Cooper.

Farina was taken away in a state of collapse and, as I passed every lap, the pile of mutilated bodies grew as helpers got to work. The official death roll was, I believe, about fifteen, but it looked more than that at the time and there were many injured. Eventually word got through to the ambulance service and the ambulance drivers set off on the wrong way round the course to show the crowd some real speed. The inevitable happened. One of them lost control, skidded into the crowd and killed two more. The victims were taken on board and he continued to the main accident.

Valiantly the police tried to restore order and some of them showed a lot of courage, though one of the mounted police paid heavily for it. In a desperate effort to clear the road he drove the crowd back with a big stock whip; for a time he seemed to be succeeding, but they turned and rushed him, dragged him from his horse and kicked him to death.

While this was going on, Fangio had retired with a broken universal joint and Manzon on the best of the Gordinis had moved up to challenge the Ferraris, but the Gordini lost a wheel—a habit they had in those days—and I moved into third place behind Ascari and Villoresi, but Gonzales was driving with terrific determination between pit stops and he eventually came past me to take third place. After all that had happened, I was quite happy to have finished fourth in my first race with the Ferrari team.

After the race, we were flown to Mar del Plata as guests of the Government and spent a pleasant few days relaxing by the seaside. I was fascinated by the amount of private flying in the Argentine and while we were waiting at the airport for President Peron's plane, which was to take us back to Buenos Aires, I accepted an invitation to go up in a pre-war Focke-Wulf sports two-seater. I was not at all encouraged when I found that I was expected to wear a parachute, but I enjoyed the flight, looking down on the fine modern buildings which fringed the beach. Eventually the Presidential Viking arrived and we went on board, but the take-off was most peculiar. The plane veered sharply before it got airborne and the whole operation felt rather precarious. We found out afterwards that the pilot was under instruction at the time.

. . . . . .

The second meeting of the Argentine season was back at the Buenos Aires Autodrome on February 1. It consisted of a Formula Libre race and a sports-car event run over a longer version of the circuit, measuring 2.9 miles to the lap. The big race produced the sort of mixed field that one could scarcely hope to see anywhere outside the Argentine. There were supercharged pre-war Alfa Romeos of 3.8 and 4.5 litres, a 4CLT Maserati, 2-litre Maseratis and Ferraris from 2 to $4\frac{1}{2}$ litres.

Some excitement was caused during the practice by the arrival of Argentina's own Grand Prix car, the Autoar. It was unloaded from its truck under heavy guard and turned out to be none other than the almost legendary $1\frac{1}{2}$-litre supercharged Cisitalia, which had been built just after the war but never raced. The car had quite a romantic history. It was designed by a team of Porsche engineers for Piero Dusio, who had made a fortune during the war and was spending a lot of it on Cisitalia. Ferdinand Porsche was at that time held prisoner by the French and the money paid by Dusio was used to put up a bond which secured the old man's release.

The car had a flat-twelve engine behind the driver, fed by two vane-type superchargers and designed to produced 500 horsepower. As the car only weighed a ton, wheelspin would obviously be a problem and there was a small lever on the steering column by which the driver could obtain four-wheel drive for maximum acceleration. It was potentially one of the fastest cars designed for the immediate post-war formula ($1\frac{1}{2}$-litres supercharged and $4\frac{1}{2}$-litres unsupercharged) but Dusio ran out of cash before it could be finished and tested. He skipped over to the Argentine, where he started the Autoar car factory making station wagons with parts of Jeeps. The Grand Prix car eventually followed, but there was no one who knew how to develop it and make it go properly; there would have been little hope of finding enough money if they had. So here it was on the Autodrome, but obviously far from ready to race. Clemar Bucci, the Argentinian driver, did a few slow laps on it and I believe Bonetto was invited to try it, but it eventually stopped in a cloud of smoke, with the engine swimming in oil, and that was the last that was seen of what Laurence Pomeroy describes in his book *The Grand Prix Car* as "one of the most ingenious design studies in the whole history of motor racing".

On race day it was obvious that the Government was not going to risk any repetition of the scenes which had taken place two weeks earlier. The army had been brought in, with all necessary means for effective crowd control, including machine-guns. But as it happened there was no particular problem, as two important football matches formed a rival attraction which drew away large numbers of spectators and the crowd was very much smaller than before. Ferrari, looking far ahead as usual, had produced 4-cylinder $2\frac{1}{2}$-litre engines for Farina, Villoresi and myself to try out, with an eye to the new Grand Prix formula due to come into effect a year later, while Ascari had one of the $4\frac{1}{2}$-litre V-12 cars.

At the start the Ferraris were all in the front row, with Fangio, Gonzales and Bonetto on the 2-litre Maseratis in the second rank. Behind them was a mixed assortment which included, besides the cars which had been brought over from Europe, two survivals of the 1936 Grand Prix racing under the 750 kg. weight-limit formula, a 3.8-litre super charged straight-eight Alfa Romeo driven by Mieres and a 4.6-litre supercharged V-12 with Clemar Bucci at the wheel. Ascari's car, which had been giving trouble in practice, soon passed out with oil-pump trouble, leaving the three 2½-litre Ferraris driven by Farina, Villoresi and myself more or less unchallenged, until Bucci, making a terrific effort on his old Alfa Romeo, passed both Gonzales and Fangio and started to chase me, but he had to slow down when his brakes started to weaken. Farina and Villoresi made it a neat finish, crossing the line only ten yards apart, and I came in third some way behind.

After the race we flew back to Italy and I motored home from there to England with John Barber in my Lancia Aprilia, which I had left at the Ferrari works.

CHAPTER SEVEN

## ROUND THE HOUSES

BY THE middle of March I was back in Italy again, preparing for the Grand Prix at Syracuse, which opened the European racing season. There were four Ferraris, for Ascari, Farina, Villoresi and me, with modified engines which we were told were safe up to 7,500 r.p.m., instead of the usual limit of 7,000 and, as there were no works Maseratis, it looked like a walk-over, but the race provided a first-class example of that glorious uncertainty of motor racing which makes team managers old before their time.

At the start we went into the lead with the four Ferraris in team order, but that happy state of affairs did not last long. Villoresi slid into the straw bales, jammed a wheel bearing and limped into the pits to investigate, Ascari soon retired with engine trouble and Emmanuel de Graffenried, the Swiss private owner, worked his Maserati into third place, behind Farina and me. We began to overtake the slower cars and as I went into a fast left-hand turn at the bottom of a hill I saw smoke, thick, black, oily and ominous, belching up into the sky. Tom Cole, the hard-trying American driver, had lost control in his brand-new Cooper-Bristol, slid into the outer wall and split the fuel tank. He got out without a scratch, but the car immediately went up in flames. As I came round the corner I found the road partly blocked by the blazing car and, in front of me, taking most of the remaining space, was de Tornaco, the Belgian independent Ferrari driver, braking hard. I moved out to pass him on the outside, but as I did so he too moved out. I tried to cut back to the inside but my car began to slide and in a fraction of a second I was skating through the flames from the burning Cooper, to finish by crashing backwards into the wall. I got somewhat knocked about by the impact, but I managed to scramble out of the cockpit to find that the back end of my own car was alight. Oil in the undertray had begun to burn and was working up a fine fire right under the fuel tank. The only thing I could think of was the fact that I must somehow get the fire out and get back into the race, so I grabbed a handful of earth, threw it on the flames, blew frantically and the fire went out.

I knew I was still second and the car was standing on a very slight slope, so I got back in and tried to get it rolling to re-start the engine, but it would not move. I implored soldiers, police, spectators, anyone to come and give me a push, but they all looked back at me blankly and kept well away from any contact with racing cars which were or even had been on fire. While I was still trying to rustle up some help de Graffenried went through. I was by then absolutely desperate and frantic with frustration, but suddenly two people arrived—I think Tom Cole was one; they gave me a push, the engine fired and I was away. By now I was probably half a minute behind de Graffenried and as I passed the pits I made a signal to let them know I had spun. I began to realise that I was bleeding from various cuts and scrapes and, when the pit waved a white flag with a red cross at me, I thought they meant me to come in, so I stopped next time round. I was sent on my way with very little ceremony. Shortly afterwards I did get a signal to come in and had to hand my car over to Ascari, but it quickly blew up. Finally, Farina's car broke up, leaving de Graffenried the winner on a privately owned Maserati against the whole Ferrari works team. It was a black day for the prancing horse, but those are the occasional breaks that repay the independent driver for years of expensive effort.

.       .       .       .       .       .

From Syracuse we moved over to the south-west of France for the Grand Prix at Pau on Easter Monday. This is a short, round-the-houses circuit of 1.72 miles through the Casino gardens and round the neighbouring streets. In three hours of racing you get to know it quite well. Ascari, Farina and I were there with Ferraris and the main opposition came from Jean Behra and Harry Schell with Gordinis, but even if their cars held together for the distance we reckoned we ought to beat them and Ugolini asked us to put on a show to make the race more interesting for the crowd. The idea was that we should change positions fairly frequently for the first two hours and then really get going during the last hour, which meant that on current form Ascari would streak away into the lead and win. However, Behra soon got into the act and he tried to overtake me on the hairpin bend just before the long curve outside the casino.

It was a cloudy day and in case it rained the Ferrari mechanics had fitted our cars with spray deflectors, flat metal sheets just behind the front wheels. Behra came close in on the corner trying to overtake me on the inside and for a moment we just touched. Neither of us thought anything about it, and we accelerated away, but as I went round the Casino bend I realised that Behra was missing. The next time round I saw his car wrapped round a tree. It was an extraordinary piece of bad luck. We found out afterwards that when he touched my spray deflector, it must have cut the tyre valve on his front wheel. As he went into the casino curve, the tyre suddenly went flat, and he lost control. Behra was badly shaken and hurt his shoulder, but fortunately was not seriously hurt.

After that Ascari, Farina and I settled down to our demonstration run as planned, but as time went on I noticed a curious thing. Sometimes I dropped back to third place and sometimes Ascari, but never Farina. It seemed as though he felt his prestige demanded he must always be in first or second place.

I was having a spell in the lead when I took a winding downhill stretch particularly fast and the tail came round rather far on a couple of bends.

I could see Farina chasing me in my mirror and I thought: "He won't like that a bit; I bet he comes screaming past."

Sure enough, as we accelerated along the avenue which provides the only straight on the course, he nipped past, tore round the left-hander at the end, braked hard for the right-hand hairpin and started into the long right-hand curve past the casino at high speed. As soon as he went into the corner I had a feeling he was not going to make it; slowly but surely the back of the Ferrari slid outwards. Suddenly it spun completely, ploughed across the grass, cut a swathe through some flower-beds, then crossed the road in front of me and finished up on the lawn in front of the casino. Next time I came by there was Farina, smiling rather ruefully, inspecting a bent wheel which put him out of the race.

After that Ascari and I had it to ourselves. I broke the lap record, but he soon knocked two seconds off my time and rushed away to win easily.

Farina was furious at having thrown away a certain second place and that evening he said: "To hell with it! I'm going to the casino. That's where I crashed and I'm going to back my race number." He did and he won £250, after which he felt better.

The Autodrome at Buenos Aires was an artificial circuit, with grass verges and devoid of gradients. Racing there was therefore very like racing on our airfield circuits at home in England, but Syracuse and Pau introduced me to the Continental type of round-the-houses circuit, run over public roads and streets closed for the occasion. I had encountered narrow roads between earth banks at Dundrod, but here the road was lined with stone walls and big trees, with complications like railway-crossings and bridges. All this demanded precise and accurate driving. If the grass verges are wide a driver is tempted to take a chance on a corner, with the idea at the back of his mind that he can always slide onto the grass if he overdoes it; but there is no future in this kind of driving if the corners are bordered by solid walls of brick and stone. It was a challenge which I enjoyed meeting and I have a feeling that if I am enjoying myself I drive better.

· · · · ·

I had now come fourth, third and second in my first three races for Ferrari and it would have been a neat arrangement to win the next one. However, I knew that was out of the question, for my next engagement was the Mille Miglia. Commendatore Ferrari had told me after the Syracuse race that he was entering me for it and he was surprised at my glum expression when I heard the news. I really was not looking forward to it with much pleasure, as I could not see much hope of doing well in the circumstances.

The accident in which the Marquis de Portago was killed in 1957 has made people all over the world familiar with the problems and perils of this unique event, which carries on the tradition of the great town-to-town races of the first golden age of motoring—an age that ended abruptly when the disastrous Paris–Madrid of 1903 was stopped at Bordeaux. At the time when I was to do my first run, the Mille Miglia was at the peak of its popularity, with somewhere around 600 cars containing over 1,000 drivers and navigators strung out over almost a thousand miles of road, thickly lined with spectators. It seemed to me that to stand any chance of success one must spend months learning the course and, even then, it would probably mean several attempts, gaining experience the hard way before one could hope to win. Even after all that there are so many possibilities of trouble outside the control of the driver that one needs a lot of luck (Taruffi only won at the fourteenth attempt). For a driver who was still unknown it would be easy to learn about the race as he went along, but Ferrari had won the last five Mille Miglias in succession and, as a member of the official Ferrari team, I had to put on a good show first time out.

However, it was no use arguing about it so I set out to learn as much as I could about the course in the short time available. By now I had a Ferrari coupé of my own, so I used this and took with me Hans Tanner, who is extraordinarily well informed on all aspects of motor-racing. With his wavy black hair, black moustache and his habit of wearing South American riding-boots, Hans has a distinctly Latin appearance, although I believe he is really Swiss, and he speaks most European languages. He spent a lot of his time at Modena while I was driving Ferraris, but he usually turned up wherever there was a motor race, either working as a journalist, or lending a hand with the organisation of one of the racing teams.

We spent three days doing one complete run round the course, starting from Brescia and going out across the Lombardy plain through Verona and Vicenza to Padua, then southwards via Rovigo, Ferrara, Ravenna and Forli, to join the Adriatic coast at Rimini. From there it was fantastically fast coastal road all the way through Pesaro and Ancona until we turned inland at Pescara to cross the Apennines en route for Rome. Northwards again from Rome it was hard going most of the way to Bologna, with the 12-mile run over the Radicofani Pass, where there never seems to be a straight of any length, coming before Florence, and the two ascents to over 3,000 feet on the Futa and the Raticosa afterwards. Then it was flat and fast through Modena, Parma, Piacenza and Cremona, back to Brescia. We went back to Modena, had a night's sleep, and got up at 4 a.m. to start again, intending to go direct to Forli and omit the northern part of the course, but the radiator started to boil and there were signs of water in the sump. We struggled back to Modena and that was all the practice I had. However, even that much was better than nothing, as it gave me a general idea of the location of the most difficult sectors of the course and enabled me to note three or four points which could be particularly dangerous at racing speeds.

In Brescia the race dominated the life of the town as the day came near. The red arrow, which is the symbol of the race, was stuck on walls all over the town and cars with race numbers on their sides went blaring about with open exhausts as though the race had already begun.

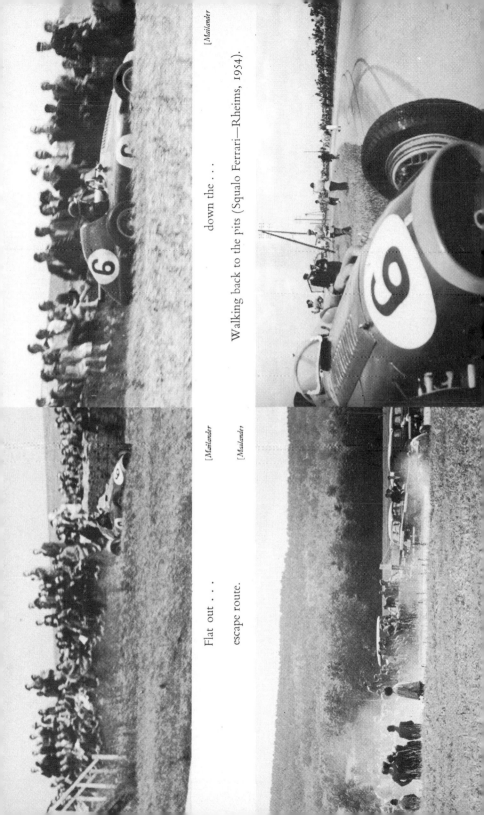

Flat out . . .

[Mailänder]

down the . . .

[Mailänder]

escape route.

[Mailänder]

Walking back to the pits (Squalo Ferrari—Rheims, 1954).

Badly gassed by a broken exhaust pipe at the Belgian [*United Press*

A proud moment in a racing driver's life: standing to [*Klemantaski*

The great square, the Piazza Vittoria, was decorated with flags and banners and on the Friday of race week it was packed with people who jammed themselves all round the enclosures where the fastest cars were presented before the scrutineers. As each new arrival came roaring round the corner he was engulfed by sightseers and autograph-hunters, and the *carabinieri* had to struggle to make a path for him to enter the enclosure. Meanwhile loudspeakers boomed out the names of the drivers and details of the cars, and proclaimed the sporting and technical significance of the *Grande gara Bresciana*.

There was plenty to see for the 1953 race produced a bumper crop of cars in the unlimited sports category. Ferrari's main hopes lay in the big 4.1-litre V-12 two-seaters driven by Farina, Villoresi and Giannino Marzotto, one of the four famous racing sons of an Italian textile millionaire. Backing them up were Tom Cole and Castellotti, with Bracco, the previous year's winner, Paolo Marzotto and myself on V-12 3-litres.

Alfa Romeo had produced new coupés developed from the famous but elusive Disco Volante model with 3½-litre 6-cylinder engines and five-speed gearboxes, which were to be driven by Fangio, Sanesi and Kling.

The cars which created the most excitement among the journalists and the international gathering of enthusiasts in the scrutineering bay were the completely new 3-litre Lancia coupés with V-6 engines employing four overhead camshafts. There were five of them, to be driven by Taruffi, Bonetto, Biondetti, Maglioli and Bornigia; people were soon lying flat on the ground in front of them looking at the front suspension by trailing links and transverse leaf spring—a complete departure from all previous Lancia practice. Nor was that all, for the front brakes were carried on the chassis and connected to the wheels by shafts with two universal joints, a feature which was later adopted by Daimler-Benz as a means of cutting down unsprung weight while employing really big brakes. They were all coupés, quite well streamlined, but somehow husky and muscular in appearance. Through the rear window could be seen an arrangement of wires running over pulleys, which enabled the driver to adjust the auxiliary friction-type dampers at the rear, and in the right rear wing was an oil cooler, with the tail lamp placed in the centre of the outlet.

I went to bed early on the Saturday night, while the small touring cars were dashing away one after the other down the starting ramp

which stood out under the glare of the floodlights in the Viale Rebuf-
fone. They were sent off on their long drive at intervals of thirty
seconds until midnight. Then the small sports cars and gran turismo
models went off at minute intervals throughout the night, until the
turn of the big sports cars came with the dawn. My number was 625,
which meant that I started at 6.25 a.m. I had with me as riding mechanic
a young chap named Tati, who had only been in one motor race before;
that was a Tour of Sicily, during which his driver had smartly rolled
the car over several times. He was very game and quite cheerful as
we climbed up the starting ramp so that the crowd could see us depart.
There we sat, with flash-bulbs going off in our faces, as the seconds
ticked away. Beside us were the Mayor of Brescia and Commendatore
Castagneto, the Clerk of the Course, in the famous bowler hat in which
he has started every Mille Miglia since it began.

At last the flag dropped and we were away; slowly down the ramp,
to avoid catching the tail of the car as we reached the road, and then
full bore down the long avenue out of the town. The long build-up of
excitement, the general circus atmosphere in Brescia did not suit me
psychologically and I was not feeling very keen about the race as we
drove to the start, but once we started racing I began to enjoy it. The
weather was good, an unusual thing for the Mille Miglia. It did rain a
little and the road became terribly slippery, with a shiny black surface
like ice, but it soon cleared up and I steadily increased speed. All the
same, it was a bit disconcerting to see the wrecks of earlier cars littering
the course. There they were, perched at crazy angles on grass banks,
upside down in ditches, crumpled against the walls of houses or
wrapped round trees.

After about two hours I noticed a faint vibration coming from the
back of the car and next time I tried to use the brakes I found that they
had almost disappeared. I decided to press on to our first control point
at Forli, about 205 miles from the start, where some Ferrari mechanics
were waiting and I kept going by using the gears to slow the car down
on corners, or putting it into a slide when all else failed. I told Tati
what had happened and he must have begun to think there was no
future for him in motor racing, for as each bend approached he got
right down under the scuttle and almost disappeared from view.

At Forli, Ferrari was there himself with the mechanics. They
could not see anything wrong, so they bled the brakes and I did a short
run down the road, but only the front brakes were working, so I went

back and then they found that one of the master cylinders had failed. There was no spare available and Ferrari said he would rather I did not continue in that condition, so we decided to drive slowly over to Modena. We had only gone about 50 miles when the rear-axle pinion bearing failed, which explained the vibration I had noticed earlier, so we were completely immobilised. Luckily Peter Aston, the competitions manager of Mintex, happened to come by and he gave us a lift into Brescia.

The Ferrari outfit had its full share of misfortunes that day; Villoresi dropped out with brake trouble, Farina hit a wall, Bracco's differential broke and Paolo Marzotto's car was destroyed by fire when he was lying third, only about 50 miles from the finish. But Giannino Marzotto saved the day by winning his second Mille Miglia victory at 88 m.p.h., 11 minutes in front of Fangio on the 2.6-litre Alfa. Bonetto was third on the only surviving 2.9 Lancia, Tom Cole on another privately owned Ferrari was fourth and Reg Parnell was fifth on an Aston Martin.

## CHAPTER EIGHT

## MY FIRST LE MANS

FOR Ascari, Farina and Villoresi the next fixture was the Naples Grand Prix, but I was being allowed to go alone to England, to compete in the Daily Express International Trophy meeting at Silverstone, and on to Northern Ireland for the Ulster Trophy at Dundrod. Tom Cole was also going to Silverstone with his 4.1 Ferrari, but he wanted to have his Fiat 500 with him as a runabout. As my cars, a 2-litre single-seater and a 4.1 two-seater, were going in the Ferrari van, I offered to drive the Fiat to England for him. Personal transport is always a problem for the racing driver. We spend our working hours driving, but off the circuit we are perpetually thumbing lifts. We use our own cars whenever we can, but we often have to hop on an aeroplane to save time and when the car is needed it is usually standing forlorn and deserted on an airfield, or hidden away in a garage in some other country far away. The little Fiat was only just run in, but we did not have much time to waste, so it went from Modena to Paris just about as fast as it was able and I only remember being passed once on the way. After making a few calls in Paris, I decided to fly to England and Hans Tanner, who had driven up with me, promised to bring the car over later.

When I saw him at Silverstone I asked: "Did you get the car over all right?"

"No," he said. "Amazing thing happened. It ran perfectly from Modena to Paris, but when I got it about ten miles out of Paris the engine completely disintegrated under the strain."

Most surprising.

Like all the season's main events for single-seaters, the Daily Express International Trophy was run under Formula 2 for 2-litre cars, which had become in effect the main formula as Formula 1 had been abandoned by constructors and race organisers, although it was not yet time-expired. The event was in two heats of 15 laps and a final of 35.

My Ferrari did not seem to have found its peak form in the Silverstone climate and in practice I was beaten by de Graffenried on his Maserati and Ken Wharton on a well-tuned Cooper-Bristol with preselector gearbox. De Graffenried won the first heat, Stirling Moss coming second in a new Cooper-Alta with coil-spring suspension which he had had constructed to his own requirements. By normal standards he should have been in bed, as he had crashed badly the day before in the Jaguar he was to have driven in the sports-car race.

Ranged against my lone works Ferrari in the second heat were Bobby Baird's privately owned car, a trio of Cooper-Bristols driven by Wharton, Bryde and Sanderson, the Connaughts of Salvadori and Coombs, Gordinis driven by Trintignant and Schell, H.W.M.s with Macklin and Collins and Whitehead's Cooper-Alta, inter alia. Ken Wharton harried me from start to finish with his yellow-nosed Cooper and crossed the line only a second behind me. I knew then how Villoresi must have felt when my Cooper-Bristol was chasing his Ferrari at Boreham.

Before the final we had the sports-car race over 17 laps. In the unlimited category, Tom Cole and I on 4.1-litre Ferraris were opposed by three works-entered XK 120C Jaguars driven by Moss, Walker and Rolt, and two Allards handled by Sidney Allard and Philip Fotheringham Parker. Smaller, but very fast, were the 3-litre Aston Martins driven by Reg Parnell, Collins and Geoff Duke. Stirling, who must have spent hours practising Le Mans starts, vaulted into the Jaguar and was first away, but I got past on the first lap and he dropped back, obviously far below his top form. Tom Cole came up into second place and the two Aston Martins driven by Parnell and Collins beat all the Jaguars to take third and fourth places. My Ferrari was the one which Farina had crashed in the Mille Miglia. The bent front suspension had been replaced, but the axle ratio had not been changed and I could only just get into top for a moment on Hangar Straight before it was time to change down again, so I practically drove the race in third and fourth gears.

Twenty-seven starters lined up for the final of the main event, myself, Wharton, de Graffenried and Moss in the front row. Behind us were Salvadori (Connaught), Bira (Maserati) and Whitehead (Cooper-Alta). As the last minute ticked away and we sat there with engines roaring Kenneth Evans raised the starter's flag and held it there for what seemed an unusually long time. There had already been a false start in the first heat and now de Graffenried seemed to mistake a flicker of the flag for the real thing. In a flash the Maserati leapt forward, leaving us all standing on the line, then he realised his mistake and stopped just as the rest of us surged forward in a thunder of exhausts. Stirling shot ahead at the start, but I took him at Copse, only to be passed by de Graffenried before the end of the first lap. On the fourth lap I managed to get into the lead again and stayed there for the rest of the race.

Just before half distance, de Graffenried learned from a pit signal that he had been penalised a minute for jumping the start and at once retired in a fury. A rear hub broke on Trintignant's Gordini as he drifted round Woodcote and the wheel flew through the air to land in the tea tent, where it probably interrupted the gentle flow of conversation, but fortunately only inflicted slight damage on one inmate. Meanwhile Trintignant, finding himself driving a tricycle, had neatly dumped in on the grass verge. Stirling was worried by oil on his brakes, Chiron's Osca split its fuel tank and the engine of Ken Wharton's Cooper began to sound rather tired, so that when I crossed the line for the last time, I had behind me two of the Connaughts which so often turned up trumps, driven by Roy Salvadori and Tony Rolt.

· · · · ·

The next week most of us moved over to Ulster to renew the struggle on the Dundrod circuit, in the Ulster Trophy event. There was a good deal of mist about in practice, but I managed to get the Ferrari round the 7.3-mile circuit in 4 min. 51 sec., at an average of 91.74 m.p.h. The race was run in two 10-lap heats and a 14-lap final and the first heat provided a fine struggle between Duncan Hamilton on an H.W.M. and Stirling Moss, who was driving one of the works' fuel-injection Connaughts, as his own special Cooper was being modified in the light of experience gained at Silverstone. Stirling had been held up by gearbox trouble and Duncan just managed to stay ahead after an epic chase by the Connaught. In the second heat I managed to get ahead on the first lap and stayed there. De Graffenried retired early with transmission trouble and there was a great tussle for second place between Ken Wharton on the Cooper-Bristol and Bobby Baird, the local newspaper director, on his privately owned 2-litre Ferrari; Wharton just won. The gearbox had been changed on Stirling's Connaught, but it was not ready to start in the final, so the story of the second heat repeated itself, with Wharton and Baird fighting for second place behind my Ferrari.

. . . . .

My memories of the next event, the Dutch Grand Prix, are not very happy for two reasons. It was a very uncomfortable race as the Zandvoort circuit, among the sand dunes on the Dutch coast, had just been resurfaced with tar and granite chippings and the sharp stone fragments, flung up by the wheels, stung our faces like angry bees.

Secondly it produced the first friction between myself and the Ferrari team manager, Ugolini.

The Maseratis were fitted with wire screens to provide some protection and some of the drivers wore improvised face masks. Ascari, Farina, Villoresi and I had the works' Ferraris, and Rosier was there with his own car. Fangio, Gonzales and Bonetto made up the Maserati team, with de Graffenried as independent; there were also two Gordinis, four Connaughts, two H.W.M.s and Wharton's Cooper-Bristol.

The loose surface made driving extremely tricky and this was the only major event of the year in which lap speeds were heavily down compared with the previous year. Ascari went out in front at the start, but positions were changing fast behind him. Farina, Villoresi and I followed him up and then Fangio passed me. At 22 laps I saw Gonzales fall out with a broken back axle. I carried on in fifth place for a long time and as I got no pit signals I thought I must be keeping well ahead of possible opposition. At 67 laps, Villoresi dropped out with engine trouble and then, to my astonishment, Gonzales, who had taken over Bonetto's car, caught me and passed, showering me with sand and small stones.

Fangio had retired with a broken axle, so Farina and Gonzales were now second and third behind Ascari, with myself fourth, and I simply could not catch Gonzales. Ugolini, our team manager, felt that Ferraris should have been first, second and third and he said so, pretty pointedly, at Zandvoort that night, suggesting that I had not tried hard enough. I in turn felt I had been let down by receiving no pit signals to show that Gonzales was overhauling me and said so. In all the teams I have known, these differences of opinion are sorted out informally in man-to-man talks; only Mercedes-Benz seem to hold full-dress inquests into every aspect of a race but then their methods are unique in many respects.

. . . . .

Three days later I was at Le Mans preparing for my first 24-hours race. It was something I had looked forward to for years, but as so often in the life of a professional driver, there just was not any time to savour it in anticipation. My own Ferrari coupé was supposed to be ready after an engine overhaul to put right the trouble which had cropped up during practice for the Mille Miglia, so I took a train from Holland down to Modena, only to find that the car was not ready. This was by no means an unusual occurrence during the racing season. The racing cars got priority and other things tended to be postponed until the mechanics had more time. I was not as badly off as an American owner who once flew from Mexico to Modena on the day repairs to his badly damaged car were due to be completed. He got to the works to find the bits still in the packing case, just as he had sent them.

Hans Tanner promised to drive my car up to Le Mans and I set off with Phil Hill and two other Americans in a Ford with a Chrysler engine belonging to Luigi Chinetti, former racing driver, and Ferrari representative in the United States. I thought Chinetti had lent the car to me and Hill thought it had been lent to him. I hated the idea of being driven for long distances by other people so I announced that I was going to drive and anyone who wished could sit in the back. The announcement did nothing to further amicable Anglo-American relations, but to my relief the others did not argue the point. We started off at ten o'clock that night. The engine did not seem to be running on more than six of its eight cylinders and we did eventually share the driving as it took us about 24 hours to make the trip.

On paper Le Mans looked like being a terrific race and it looked more than usually difficult to forecast the winner. Our Ferraris were all coupés, a 4.5-litre engine for Ascari and Villoresi, and 4.1-litre for Farina and myself and the smaller two again for the two Marzotto brothers, Giannino and Paolo. In addition, Tom Cole was sharing the wheel of his own open 4.1 with Chinetti. Alfa Romeo had a team of three 6-cylinder 3½-litre 230 b.h.p. cars driven by Fangio-Marimon, Sanesi-Carini and Kling-Riess. Lancia had three of the V-6 2.9-litre coupés, fitted with superchargers to give 240 b.h.p., with the drivers paired off: Taruffi-Maglioli, Manzon-Chiron and Gonzales-Biondetti. Briggs Cunningham had three cars with beam axles front and rear—a retrograde step made possible by the unnaturally smooth surface of the Le Mans circuit—and powered by 5½-litre Chrysler engines; drivers were Briggs and Bill Spear, Walters and Fitch and Moran and Bennett. Aston Martin had a team of 2.9-litre cars and Gordini had three, a 2.9-litre 8-cylinder and two 2½-litre sixes. Then there were the Jaguars, anxious to wipe out the memory of their failure the previous year; they had three works' cars fitted for the first time with disc brakes, in the hands of Moss-Walker, Rolt-Hamilton and Peter Whitehead-Ian Stewart, with a private entry from Belgium handled by Swaters and de Tornaco.

Yet in a few hours the costly and impressive Italian offensive had dwindled away into defeat, leaving Jaguars to finish first, second and fourth, with a Cunningham in third place. The only modest satisfaction left for the Ferrari team was a fifth place by the Marzotto brothers and a new lap record at 112.8 m.p.h. established by Ascari before his clutch failed.

My own experience of the race was brief enough. After 12 laps I suddenly found the front brakes were out of action. I stopped at the pits and we found one of the brake pipes had fractured. It was repaired, the brakes were bled, the reservoir topped up and I re-started, but two laps later I was called and told I had been disqualified for taking on replenishments before the permitted time. Obviously no pit manager could permit a car to re-start after bleeding the brakes without topping up the reservoir, and this was forbidden by the rules. Since then the regulations have been changed, so that brake fluid can be added when required and not only at the permitted intervals for petrol and oil replenishments.

Farina and I went into Le Mans for a night's sleep and when we got back to the circuit on the Sunday morning it was to learn the sad news that Tom Cole had just been killed at the White House. Tom was a popular and courageous driver who drove extremely fast, but some of us had been wondering whether perhaps his will to win was not forcing him to drive a bit faster than he should have done. Now he had made a fatal mistake on the one corner where there is no margin for error.

With no driving to do, the hours of that Sunday morning and afternoon dragged interminably, but I stayed on to see Tony Rolt and Duncan Hamilton win at an average of over 100 m.p.h. for the first time in the history of the race. After all the ritual of verification of seals, tools and spare parts on the cars, the garlanded finishers eventually escaped from the photographers and autograph-hunters and I got entangled in some of the British victory celebrations.

73

Some time later I emerged onto a deserted circuit, whence drivers, mechanics, spectators and officials had fled long since, and then I remembered that I had no transport. Our crippled race cars had been taken away in the vans and my own car was at that moment standing outside the Le Mans railway station, as I had lent it to Farina who had wanted to catch a train before the race ended.

There was nothing for it but to start walking. After about a mile I heard an old 2-litre Lagonda hurtling up the road behind me, so I thumbed a lift. The car screeched to an abrupt stop and I got in gratefully.

By way of conversation I said: "My father used to have one of these cars. They're jolly good, aren't they?"

It was a mistake; thus encouraged, the driver tried to demonstrate that what I had said was indeed true and went weaving in and out of the traffic at a furious pace. We went hurtling up to the backs of trucks, braking late, with all wheels locked, and it dawned on me that he too had been celebrating—and rather too well. Sweating with fear, I frantically tried to keep the conversation going in the hope it would slow him down.

"Jaguars did a good job, winning at that speed," I said.

"Yes, old boy," he replied, snatching another gear. "Drove those damned Ferraris right into the ground. Showed 'em how to drive."

I had struck the right note and for the rest of the way into Le Mans he told me with much elaboration and adjective and expletive how Jaguars had ground the pride of the Italians and their drivers into the dust. He got so interested in this that he forgot to drive so fast, which made me very happy, and I kept on agreeing with everything he said.

He was kind enough to take me back to my hotel and as I staggered out of the car, surprised but happy at having arrived in one piece, he said:

"Hope we meet again some time. We might have a drink."

"Yes," I said. "We might. Remember the name, it's Mike Hawthorn."

The effect was wonderful. His face seemed to subside like a load of cement sliding out of a wheelbarrow. Oddly enough we did meet again that same night and we had several drinks together.

Four days later the international racing circus reassembled at Spa for the Belgian Grand Prix, on the lovely circuit in the forests of the Ardennes. This is a circuit I enjoy for its immense variety of corners, from the slow hairpin bend to the fast sweeping bends taken in a drift at over 100 m.p.h., and also for the variety of up-and-down grades, which add to the interest.

This time my luck was out. Gonzales led for 11 laps, putting in one lap at 115 m.p.h., which showed that the Maseratis had found speed at least equal to that of the Ferraris, but he then retired with smoke rising from his engine, and soon Fangio also retired, leaving Ascari in the lead. This let me into second place, with Fangio somewhere behind us taking up the pursuit in Claes's car. I had been worried for some time by fumes from the fuel which were making my eyes smart and at 29 laps, with seven laps to go, signs of fuel starvation forced me to stop for a quick fill-up. This dropped me five places, but I got past Trintignant's Gordini and de Graffenried's Maserati again, only to run out of fuel again five laps later. I managed to pop and splutter my way back to the pits for another fill, but by now it was obvious that one of the flexible fuel pipes was leaking badly and I should be lucky if the car finished the race without catching fire.

It was a great relief as I braked for the hairpin at La Source for the last time. I was just sixth and then ahead were Trintignant and another driver. Trintignant waved me on and as we went into the corner I tried to nip by on the inside. Suddenly he realised who was driving the Ferrari; he knew that if I passed him he would be robbed of fifth place. He changed his mind about letting me pass and tramped on the accelerator as he came out of the corner. I did likewise, but there was a good deal of oil on the road; the tail came round and for a moment I had visions of charging ignominiously through the fence on the inside within sight of the finishing line; I eased up and had to be content with sixth place.

Fangio had a lucky escape nearly at the end of the last lap; trying to make up time on the Claes car, he lost control on a very fast right-hand curve and the car overturned in the ditch. He was extremely lucky to get away with cuts and bruises, for it is never a good thing to leave the road at Spa; there is always the little stone marking the spot where Dick Seaman's career ended in 1939 to remind us of that.

The next week-end was a busy one for I had to drive at Rouen, in a race which was a combined Formula 1 and 2 event, and then travel by night to take part in the sports-car Grand Prix at the Autodrome at Monza next day. At Rouen Ferrari took the opportunity of trying out the new 2½-litre cars which he was developing for the new Formula 1 starting in 1954. Farina and I had one each and, with no Maserati opposition, it was practically a walk-over. I went into the lead at the start, but Farina came screaming past and went into a winding down-hill stretch at terrific speed. He was almost broadside on three corners in succession and I held back expecting another Pau casino episode, but he held it and drew away. Later I caught up again and we finished only 1.2 sec. apart, which did not seem to please my friend particularly. However, he was overjoyed at having scored his first Grand Prix win for Ferrari and dashed straight off for the train to Paris without even changing out of his overalls.

Third place was taken by the veteran French driver Etancelin, driving what he said was his last race before retiring, but few people believed him as he had announced his retirement almost as many times as an opera prima donna. He wore a tweed cap back to front, as he had throughout his racing career, but to comply with modern regulations, he had a cyclist's crash helmet perched on top of it, which looked rather peculiar.

.   .   .   .   .

From Paris we travelled down by overnight sleeping-car to Milan for the Monza race. This was an event for sports cars up to 3-litres, run in two heats, the times being added to obtain the final result. The first four placings were the same each time; Villoresi, Bonetto (Lancia), Farina and I. Ascari was leading the first heat when he collided with an Italian woman driver and his car rolled over onto its side. Both cars were damaged, but not the drivers. The other members of the Ferrari team had 12-cylinder engines of 2,930 c.c., but I had a 2½-litre 4-cylinder, so two fourth places were the best I could do.

## CHAPTER NINE

## IN THE STEPS OF SEGRAVE

AFTER Monza, we went straight back to France for the French Grand Prix on July 5 at Rheims, where I was destined to become the first Britisher to win this great classic since Segrave won in 1923. I suppose whatever else I do, this will always be regarded as one of my greatest successes—indeed, a lot of people seemed to think it was one of the most exciting motor races ever run—yet it simply did not occur to me at the time; I was much too busy to think about it.

Up to a short time before the start it was very doubtful whether Ferrari would let us start at all, owing to an unfortunate incident during the 12-hour sports-car race which preceded the Grand Prix. The 4½-litre V-12 Ferrari driven by Maglioli and Carini was in the lead, and had set up a new sports-car lap record at 114.7 m.p.h. for the circuit which had just been increased in length to 5.19 miles.

In the early hours of the morning the car was seen to be running without side-lights before the permitted time for switching off and after a re-fuelling stop it was pushed for a short distance when it re-started. The Ferrari personnel argued that other people had also switched their lights off and the pushing at the re-start was simply to get the car clear of spilt fuel which might have started a fire. However, the organisers took the extraordinary course of announcing that no further times would be taken for the car, while still permitting it to go on running.

Eventually, after an extraordinary series of half-hearted—and incorrect—efforts to stop it the car was called in and withdrawn. Whereupon the French crowd booed and hooted and jeered in an extraordinary demonstration against the race officials. The decision was final, however, and the race was won by Stirling Moss and Peter Whitehead, driving one of the disc-braked C-type Jaguars which had won at Le Mans and that at almost the same average speed.

The incident aroused extremely bitter feelings and right up to the start of the Grand Prix we were uncertain as to whether we would be instructed to withdraw or not. Fortunately we got the go-ahead. The usual Ferrari team, Ascari, Villoresi, Farina and I, faced Maseratis driven by Fangio, Gonzales, Marimon, Bonetto and de Graffenried, and the ranks were filled up by H.W.M., Connaught, Cooper-Bristol, Gordini and Osca. Gonzales, who had started with his tank only half full, rushed off into the lead as pace-maker and in chasing him Ascari, Villoresi and I got involved in a private duel among ourselves.

At one point I passed Ascari and he shrugged his shoulders as if to say: "Take it away; I can't go any faster!" Positions were changing several times a lap. I had the lead and then Villoresi came past, and sometimes we would be hurtling along three abreast, at 160 m.p.h., down an ordinary French main road. It was a bit frightening to see the nose of one of the other cars come alongside, then drop back again as the driver decided he could not make it before the next corner. The cars were evenly matched and we could only get past each other by slip-streaming. The trick was to tuck in close behind the other man, get a tow from his slip-stream, ease back the throttle as far as possible without losing position, and then suddenly tramp on the pedal and use the sudden surge of urge to nip out and pass him. Whereupon he would try to get into position to return the compliment.

Shortly before half-way mark, Fangio and Farina caught up with us and then we really started mixing it. It was a situation in which the slightest misjudgment by one driver could have meant disaster for everybody, but even so, we usually managed a quick grin at each other when we passed—all except Farina, who sat scowling with concentration.

After 28 laps, Gonzales had to pull in for fuel and lost his lead to Fangio and I. We saw him just preparing to re-start as we passed the pits. Fangio and I now drew ahead of the rest of the group and began a private scrap which was to last without a second's respite for the remaining 32 laps of the race. At the time I did not dream that I had any chance of winning the race; I thought Ascari, Farina or Villoresi were just letting me keep Fangio occupied and were watching for the moment to come up and take over nearer to the end of the race. At one time I got in front of Fangio and as we accelerated away from the Thillois corner he dropped back several hundred yards, as though he had missed a gear change.

I thought: "Good, now I can disappear!" but as I went round the long, fast right-hander under the bridge after the pits, I found Behra right in front of me in the Gordini. I had to slow down for a moment and as I went past I spotted Fangio right on my tail again; the old wheel-to-wheel struggle began once more. Officially we were limited to 7,000 r.p.m with the Ferraris, but lap after lap I was getting 7,600 on the straight and the engine stuck it without missing a beat.

We would go screaming down the straight side by side absolutely flat out, grinning at each other, with me crouching down in the cockpit, trying to save every ounce of wind resistance. We were only inches apart, and I could clearly see the rev counter in Fangio's cockpit. Then once, as we came into Thillois, he braked harder than I had expected and I shunted him lightly, putting a dent in his tail. That shook me for a moment, for I thought it would take some living-down. "New boy shunts Fangio," they would say. But he showed no resentment at all; he just kept on fighting every inch of the way, according to the rules, in the way that has earned him the admiration and respect of everyone in motor racing.

I did have one anxious moment when he pulled across fairly sharply just as I was trying to come past on the right but I was quite sure it was unintentional. Another time we were running abreast when we came up behind a much slower car and I pulled right over, clipping the grass, so that we could pass him in line abreast. All this time I had no idea what was going on behind us, for the pit had ceased hanging out signals. I heard afterwards that the mechanics were jumping around gibbering with excitement and even Ugolini seemed ready to throw his pencil away.

About ten laps from the end, I suddenly thought: "Good heavens, I could win this race!" and I began to think out ways of crossing the finishing line first. If I came out of Thillois first, with Fangio in my slipstream, he could always find the extra spurt to beat me over the line. If I tailed him round the corner and stayed in his slipstream, I could probably spurt past him at the critical moment; but he was too old a hand to be caught by a simple trick like that. The only hope was to stake everything on getting into Thillois first and pulling out with a sufficient lead to keep him out of my slipstream.

Then I had a totally unexpected bit of luck. As we swung into the last lap, it suddenly dawned on me that Fangio had not changed down into first gear for the Thillois turn. Perhaps he was having trouble with the gearbox and could not get the gear in. Wheel to wheel we flashed round for the last time and I knew that everything was going to depend on perfect timing of that last change into first gear on the last corner. We were only inches apart as we braked, changed down and down again. Then I slipped into first, cut round the apex as close in as possible, straightened up the wheels and simultaneously slammed the throttle wide open. The engine screamed up to peak revs, but the tyres gripped; I gained the precious yards I needed and I was leading by a second as the chequered flag came down.

During the last lap I had realised, almost subconsciously, that we were no longer alone. Gonzales and Ascari had been fighting a second duel only a short distance behind us and on the last sprint for the line Gonzales, driving with colossal determination, had closed the gap so that he finished only a few feet behind Fangio. Ascari was only 3.2 sec. behind Gonzales!

Just to show how remote the driver, concentrating on his job, can be from what is going on round him I will quote what Rodney Walkerley wrote in *The Motor* about the end of the race:

"I shall not attempt to describe the final laps. The whole thing was fantastic. The crowd was yelling, the commentators were screaming. Nobody paid much attention to the rest of the drivers at all and the drivers themselves slowed up to watch this staggering display."

And *The Autocar* said: "It was a battle which exhausted even the spectators with its intensity and duration."

Yet, whenever I was able to give it a thought, I was chiefly worried because it must be rather a boring sight for the spectators, just watching two cars passing and re-passing. I was still concerned about having shunted Fangio earlier in the race, but as we coasted down the road after the finish, he came alongside grinning broadly and gave me the boxers' handshake, which made me feel a lot better. Then we stopped and I was engulfed in a fantastic reception. Maybe it had not been so boring after all.

I was not in particularly good form at the start of the race, because of the sports-car race dispute and the uncertainty about permission for us to start in the Grand Prix. Nor is the Rheims circuit one of my favourites. Made up of French main roads closed for the occasion and linked by sections of private road, it measures 5.19 miles to the lap. Its main features are two long straights, two acute slow hairpin corners and some very fast curves where spectacular four-wheel drifts are

My father and I reading an account of my victory in the 1953 French Grand Prix. [*Klemantaski*]

Mike Currie changing the plugs of his Frazer-Nash and (in the background) Don Beauman and Brit Pearce, my mechanic, with the Riley Sprite preparing for the Leinster Trophy Race.

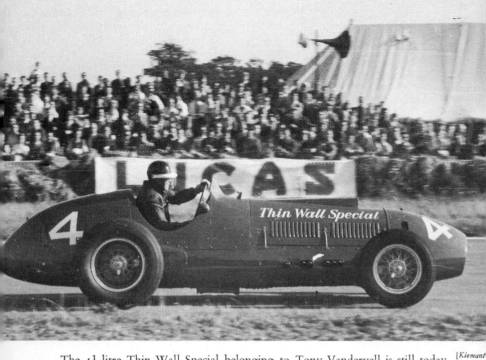

The 4½-litre Thin Wall Special belonging to Tony Vandervell is still today
potentially the fastest car for the Goodwood circuit; a beautiful car to drive.

[Kiemant

Winning the 1954 Spanish Grand Prix in the Squalo Ferrari, the first of this
model to be fitted with coil-spring front suspension.

[Su

possible at about 120 m.p.h., but the advantage gained on the fast corners can easily be lost if someone manages to get into your slipstream on the straight.

A lot of people concluded from the way I was crouching down in the cockpit that I must have been as excited as the spectators seem to have been. The possibility of beating Fangio was exciting enough for anyone, but during a race like this you have to concentrate so hard on saving every fraction of a second and on thinking out the next moves that there is no time to feel excited. I adopted a rather hunched driving position quite early in my driving career as most of the cars I drove were too small for me and I had to keep down to keep out of the wind. Gradually it became a habit and I tend to do it even when I am in a car which gives me room to sit back in the conventional modern position.

## CHAPTER TEN

## THE NUVOLARI CUP

TWO weeks later there was a full turn-out for the British Grand
Prix run over 90 laps at Silverstone. It was a Formula 2 event
and Ascari, Farina, Villoresi and I were there with 4-cylinder
Ferraris, opposed by the works 6-cylinder Maseratis in the hands of
Fangio, Gonzales, Bonetto and Marimon, with de Graffenried as independent, and teams of H.W.M.s and Connaughts, plus Cooper-Bristols
to make up the bulk of the field.

At the start Ascari, Gonzales, myself and Fangio made up the front
row and Ascari shot into the lead. He was never passed and finished a
clear minute ahead of Fangio, with Farina and Gonzales two laps
behind. I was still finding it difficult to make a good start and found
myself lying fourth, behind Ascari, Fangio and Gonzales. On the
second lap I was trying hard to catch up with them and came into
Woodcote Corner very fast. In a flash the tail whipped out so fast that
I felt I must have hit a patch of oil. It was no ordinary skid and, although I corrected mechanically, I was resigned to spinning. Then the
back suddenly held and as it whipped back I was taken by surprise.
Out it went again, but fortunately the car slid outwards, and not round
into the pits where there were quite a number of people standing. I
remember seeing a front wheel lift and praying that the car would not
turn over as it slammed through the little low marker fence, scattering
slivers of white-painted wood in all directions. Fortunately it stayed
right way up and continued gyrating on the grass right in front of
the crowded grandstand, while photographers ran for their lives. I
had managed to keep my engine going through all the excitement and
rejoined the race as quickly as possible, but fuel was splashing onto my
visor and getting into my eyes; I thought a fuel pipe had been broken.
Next time round, I stopped at the pits for a quick check, and the
mechanics closed the fuel filler which had been sprung open by the
impact. Fuel had been thrown into the cockpit and was swilling

about, but otherwise the car was quite undamaged, and ran perfectly.
I had lost a lot of time, but made up most of it and finished fifth.

.        .        .        .        .

It was one of those full-day programmes of racing which the
B.R.D.C. organize and the *Daily Express* sponsors so efficiently at
Silverstone and the finale took the form of a 17-lap Formula Libre
event. Fangio and Wharton were driving two of the supercharged
16-cylinder 1½-litre B.R.M.s and Fangio had made fastest lap in practice, but last-minute engine trouble had caused one of the familiar
B.R.M. all-night repair sessions and they were going to need a lot of
luck to beat the modified 4½-litre V-12 Ferrari, with Goodyear disc
brakes, called the Thin Wall Special, which Tony Vandervell was using
as an experimental vehicle before embarking on the construction of the
Vanwalls.

I was driving one of the 2½-litre 4-cylinder Ferraris which were
being developed for the next Formula 1 and I got away in the lead,
with a better start than I had made in the Grand Prix, but after Copse
Corner Farina came past in the Thin Wall and set a very hot pace. My
car quickly began to overheat and Fangio came past. On the fourth
lap the engine started to make terrible clanking noises, and as I stopped
at the pit it seized in a great cloud of smoke. The 2½-litres always ran
hotter than the 2-litre cars and we used to run them up to 130 deg. C.,
although we tried to hold them down to 120 deg. as far as possible.

The next lap Farina raised the Silverstone lap record to over 100
m.p.h. for the first time and stayed ahead of the two B.R.M.s without
difficulty until the finish.

.        .        .        .        .

I had to leave England almost immediately to drive in the Belgian
24 Hours at Spa on July 25-26. The Ferrari contingent were far the
strongest, with three 4½-litre cars and some closed models, opposed
mainly by Fangio and Sanesi on an Alfa Romeo, and some C-type
Jaguars. Everything went our way until the Marzotto-Maglioli
Ferrari broke its final drive during the night. When my turn came
to take over from Farina during the night hours, he came in very
depressed and announced that the magnetos were failing and causing
misfiring. He also thought that the battery was low and suspected
that the dynamo was not charging. I went off a lap behind the Ascari-

Villoresi car, and kept going as well as I could, until I caught up with Villoresi. I then switched out my headlamps and followed him on side lamps only. Sometimes he would draw ahead a little, and then I had to switch on the headlamps for a second to see where I was, so that I could spurt ahead and catch him again. As we were touching 170 m.p.h. in places, it was not very pleasant. I was also receiving signals from the pits telling me to put my lights on, so I had to remember to switch them on as I approached the pits and put them out again afterwards.

I was very glad when dawn came, but we found out afterwards that it had been a lot of wasted effort as the battery was quite all right. The magnetos were quite sound, too. The engine trouble turned out to be due to maladjustment of the new four-barrel Weber carburetters which we were using for the first time.

In spite of this we had built up a big lead and when I saw Villoresi standing by his car at the Stavelot Corner, I stopped to ask what the trouble was. He said his final drive had broken, and asked me to tell the pit and have mine checked at the same time. I was very lucky, for there was very little oil left in my axle and after it had been topped up I had to be careful with it.

Towards the end of the race I caught up with Guy Gale in the Ecurie Ecosse Jaguar which was in second position. They were many laps behind and had no hope of catching us and Guy had been told to take it easy so as to make sure of second place, so he waved me on. But I was nursing my axle and so I made no attempt to pass. Because I was behind him, he automatically speeded up and every time we passed the pits "Wilky" Wilkinson, who looks after the Ecurie Ecosse cars, was going nearly frantic trying to slow him down. We kept going that way until just before the finish and as I went into La Source hairpin I thought I would give one last burst of throttle to cross the finishing line, but just at that moment I caught up with a group of 1100 Fiat saloons. One of them pulled out in front of me and I nearly hit it. That made my second awkward moment at the finish of a Spa race within a few weeks.

. . . . . .

The following week we moved on to the Nurburgring for the German Grand Prix on August 2; it was one more stage in the ding-dong battle between Ferrari and Maserati which dominated the season's events. Ascari, who was always brilliant on this terribly difficult 14¼-miles mountain and forest circuit, had made fastest practice lap, getting down to a fifth of a second under 10 minutes, Fangio had lapped in 10 min. 3.7 sec., Farina in 10 min. 4.1 and myself in 10 min. 12.6, which put the four of us on the front row of the starting grid with Trintignant (Gordini), Villoresi and Bonetto (Maserati) behind us, then Marimon (Maserati), Behra and Schell (both Gordinis) and de Graffenried (Maserati). Moss had a new hastily built Cooper Alta, replacing the unsuccessful private-venture de Dion-axle car with which he had been struggling for some weeks; there were also two Connaughts and a collection of Veritas and A.F.M.

Fangio led at the start, with Ascari and myself right on his tail. Ascari was determined to get ahead and during the first few miles he nearly rammed Fangio as he braked for the corners with smoke pouring from the car. He managed it and had a useful lead by the end of the first lap, leaving Fangio and I to fight it out once more. I passed him in front of the grandstand, but he got past again and we went on passing and re-passing right round the course. At five laps I spotted Ascari at the pits and there seemed to be a certain amount of excitement, but I only learned afterwards what a narrow escape from disaster he had had, right in front of the grandstand. Coming up towards the pits on a part of the course which is fortunately fairly straight, he had lost a front wheel at about 140 m.p.h. and saw it go bounding away into the blue. He managed to hold the car straight and went screeching past the pits on three wheels and a brake drum. I think it was due to a hub nut coming loose. A mechanic ran after him with a jack and another wheel was fitted, but the braking was uneven after that and Ascari soon took over Villoresi's car; he set up a new lap record in 9 min. 56 sec. and was catching me up very rapidly indeed when the engine disintegrated.

I managed to stay in the lead for the fifth, sixth and seventh laps, with Fangio pressing me hard and then, as I glanced in my driving mirror, I spotted Farina passing Fangio. He was going like a rocket and passed me too, to take the lead, driving right on the limit. Then Fangio came past, too, and I simply could not match his greater experience on such a difficult circuit; I kept going as hard as possible to make sure of third place ahead of Bonetto and de Graffenried.

I like driving at the Nurburgring, which is the toughest all-round test of car and driver among the regular racing circuits. It has every kind of corner, from flat-out bends to the banked hairpin of the Karussel, and as it winds up and down among the Eifel mountains, one minute soaring towards the sky and the next diving steeply into the forest, with gradients up to 1 in 5, it gives transmission and suspension continuous punishment. Sometimes you cannot see where the road goes next until you are committed to the corner and the line you take on a given corner has to be modified to suit the next corner, and the one after that. Yet, from the point of view of spectator safety, I think there is a lot of room for improvement. After the Le Mans disaster of 1955 the Germans freely criticised safety arrangements at other peoples' circuits, but there are many points on the Nurburgring where a car could easily go through the fence into the crowd and in recent times two cars, Titterington's Jaguar, and a Mercedes 300 SL, have crashed into the car parks.

.    .    .    .    .    .    .

Mid-August saw us down at Pescara in extremely hot weather for the 12-hour sports car race. This was run over a long (15.89-mile) and varied circuit composed of main roads closed for the race. There is a very fast section by the sea, on the main road from Ancona to Pescara, and then the road climbs into the hills through a number of villages. The surface is asphalt and the heat of the sun had made many of the corners very slippery, so that the cars were sliding about quite a bit. It was an event for sports and gran turismo cars and we had two of the big 4½-litre works Ferrari saloons; one driven by Villoresi and Marzotto, the other by Maglioli and myself. Duncan Hamilton driving Peter Whitehead's C-type Jaguar led at the start, but by the end of the first lap our two Ferraris were in the lead and we kept them running close together. Progress became slightly erratic at times, as the heat was causing vapour lock in the fuel systems and the engines would cut occasionally. Eventually Villoresi had to retire with axle trouble and we went on to win.

Tazio Nuvolari, the indomitable little Italian whose exploits form some of the most dramatic pages in the history of motor racing, had died a short time before and a very handsome cup had been given in his memory. We had no firm arrangement among ourselves as to how we should share the trophies of this victory and at the prize distribution I managed to be at the receiving end when this one came up. It is one of those I prize the most.

A professional driver collects a great quantity of utensils of various shapes and sizes, not all of them made of silver or gold. After the first thrill has worn off, the collection becomes something of a liability. It takes up a lot of space, consumes many hours in cleaning and polishing and the best items offer such a temptation to light-fingered collectors who operate with jemmies instead of gear levers that they often end up hidden away in the strong-room of the bank. No one has hit on any generally acceptable alternative, although my collection now includes candlesticks, cocktail shakers and ashtrays. After many years of competitions some drivers have had their cups melted down and converted into something else. I believe Stuck made them into a top for a coffee table and a model racing car is another idea. Foreign silversmiths produce some striking modern designs for cups and trophies, but the English awards are unbeatable for quality and craftsmanship.

The biggest disappointment I have had over trophies has been at Spa. There is a magnificent silver statuette of an angel blowing a trumpet which is called the Winston Churchill Challenge Trophy, and goes to the first British driver home. The first man to win it three times keeps it. I won it with the Cooper-Bristol, and again with a Ferrari, but the third time I dropped out with exhaust gas poisoning. It was valued for insurance purposes at £500, but it would probably be a lot more today. Since then, Stirling Moss has won it twice and then Peter Collins won it once, so it is still circulating.

## CHAPTER ELEVEN

## THE PRANCING HORSE SHIES

BUT TO get back to the 1953 season; our next assignment was the Swiss Grand Prix on the difficult Bremgarten circuit at Berne. It is a fast winding main-road circuit through a forest which has seen many spectacular crashes. There are various changes of surface, it is often wet and the trees keep some parts of the course damp long after others have dried out; if you leave the road you are almost certain to hit a tree or some other solid object and on fine days the rapid changes from light to shade make it difficult to see clearly.

Personally I like the circuit, but the full two-day programme with motor-cycle and sports-car events before the Grand Prix meant that apart from the rubber and drops of oil which made the corners slippery, our race finished late, and we had the setting sun right in our eyes on the most dangerous part of the course. It was blinding on the straight past the pits and came filtering through the trees past Bethlehem Corner and the chalk pits which followed and on up the hill to the Eicholz bridge.

Before going to Berne I had spent a couple of days with the Maglioli family in their pleasant new apartment at Biella. Umberto was not married in those days and was living at home with his mother and father, sister and young brother. Unfortunately I had caught a chill on my stomach which was giving me a lot of trouble and the journey to Berne was a misery. I went to bed as soon as I got there and only got up to do a couple of laps' practice, so I had to be content with a place in the third row on the starting grid.

The race was one more Ferrari–Maserati duel, with H.W.M. and Gordini teams and various independents making up the entry. Earlier in the day there had been three motor-cycle races, every one of which had been won by a British rider, and a lot of British visitors were hoping I would win the car Grand Prix to make a day of it, but I had made a bad guess which made it almost impossible.

'It rained heavily during practice, as so often happens at Berne, and I found the axle ratio exactly right, but Ferrari wanted to put in higher gears to give us more speed for race day. I had talked to a lot of people and the general opinion was that it was almost certain to be wet on race day, so when Parenti, our massive chief mechanic, began changing the transmission gears, I insisted that I wanted mine left as it was. The matter was eventually referred to Ferrari, who said: "All right, so long as Hawthorn takes the responsibility for it."

To most people's surprise and my disgust, race day was brilliantly sunny and one of the hottest of the year. With my low ratio I fairly rocketed away from the slow corners, but the others could leave me on the straights. Ascari quickly took the lead, and I hung on in second or third position. After 40 of the 65 laps, Ascari had to stop at the pits for a few moments to have a magneto adjusted, which let Farina into the lead, followed by Marimon (Maserati) and myself, with Ascari fourth. Five laps later I passed Marimon and two laps later, when Ascari had passed him to put Ferraris in the first three places, the pit hung out the blue and yellow flag which means: "Stay as you are."

Up to then I had had practically no signals, but I was fairly pleased, as I seemed to be gaining slightly on Farina, despite the handicap of the wrong axle ratio. I now settled down to tail Farina home, instead of making a fight of it for first place, when suddenly Ascari, ignoring the pit signal, came screaming past both of us. Farina was furious and I was annoyed at being robbed of a certain second, and possible first, place, but by turning a blind eye and winning the race Ascari gained the points he needed to make sure of his second World Championship in succession. From his point of view he was probably wise, because he crashed in the last event of the series at Monza, and got no points at all.

The Ferrari team did not generally work out a detailed race strategy in advance. It was every man for himself from the moment the flag fell, but if the team established itself in a favourable position as the race developed, the team manager would hang out the "Keep Station" signal so that we did not risk breaking up the cars and throwing away the victory by competing against each other.

. . . . .

The end of August brought the 1,000-kilometre sports car race at the Nurburgring, where Ferrari had entered two 4½-litre cars; an open one for Ascari and Villoresi, and a closed one for Farina and I. However, the engine of the open car broke in practice, so the engine was taken out of my car and put in the open one; Ascari and Farina were nominated as drivers. This left me without a drive, but two great friends of mine, Don Beauman and Mike Currie, were there with a Frazer-Nash and one of our people from Farnham, Brit Pearce, was looking after the car for them. It was one of the Le Mans Replicas, with cycle-type wings, and the scrutineers refused to let it start until aluminium shields were fitted to join the wings to the body. With this and the usual last-minute adjustments, there was a lot of work to do, so we sent the drivers to bed the night before the race, while Brit and I settled down to work all night on the car in the Veritas workshop just behind the grandstand.

Amorotti, assistant manager of the Ferrari team, looked in and could hardly believe his eyes when he saw Hawthorn, thoroughly smeared in oil, putting in an all-night session of real work on a car. We got it finished soon after dawn and wakened the others, as the race started at the unusual hour of 7.30 a.m. so that it could be run entirely in daylight. It was a complicated event with a general classification and classes split up according to engine size for sports and production sports models; they all had to complete a certain number of laps, so that the race went on long after the winners had crossed the finishing line.

Morale was not very high in the Ferrari camp, as the three works Lancias, with Fangio, Taruffi and Castellotti among the drivers, had moved very fast in practice and were definitely quicker than the Ferrari round the corners. To make matters worse, the newspapers carried startling stories to the effect that Ferrari had decided to give up motor racing, but he had not informed any of the team personnel at the Nurburgring of his decision and they were left wondering what the future might hold.

The Lancias went away into the lead, but Fangio's was soon in trouble with a fuel pump, and when the other two cars came in to re-fuel, the batteries, which had taken a severe hammering, failed to work the starters. The Lancia mechanics tried to push-start the cars, but the officials stopped them and said they were disqualified. I believe Lancia found out after the race that they were permitted to push and a big dispute started up behind the scenes. The Ferrari then went on to win, about 15 minutes ahead of one of the Ecurie Ecosse C-type Jaguars driven by Ian Stewart and Salvadori. The Frazer-Nash was easily leading its class; but shortly before the Jaguar finished,

Beauman failed to appear and Salvadori told me the car was stopped at the roadside somewhere past the Karussel turn. We had an Aston Martin ready on the public roads inside the circuit, so Mike Currie, Pearce, Bob Chase and I got in and tore round to find Don sitting there disconsolately drinking a glass of water. He said the A-bracket locating the rear axle had broken, but I practically knocked the glass out of his hand and told him to get in and keep going. They had lost the chance of fourth place in the general classification, which had seemed possible, but he limped home fast enough to win the class.

I then left them and went back to Paris in my own Ferrari coupé, but on the way I had an encounter with a truck which stove in the side, so I left the car in Paris and came on to England by air.

My father met me and said: "I have some bad news. Mike has been killed."

Don Beauman was driving back to England in his Lancia Aprilia with Brit Pearce, and Mike Currie was following in the Frazer-Nash. Soon after crossing from Germany into Belgium, at night, they found an American car wrapped round a tree with the headlamps still blazing. It had gone off the road only a few seconds before. Two of the Americans had died almost immediately, but there seemed to be some hope for the third, so Mike said he would go back to the frontier post to call a doctor. The doctor eventually arrived, but after a while Don and Brit became worried about Mike who had still not returned. In the end they went back to look for him. At the frontier post they found the Frazer-Nash wrecked. Mike had failed to see the unlit pole barrier across the road and had crashed into it with fatal results.

I had known him for quite a time; we were good friends and he had bought the car from my father. Now he was gone.

It now began to look as if I was out of a job. Ferrari seemed determined to retire from motor racing, though the press commentators agreed that it would be disastrous for the sport. He pleaded that he was tired and needed a rest; he was known to be worried about his son, who suffered from chronic ill-health, and he even alleged that one of his draughtsmen had been smuggling drawings out of the factory for use by his rivals. But the real reasons only came to light later. He saw the possibility of having to compete against works teams from Alfa Romeo, Maserati and Mercedes before long, probably during 1954, and he particularly resented having to struggle on as an independent when Alfa Romeo was virtually state controlled. In his astute way he was putting on pressure to secure more tangible support for the Ferrari organisation, but we could only guess at the outcome.

. . . . .

My last event of the 1953 season as a member of the team was the Italian Grand Prix at Monza, that fabulous race in which Ascari, Fangio, Farina and Marimon went round in a tight bunch for hours on end with rarely more than inches between them. The two Maseratis had a very slight advantage in speed on the straight, but the Ferraris were just a little better on the corners and so they fought every inch of the way until the last lap of all when Ascari slid, Marimon rammed him, Farina swung wide and Fangio nipped through to win.

I had no part in all the excitement, as I had a bad car with a poor engine and was more or less pottering round. At one time I was even passed by one of the Gordinis with Trintignant at the wheel, but I got past him again, to take fourth place.

The prototype of the new Ferrari, later known as the "Squalo", which had been designed for racing under the 2½-litre limit in 1954, was fitted with a 2-litre engine and entrusted to Carini, but it proved very disappointing and it was a long time before the road-holding was right.

From Monza I went down to Modena where Ugolini asked me if I would sign up for the 1954 season. This was a bit of a surprise, coming so soon after Ferrari's own announcement that he was retiring from racing, but I agreed and after I had signed the contract I asked Ugolini what all these reports of retirement meant. He just smiled and shrugged his shoulders. In fact something was arranged, as it so often is in Italy. Official and unofficial interests got busy, Ferrari received some financial support, the preparation of the Squalos went ahead and the "retirement" was quietly forgotten.

. . . . .

I wound up the season by driving the Thin Wall Special for Tony Vandervell at Goodwood. It was fun to be driving this powerful machine on the track where I had had so much success with the Rileys and the Cooper-Bristol; I managed to defeat the B.R.M.s driven by Fangio and Wharton in two events, setting up a new lap record in the process, but very few people knew how narrowly I missed spending the day as a spectator with no car to drive.

During practice the previous day I was taking it fairly gently, as the engine had not been fully run-in after being rebuilt. Mr. Vandervell said I could open it up a little. I did—and it started smoking badly; when they opened up the engine, they found that the piston rings had seized in their grooves. No new rings were available, so they had to make do with a used set which had already been discarded and it became an all-night job.

I got to the course next morning to find no car in sight and it eventually arrived during the race previous to mine. The car was unloaded on the outside of the track and pushed across to the paddock, where it still had to have its plugs changed and oil level checked. With twenty-four plugs to change, this took time, and the other cars were already assembled on the starting grid for the Goodwood Trophy event.

The starter was about to raise his flag as I was pushed out at the bottom gate. We stuck the car onto the track at an angle slightly ahead of my mark; I stuck my thumb up to Fangio to see if he was happy about it; he grinned and nodded his head, the starter dropped his flag and we were away. My engine had three new pistons which had not been run in at all and we all wondered how long it would last, but the car went like a rocket, and set up a new lap record in 1 min. 31.4 sec., at 94.53 m.p.h. Fangio, who was having trouble with the gearbox, spun and retired, leaving Ken Wharton to chase me for the full 15 laps. The engine still held together for the Woodcote Cup 5-lap event and allowed me to beat Fangio on the B.R.M. by 6 seconds, although it was sounding rather rough towards the end.

It had been a wonderful year; in only my second full season of motor racing I had managed to keep up with the world's best drivers, on the fastest cars then running, I had won the British Racing Drivers' Club's Gold Road Star and the Seaman Trophy and Ferrari was telling people that I could be World Champion within two years. But it was going to be some time before things ran my way quite so smoothly again.

PART III

ILL-FATED YEAR

# CHAPTER TWELVE

## SOUTH AMERICAN PRELUDE

THE first race under the new Formula 1, which allowed engines up to 2,500 c.c. unsupercharged or 750 c.c. supercharged, and the first event counting for the 1954 World Championship, was the Argentine Grand Prix—three hours long, on a 2.4-mile circuit at the Buenos Aires Autodrome on January 17. I flew out and arrived in the late evening, and there were thunderstorms going on, with a great display of forked lightning, which seemed to be the normal weather whenever I arrived for the South American *Temporada*.

Farina and myself were driving Ferraris with Maglioli, who was being given a trial after some fine sports-car successes, and we had Gonzales in the team after his two years with Maserati. Fangio led the Maserati team, with Musso and Giletti; Behra, Bayol and Bordoni drove Gordinis; Mieres, Schell and de Graffenried had independent Maseratis, some with 2-litre engines; and Rosier and Trintignant had independent Ferraris. Ascari and Villoresi were under contract to Lancia whose new cars were not yet ready.

The new Ferrari Squalo with side tanks and a short chassis had been held back for further development after its disappointing appearance at Monza and the cars we had were the 95-inch wheelbase model developed from the Formula 2 2-litre cars, with the bore and stroke of the 4-cylinder engine increased from 90 × 78 to 94 × 90 mm., to give about 235 b.h.p. at 7,000 r.p.m. As usual, the four-speed gearbox formed a unit with the differential, behind which passed the tube of the de Dion axle. Front suspension was by double wishbones with a transverse leaf spring, which took no part in locating the wheels. Dry weight was about 1,430 lb.

Maserati had new cars using an enlarged 6-cylinder engine, with the same stroke of 72 mm. and bores increased from 76.2 to 84 mm., and they were said to be getting 250 b.h.p. at 7,400 r.p.m.

The Gordini 6-cylinder engine had been enlarged from 75 × 75 mm.

to 80 × 82 mm. and still retained its unusual valve gear, with the twin overhead camshafts operating the valves through rockers.

The weather was very hot and I was wearing my visor as usual, although it is often advisable to wear goggles in the heat. I was feeling thirsty and my throat was drying up; it was a great relief when it started to rain after about five laps. By this time, Farina, Gonzales and I were in the lead on the Ferraris, ahead of Fangio. Some of the other drivers had to stop for visors, and I went ahead and built up a lead of about 30 seconds in the wet.

On the corners, which were all fairly slow, I was lifting up my visor and letting the front wheels spray water over my face, which felt wonderful. We were using the same circuit as we had the year before, but driving the opposite way round. Going clockwise, as we did in 1953, there is a left-hand bend just at the end of the pits, coming after a fast straight, so the cars drift right up to the pits, which is very dangerous. When Ascari drove a Ferrari he was actually drifting flat-out under the canopy of the pits. Going round the other way, there is a climb from a left-hand corner which slows the cars down before they get to the pits.

Unfortunately we were not using rain tyres, with extra cuts which increase grip, and the course was flooded nearly two inches deep in parts. I came out of a corner at the beginning of the straight, thought I was clear of the flood water and put my foot down, but the car spun and the engine stopped. I coasted downhill to try to start it, but without success. Then some people arrived and gave me a push. I had lost half a lap, so I really pressed on, but going past the pits I slid again; a great gush of water went into the carburetters and the engine stopped once more. I walked back to the pits to find that instead of being listed as a retirement I had been disqualified for receiving outside aid. I had made the fastest lap of the race, but this was not credited to me either. I did nothing about it at the time, but at the end of the year I found that this single point would have enabled me to beat Gonzales by half a point for second place in the World Championship.

There was more trouble to come. While Farina was leading, Fangio stopped at the pits to put on rain tyres and the car was hidden among the helpers. There were certainly more than the permitted three mechanics. The Ferrari team manager protested and was assured that Fangio would be disqualified; Farina was slowed down, as there was no other challenge in sight. Fangio then shot past him and was acclaimed as the winner. The Ferrari protest was disallowed, first by the Argentine stewards and later by the F.I.A.

I did not drive in the 1,000 km. sports-car race the next weekend and I did not watch it as I was spending the time learning to fly at an aerodrome about 15 miles from Buenos Aires. This was the event in which Eric Forrest Greene was killed. His Aston Martin slid off the course early in the race, overturned with a full tank, and, before he could release himself, the fuel went up in flames. He got out with his clothes alight, but no one had the presence of mind to help him and he died from his burns the next day.

The *Temporada* concluded with the Buenos Aires Grand Prix, a Formula Libre event which brought out some locally-owned large cars like Landi's 4½-litre Ferrari, a 4½-litre blown Alfa and an old 4 CL 1½-litre Maserati to compete with the Formula 1 machines. The race began with Maglioli leading, Farina second and myself third, but after a few laps I managed to get past them both on the inside of a corner and stayed there until the last lap, with a comfortable lead. About an hour from the end the throttle started sticking, and, instead of closing as I approached a corner, it would stay slightly open so that I had to press like mad on the brakes and heave at the steering wheel to get it round. The heat was terrible, and I was rapidly getting exhausted, as were most of the other drivers.

Once as I approached the pits, I found several people waving at me and caught a glimpse of a shoe lying on the track as I went past. An Argentino driver had got into a slide there coming into the pits, got out of control, and struck Enrico Plate, the popular little Italian who ran a private team of Maseratis, killing him instantly.

I was wondering how much longer I could hold on and with great relief I began the last lap, still with a 20-second lead over Trintignant, who was driving one of Rosier's privately owned Ferraris. For some reason I started thinking how Ascari must have felt when he spun while leading on the last lap at Monza the previous autumn, and I thought how terrible it must be to have that happen to you. I only had one more corner to take before the finish; I changed down into third and then tried to change into second; but as I did so there was a horrible clanking noise. A connecting rod had broken, the back wheels locked and the car started to spin, sliding on its own oil. I missed the corner and slid off the course. I got out of the car and, dazed with heat, exhaustion and disappointment, I just fell on the ground.

I picked myself up eventually and staggered to the edge of the circuit, hoping to get a lift back to the pits. Just then Harry Schell's Maserati hit the oil I had dropped on the track and started to slide straight at me. Dizzy and dead-beat, I just stood there, thinking: "Now I'm going to be written off by another car", but he just managed to stop it in time.

Down the road, the man with the chequered flag had been waiting to flag me in as the winner and when I failed to arrive he was so surprised that he nearly let Trintignant go by without showing him that flag at all. Derek Davis, the Shell competitions manager out there, had my ciné camera to take me crossing the finishing line. He got the picture of the winner, but it was only later that he realised he had taken Trintignant and not Hawthorn. I had had a long run of luck, but it was beginning to give out.

. . . . .

Maglioli and I were hoping to drive a Ferrari at Sebring, so we decided to spend the intervening weeks travelling slowly up South America seeing something of the country. As we had no car, we had to use whatever transport we could find locally and at one seaside resort—I think it was called Punta del Este—the hotel kept a line of horses for the use of guests.

Maglioli and I decided to risk a trip on a couple one day; he selected a low-built job which kept his feet near to the ground, but I had a normal job. We went off into the woods, but after a while I missed him and found that his steed had taken him up the drive of a private house to the front door. The owners did not seem to find it very funny, but Maglioli knew a little Spanish and talked his way out of it. I was roaring with laughter, but in the middle of it my mount started walking backwards—and kept on, no matter what I did. In the end I had to jump off to stop it and get it started up in the normal way.

We got them back safely eventually, and although we were both feeling a bit stiff and sore I suggested we try again a few days later. Maglioli refused, as he was going to visit some friends in town, so he took a pony and trap and I followed on a horse; it went lame fairly soon and I had to take a stone out of its hoof, after which it refused to do anything but take me back to the hotel. I tried tempting it with bits of sugar, but it simply stretched out its neck for the sugar and then doubled back every time, so after a lot of pulling and tugging I gave up and asked for another horse which would really take me where I wanted. They gave me another, something quite different. No sooner had I set foot in the stirrup than it was off and nothing I could do would slow it down. Down the road we went, thundering past a Ford and a Jeep, with me, very frightened, holding on like grim death. It only slowed down when it got tired. I rested it—and myself—and then tried to start back for the hotel. It soon began to accelerate again, so I jumped off and led it the rest of the way, which must have been a couple of miles. That was the last time I rode a horse.

In Uruguay we spent most of our time on the beach or in the casino, where I lost money regularly, but we made an interesting excursion to an island just off the coast which was absolutely covered with seals. In small numbers, seals are amusing creatures, but among this vast mass— it was the mating season and fantastic battles were going on among the males, with bodies of former losers lying rotting on the beach and creating an appalling stench—we quickly lost our enthusiasm for nature study.

Like most fair-haired people, I get sunburnt very easily and suffer agonies from the blisters, so I used these weeks in the sun to try to build up a resistance to it, gradually lengthening the exposure. I put up with weeks of pain and eventually acquired a dirty colour which I hoped was the foundation of a handsome tan, but it all disappeared on the plane coming back to Europe and by the time I reached Italy I was my normal pink self.

In Mexico City we borrowed a car, and Maglioli was driving when a local driver cut us up rather badly and I shook my fist at him.

The character seemed quite annoyed and started to follow us, which upset Maglioli considerably.

When we had shaken off the pursuit, he said: "You must never shake your fist at anyone here, and never, never do this on your horn", playing a tattoo which is widely used as a friendly greeting in Europe.

I thought I was having my leg pulled and said: "Nonsense, old chap", but he was deadly serious, and went on to tell me about a friend of his who had got involved in a friendly scrap with another car the previous year. As they were rushing along, he played this tattoo on his horn and soon afterwards the other car stopped. When Maglioli's friend stopped too, the first driver went over, pulled out a knife and killed him on the spot. According to the story, the character was taken to court, where he explained what had happened. It was accepted that the horn signal was an insult which constituted a perfectly good reason for murdering someone and he left the court without a stain on his character. I found the whole thing fantastic, but I decided not to put it to the test.

From Mexico City we flew up to Miami, and then on to Palm Beach, where we were the guests of Isabelle Haskell, the American girl who has raced Oscas with considerable success. She lent us a Ford shooting brake to drive over to Sebring, which takes about 1½ hours. Ferrari had decided not to send a car over for us and had given us permission to drive another car if there was one available, but we could not find anything suitable, so decided to watch the race as spectators.

I was not very impressed with my first view of Sebring. It is an aerodrome circuit out in the wilds, with only two hotels, which were fully booked and very expensive anyway. The organisation was not very good and very few spectators arrived. In subsequent years the organisation was greatly improved by experience and much larger crowds turned up to watch. Stirling Moss had a room in a motel with a spare bed, so I moved in with him for the night, but we had an unhappy time as the sanitary system gave off a vile chemical smell.

The race was an amazing spectacle. A full works team of Lancias was there, with Ascari, Villoresi, Fangio, Manzon, Taruffi and Rubirosa as drivers, but they all retired, and Stirling came home the winner with a little Osca.

CHAPTER THIRTEEN

## FLAMES IN SYRACUSE

D URING this time a storm was blowing up in England over the
fact that I had not yet done my military service. I first heard
of it when I was in the Argentine, where the *Daily Mirror's*
New York office rang me to ask if I was going back to England. My
plans were to race at Sebring, if possible, and then return to Italy in
time for the Syracuse Grand Prix early in April, but I was told that
questions had been asked in the House of Commons as to why I had
not been called up. This came as a complete surprise to me as I was
on indefinite deferment and had heard nothing new about it during
several long visits to England.

"I have been given deferment," I said, "and I've had no call-up
papers."

The reporter replied: "Is that all you can tell me?" and I said "That's
all I know", but the debate was on and my case was soon being discussed with the utmost freedom in Parliament and in the press, by
people who knew nothing at all about it.

During my apprenticeship at Dennis I had the usual deferment which
was granted to all trade apprentices, but when I left the Chelsea College,
early in 1952, I had started on my season with the Cooper-Bristol and
was having more success than I had dared to hope; I applied for deferment until the end of the 1952 season and got it.

At the end of the season, of course, I had my crash at Modena, with
all the weeks in hospital which followed, and I was informed that I
would not be called up until I had passed another medical examination.
When Ferrari offered me a contract for the 1953 season, the fact that I
was joining a crack Italian team was splashed in the national newspapers, but I heard nothing more about the call-up. I left in January
for the Argentine season. When I came back to race at Silverstone,
a Ministry of Labour official came to see me and said: "We just want to
know where you are living now and what you are doing."

I replied: "I am living in Italy, and driving for Ferrari." I heard no more, although I was in and out of the country for races which were well publicised by press and radio and I was in England right through October, November and December, 1953. If I had been really trying to dodge my responsibilities I could quite easily have arranged to stay out of the country altogether.

No sooner had I left for the Argentine in January, 1954, than Mr. Kenneth Thomson, the Hon. Member for Walton, was asking how Hawthorn was able "to escape his call-up responsibilities". In view of the campaign which was being waged against me in some of the newspapers and the reaction this was producing among parents whose sons had been called up, he was only doing his duty, but I thought the reply by Mr. Harold Watkinson, the Parliamentary Secretary to the Ministry of Labour, was absurd.

"The difficulty in this," he said, "and in other cases of a similar kind is that a man has to be in this country for us to serve the call-up notice on him."

Not a word about the fact that I had recently spent three months in England and had never heard anything from the Ministry. People were given the impression that Mr. Watkinson's faithful sleuths had been watching for me at the ports and aerodromes for years while I skulked abroad, dodging the call-up.

Under continued pressure, Mr. Watkinson assured the House of Commons that he would be delighted to call me up "very rapidly indeed" if I returned to England, presenting the picture of a devoted public servant preparing to bring all the might of his Ministry into action against a persistent dodger. One question by a well-informed M.P. to ask why the Ministry had taken no action during the long periods when I was in England would have pricked this bubble, but there was no one to ask it.

Both my father and I were caught out by the speed with which I had become an international celebrity. We knew nothing about the innumerable ways in which celebrities—and politicians—become the subject of public controversies, nor were we particularly interested. I thought only of making a success of my job and proving that a British driver could beat anybody in the world.

I went on to race at Syracuse, while Father bore the brunt of the rising storm at home. Having repeated the facts to the reporters until he was tired, he tried writing and ringing up the Ministry of Labour to get them to issue a statement giving the facts of my deferment, but they blandly made the standard reply that they could not discuss details of individual cases, so the moment I arrived in Italy pressmen started pestering me to know when I was going back to England. I was justifiably upset over the Ministry's attitude and my replies were terse.

·  ·  ·  ·  ·

The Syracuse event was the first European race under the new formula and there were only eight starters; six Ferraris: including one of the new Squalos driven by Gonzales, and two Maseratis. I took the lead during the first few laps and was being pressed hard by Gonzales and Marimon when I missed a gear coming out of the hairpin bend, which I had taken in bottom gear. Having missed second, I engaged third and by the time I had built up the revs the other two had come past. I got past Gonzales again on the next lap and then went out for Marimon. I decided to follow him into one corner going a bit faster than he was and try to pass him as we came out, but seeing me on his tail he went in faster than usual and got into a slide.

There were low walls on each side, guarded by straw bales, and his back wheel churned along the bales like a chaff cutter, filling the air with dust and flying straw, which completely blinded me. I swerved to try to dodge him, but hit the wall with a bang. The filler cap flew open and fuel from the full tank slopped over me and down onto the hot exhaust pipe. With a great *whoof!* the whole lot went up and the blazing car, with me in it, well alight, slid backwards across the road and into the wall opposite. Somehow I leapt out of the cockpit, jumped over the wall into the field and rolled over to put the flames out.

Meanwhile Gonzales had arrived and, seeing the blazing car, he thought I must still be in it, so he jumped out of his car and dashed over to see if he could drag me out, although he must have known that my tank might explode at any moment. I thought he did a fine thing and we became great friends afterwards. Fortunately he spotted me in the field before he got involved in the flames himself. When he looked round again, his own car had slowly rolled into mine and they were both ablaze.

By the time they got me into the ambulance I was in shocking pain, but there did not seem to be anything to do to relieve it, so I had to stick it. I began to worry about the speed at which the ambulance was hurtling along; convinced that we were going to have another crash,

I yelled to the driver to slow down. Luckily he had to reduce speed anyway, because the road was jammed with the cars of spectators who were still arriving to see the race, which continued, with the drivers running the gauntlet of smoke and flame past the two burning cars.

Eventually, with the aid of the screaming sirens of a police escort, we got through to the hospital, where they rushed me to the operating theatre and found that I had second-degree burns on my left hand, wrist, elbow and both legs. They did not waste time cleaning anything, but simply covered everything with sheep's fat, a medicament that looks like Vaseline, and wrapped me up in bandages. I was then put in a private room and sank into a wonderful feather bed about two feet thick. But not to rest.

Just before the race there had been a lot of excitement in the papers about a statuette of the Madonna in a working man's home which was supposed to be weeping, and I had been taken along to see it on exhibition in one of the public squares. There was an old woman there selling white flowers and she had presented me with a sprig, saying: "Carry this with you while you are racing." I put it in my breast pocket and when I survived the crash word got around that it was because of the flower. People came streaming to the hospital to see me. No one stopped them and whole families crowded into the room, father, mother and the children, just standing there silently gazing at me. I was finding it rather a trial, but the strange thing was that the pain suddenly drained out of me through my legs and feet and I felt no more.

All the drivers came to see me, except Farina, who had won the race. He dismissed the whole thing with a shrug, saying that a few burns were nothing. He was not shooting a line, probably, for in the course of a long and brilliant career, interspersed with forty or fifty serious crashes, painful spells in hospital had become a matter of routine to him. He had broken most of the bones in his body at one time or another and I believe that when Piero Farnè, the Italian journalist, tried to get him to list what injuries he had suffered in each accident, he had to admit that there were three crashes where he could no longer recall just what he had broken. Oddly enough, at Monza a few weeks later, his propeller shaft broke loose, cutting through the fuel pipe and battery lead, and he found himself travelling at about 100 m.p.h. in a cockpit which was rapidly filling up with blazing petrol. He climbed out smothered in flames, had to jump for it while the car was still travelling quite fast and had a very bad time as a result of the burns and the injuries he suffered in skidding along the track.

Among those who did come to see me was Jenny Crosse, an English journalist who had been out in Sicily covering the weeping Madonna story, and she was a tremendous help in organising my removal to Rome and getting in touch with my father. She writes under her maiden name of Jenny Nicholson and was originally married to the late Alexander Clifford, the famous war correspondent of the *Daily Mail*, and later married Patrick Crosse, head of Reuters in Rome.

After one night in the Syracuse hospital I was put on the boat for the mainland and then handed in on a stretcher through the window of a sleeping compartment of the night train for Rome. Here I was taken to the Salvator Mundi hospital and wonderfully looked after by Dr. de Stefano, a dashing Neapolitan bachelor and a great car enthusiast, aided by a devoted staff of nuns. Several of the nuns were English and some of the young novices were Irish girls, so there was no language problem. Apparently the emergency treatment in Sicily had been exactly right and in Rome my legs were eventually patched up with skin taken from my back. My mother came out on the third day, but the shock affected her rather badly and they had to put her to bed in the hospital and look after her too.

As I got stronger I was given a pair of crutches so that I could hobble about a bit, but the pain under my armpits was excruciating, so I had a wheelchair instead. I soon worked out a few circuits round the corridors of the hospital and started timing myself round them with my wrist stopwatch, but it was decided that I was a menace to hospital staff, who might be carrying bottles or bed-pans, so the wheelchair was taken away and I had to persevere with the crutches.

I had a steady stream of visitors, and I used to go up to the ward above to chat with an English family named Hall, father, mother and two daughters, who had been particularly unlucky in a car crash. The husband had a cut leg, but all three women had fractures of the pelvis.

Isabelle Haskell came to see me and one day Reg Parnell looked in while on a reconnaissance run for the Mille Miglia. On the day of the race there was a knock on my door and in came Reg, saying: "I've done it, Mike." And so he had. Driving an Aston Martin, with Louis Klemantaski as passenger, he had lost the front end on loose gravel on a mountain hairpin and had slid into a concrete barrier, smashing the car to bits.

Signor Ferrario, the owner of the Quirinale Hotel, whom I knew quite well, used to come and visit me with his wife and when I was fit enough to move he very kindly invited me to go and stay at the hotel as his guest, returning to the hospital each day for treatment. My face had been scorched by the flames, and I had grown a beard and moustache, but they were not very successful, so I shaved them off when I was fit enough to move about again.

Jenny lent me a Guzzi motor scooter, which enabled me to get around and see a number of people I knew, but after one late party with Captain Johnny Johnson of B.O.A.C. and some other airline pilots, I found I was not nearly as strong as I thought and had some explaining to do to the doctor next day.

I rang my father from Rome and asked him if he thought I should come home. He asked how I felt and I had to admit that I was still far from well, so he advised me to stay on for another couple of weeks. That was the last time I was ever to speak to him.

I was learning that whatever its advantages, motor racing is a precarious occupation. The cost of putting me right after this accident was pretty high. The insurance company paid out something on my personal accident policy and Ferrari helped, but I was left with bills for several hundred pounds to settle, which were paid by Ferrari on condition that they were to be deducted from my earnings. As I had no retainer at that time, my income stopped while I was in hospital and I was anxious to start earning again as soon as possible; I went down to Modena and tried to persuade Ferrari to let me drive at Le Mans. He was not at all happy about it, but as they were just going up to Monza to try out a 4½-litre sports car and one of the Grand Prix cars, he invited me to come along and see how my legs reacted. I put up some good times on the sports car, and was getting round quite fast in the Grand Prix car, with no adverse reactions, when suddenly, as I was going down the back straight, fuel started pouring into the cockpit. It was ghastly; I could see myself going through all the pain and misery over again. I switched off the engine, flicked the gear lever into neutral and climbed up onto the seat, ready to jump as soon as the flames started. But they did not and I coasted round to the pits very worried indeed. A union nut had come off and the fuel pipe from tank to engine had just come apart.

This was a curious blind spot in the Ferrari organisation. They just would not secure these nuts by wiring them in the old fashioned way, or by any other method, and from time to time they worked loose. After this incident I took it up with some vigour and they promised to do what they thought necessary. They merely wound insulating tape round the nuts and almost the same thing happened to me in the Swiss Grand Prix.

As a result of the Monza trials, Ferrari agreed to let me drive a 4.9-litre car with Maglioli in the Le Mans race and I drove up to Paris en route for the race, with Maglioli in his Fiat 1100, on the Whit Sunday. We spent Monday and Tuesday in Paris and on Tuesday evening I looked in at the Bar de l'Action Automobile near the Etoile. The girl behind the bar said that Reuters had been trying to find me. They soon came through again and asked if I was going to England to see my father.

"Why should I be going?" I asked.

"Don't you know?" they replied. "He's had an accident."

It was obviously pretty bad, so I got through to the garage at Farnham and learned from one of the girls in the office that my father had had a car crash the night before; there was not much hope for him. The planes to England that night were fully booked but Bernard Cahier, the journalist, got me first refusal on the last plane of the day and I rang Farnham to say I hoped to arrive that night. They told me that my father had died a few minutes before.

One passenger failed to show up, so I got on the plane and I was met at the airport by my mother, Don Beauman and Sir Jeremy Boles. Pressmen and photographers were waiting in force, but the customs people were very helpful and whisked me into a special room from which we were able to escape by a side entrance.

On the way home I heard what had happened. My father was driving back in his Gran Turismo Lancia Aurelia after the Bank Holiday meeting at Goodwood. It was a black night with torrential rain and as he went round a corner in the Golden Valley, near Hindhead, I think his vision must have been obscured, he may have been distracted by the lights of a car coming the other way. Instead of straightening up, the Lancia continued turning, hit the opposite bank, flipped over, bounced on the bonnet of the oncoming car and cartwheeled down the road to finish up a total wreck with its wheels in the air. He was thrown out and never regained consciousness.

It was a heavy blow to me and having only been discharged from the hospital a few days, I was feeling pretty grim; when a police officer arrived on the morning of the funeral to serve me with three summonses arising out of an incident in which I touched a Post Office van parked on a corner, I am afraid I was very rude and slammed the door.

The newspapers were full of speculation as to whether I would receive my calling-up papers, but some writers were beginning to say that the whole thing had been overdone and I was being given a raw deal.

Said the *Daily Mirror*: "Mike Hawthorn, the racing motorist, has returned to Britain in distressing circumstances. His father has died.

"It is a sad homecoming.

"Four months ago questions were asked in Parliament about how Hawthorn was able to escape the call-up. The answer was that he could not be called up while he remained abroad. . . . Well, Hawthorn HAS returned. Should the Ministry now act? Of course they should—much as they must regret having to do so at such a time."

They then went on to attack Peter Collins and concluded: "Some young racing motorists seem to be blinded by their own haloes. Otherwise how could they imagine that driving foreign cars in foreign parts helps their country more than soldiering for the Queen?"

But John Gordon wrote in the *Sunday Express*: "Aren't we being a little inhuman to poor young Mike Hawthorn? He made a foolish mistake by choosing to go abroad rather than do his whack of National Service. And he made an even more foolish mistake by some petulant remarks on the subject.

"But is it really decent and necessary to greet him on his return in deep sorrow to attend his father's funeral by whooping gleefully 'Now we've got you, my boy'?

"And to add further to his distress by announcing that the local police propose to plant several summonses for driving offences upon him?

"As a citizen I feel a little ashamed. And I think many citizens will share that feeling."

Well, the call-up papers did arrive and I presented myself for another medical examination. When the doctors saw my legs they did not even bother to remove the bandages; they simply instructed me to report again in three months' time.

## CHAPTER FOURTEEN

## POISON GAS

I NOW had to make a vital decision about my future career and I was not sure what to do. Should I sell the garage and continue motor racing, or retire from racing and run the garage? It was my mother who solved the problem for me. Bill Morgan had joined us only a month before from H.W.M. and was proving a great asset.

"You carry on with your motor racing," she said, "and I will run the garage with Bill Morgan."

I knew perfectly well that, having just lost my father, she would have liked nothing better than to see me give up racing immediately, especially knowing how badly she was affected when she saw me in hospital in Rome, and I shall always admire the courage with which she faced up to that difficult decision.

.    .    .    .    .

She plunged into the mass of paper work required to settle my father's affairs and a few days later I flew out to Belgium for the Grand Prix on the Spa circuit. Only three makes of car were engaged, Ferrari, Maserati and Gordini. Farina and Gonzales had the new short-chassis side-tank Squalos, while Trintignant and I had the old type. Maserati had the new 250F cars with de Dion rear-axle for Fangio, Marimon, Mantovani and Mieres, while Moss and Bira ran as private entries. Behra, and the Belgian drivers, Frere and Pilette, had Gordinis.

Several of the drivers were feeling below par. I had lost weight and my left leg was still swathed in bandages; Farina's right arm, which he had smashed up in a crash in the Mille Miglia, was still in plaster and Stirling Moss was suffering from boils which made driving painful. In practice, Fangio lapped the 8.76-mile circuit in 4 min. 22.1 sec., which equalled the lap record he had achieved with the supercharged Type 158 1500 c.c. Alfa Romeo in 1951. Gonzales piloted me round the circuit for a lap, holding up his fingers to show where he was changing gear, after which I managed to clock 4 min. 29.4 sec.

On the back row at the start was de Graffenried, the Swiss independent, his Maserati carrying the crest of the fictitious Burano and a new nose containing a ciné camera for the purposes of that lurid but exciting film *The Racer*, which was being shot on various circuits that season. The film camera-men certainly got their money's worth, for as we roared away down from the start, over the Eau Rouge bridge and up the climbing turn on the other side of the valley, flames enveloped the tail of Mieres's Maserati and started licking the driver's back. He managed to get it onto the grass safely and escaped with only slight burns.

Fangio was caught out by the indecisive way in which the starter dropped the flag, so Farina and I led on the first lap, but the Gonzales car blew up immediately, Swaters also retired and Marimon had bent a valve. Fangio passed me and got involved in a terrific scrap with Farina in which they passed and re-passed each other several times in one lap until Farina's engine broke a piston. That left Fangio in the lead, with me second and Trintignant third. I knew I could not possibly catch Fangio, unless something happened to slow him down, and was concentrating on keeping ahead of Trintignant, who was about ten seconds behind. The shield over my exhaust pipe had come loose and the wind was lifting it up at the front. I did not take much notice of it at first, but I began to smell exhaust fumes. Then the pipe began to squirt hot gas onto my arm, which I had to hold out into the slip stream to cool it off. Suddenly I realised I was doing odd things, running onto the grass and sliding round corners in a most untidy way. On the left-hander before the descent to Burneville I touched the grass on the outside and I knew I had been gassed and was passing out fast. The rest of that lap was a nightmare; I was braking late, overshooting the corners, and driving like a drunk. I knew I had to get to the pits somehow and kept going as fast as I dared. I just managed to drag the car round the La Source hairpin, pulled into the pits and had to be lifted out of the car. The pit crew thought my leg was giving me trouble and before I could explain what had happened Gonzales had nipped into the car and was away. With his short-sleeved shirt, the hot gases playing on his arm soon told him what was happening, and he came in next time round for repairs.

In the pit Ugolini poured mineral water over my head to revive me

I take over Gonzales' Ferrari in the German Grand Prix, 1954, when he was [Klemantaski]
too upset to carry on after the death of his friend Marimon.

Understeer with the Super Squalo Ferrari in the Dutch Grand Prix, 1955. [Van Wijk]

Facing the cameras after winning Le Mans, 1955, in a Jaguar with Ivor Bueb; Lofty    [Dun
England is standing to the right of the picture, head and shoulders above every one else.

Fangio (Mercedes) breathing down my neck through the Esses at Le Mans, 1955.    [Klemantaski

and I was given milk to drink, to counteract the poisoning, but the doctor said that one more lap would probably have finished me. During the commotion Trintignant and Moss had gone past and Gonzales could not catch them, so Stirling won the Winston Churchill Challenge Trophy, which could have been mine outright that year as I had already won it twice before.

·     ·     ·     ·     ·

After the Spa incident Ferrari decided that I was still not really fit and ought to take a rest, so I was made reserve driver for the Super-cortemaggiore sports-car Grand Prix at Monza. This was a 620-mile event for sports cars up to 3 litres organised by Italy's big petrol company and had a very impressive prize fund. We had two of the new 4-cylinder 750S cars for Farina-Maglioli and Gonzales-Trintignant, but this was the time when Farina's propeller shaft broke in practice and the car caught fire at high speed. Farina was taken to hospital with burns which kept him there for months and I was then teamed up to drive with Maglioli. A spare car was produced for us, fitted with the 4-cylinder engine, but with a higher chassis and body than the works' team cars. Fangio and Marimon had a new 2½-litre Maserati and Behra was sharing the wheel of a 3-litre disc-braked Gordini with Paul Frere.

During the early part of the race, rain fell in torrents and while I was ploughing through the flood water on the corner, which is now known as the Ascari corner, because he was killed there, Marimon caught me up, going much faster than I was. He suddenly caught sight of me through the cloud of spray, got into a skid, spun round several times and finished up among the trees, which can easily be fatal at Monza. Luckily he encountered nothing more than a few saplings and continued almost without a pause.

Driving conditions were very bad; it was difficult to see ahead and I could see nothing but a cloud of spray in the driving mirror, but I managed to hold the average at over 100 m.p.h., pursued by Gonzales, who put in one lap at 109. Behra was pressing us with the Gordini, which was only making one fuel stop to our two, and when I handed over to Maglioli at our first stop, the Gordini took the lead, but ultimately retired with a broken rocker shaft. Gonzales lost a lap having a sticking throttle attended to and when I took over from Maglioli for the last spell it was obvious that we must win, barring accidents, but after such a long run of bad luck, I felt something was bound to go wrong and I had a thoroughly miserable drive waiting for something to happen. Nothing did go wrong and we won at an average of 100.63 m.p.h.

The Supercortemaggiore race has since proved to be a lucky one for me and as it has such a fabulous prize fund, people think I must have made a lot of money out of it. Very little, if any, starting money is paid, but the prizes total about £23,000. What most people do not appreciate is the fact that the big money (first prize £8,300) is reserved for the manufacturers and it is only awarded to recognised manufacturers building cars for sale; it does not go to an amateur who builds his own car and happens to do well. The prizes in the general classification, from which the drivers take their cut, are only a tenth as much, but there is a prize of about 8 gns. for the leader of every lap. Half of this went to Ferrari, too, so Maglioli and I shared about £750. But for me the important thing was that I had won a race again and overcome that loss of confidence which comes when you feel that your luck is out.

. . . . .

The sole topic of conversation in motor-racing circles now was the new Mercedes which were due to make their first appearance in postwar Grand Prix racing in the French Grand Prix at Rheims on July 4. Fangio, who had been trying them out in a private test over the Rheims circuit, had already told me they were quite fantastic and when they arrived at the circuit for official practice they certainly looked it. With streamlined all-enveloping bodywork, intricate tubular chassis, 8-cylinder fuel-injection engine with desmodromic valve gear canted on its side, five-speed gearbox, vast front brakes mounted on the chassis and connected to the wheels by universally-jointed shafts and pivot swing axles at the rear, located by Watt linkages, they were infinitely more complicated than any existing Grand Prix car and soon showed themselves to be very much faster. I tried to take a look at one at the pits, but was roughly shoved aside by Neubauer, the mountainous Mercedes race director; I had my revenge by shooting him up as closely as possible when I took off to start my own practice laps, which gave the French crowd a laugh. Both Gonzales and I had the side-tank Squalos and I had not been going long when smoke started pouring from my engine. We found that an external oil pipe leading to the camshaft had broken, pouring oil onto the exhaust pipe, which had started a small fire. It happened to us twice in practice and caused Gonzales to retire in the race, when he spun with smoke belching from the bonnet. This was a bad beginning, because we needed to have absolute confidence in the cars if we were to hold off the German challenge.

Ascari and Villoresi were under contract to Lancia, whose new cars were not yet ready to race, so Gianni Lancia released them to drive for Maserati; otherwise there would have been no Italian drivers in this important event. Ascari managed to secure a place on the front row at the start, alongside the Mercedes of Fangio and Kling, Gonzales was in the second row with Marimon on a Maserati, and I was in the third rank with Herrmann on the third Mercedes and Bira on his Maserati.

The Squalos did not steer well, and felt very peculiar in the corners; from the moment the race started I felt uneasy. I had a premonition that something was going to go wrong and wished I could have stopped there and then. The three Mercedes drew away from us, with Ascari and Gonzales in pursuit, followed by me in sixth place, but my brakes were locking badly and smoking and Marimon caught up with me. Ascari's engine broke up almost immediately and at ten laps, just as I was going into the right-hand corner after the pits, I felt something go. It was not a loud noise, but the car did not feel right, and in a split second I switched into the escape road. I was doing about 150 m.p.h. and put my brakes on, but nothing happened; the car did not seem to slow down at all, but a great cloud of smoke came up, and it was obvious the engine was finished. This really shook me because I was hurtling towards a pole barrier across the end of the road and I knew I could not pass underneath it—I had tried it before the race when I drove onto the circuit that way and knew it could not be done. The left side of the road was lined with spectators, so I tried to swing the car into the field on the right, but it did not answer the steering either. I was now heading for a really bad crash, the barrier was coming towards me at a frightening speed and I could not think of anything else to do; no brakes, no engine and apparently no steering—I simply pulled the wheel over as hard as I could and held it there. Mercifully the car started to spin and stopped within a couple of feet of the barrier. The engine had completely blown up, a connecting rod had come through the side of the crankcase and oil was pouring out over the road and over the rear tyres, so that the car had just been sliding along on its own oil.

I started walking back, picking up hot bits of piston and crankcase which were liberally strewn over the road. In spite of this, various characters came rushing up to ask what had happened; I told them something had gone wrong with the brakes.

Two laps later Gonzales was out with a broken oil pipe and one by one the remaining cars capable of challenging the Mercedes dropped out, leaving Fangio and Kling to win easily.

This first brief encounter had shown that the Mercedes, with their streamlined bodies, possessed marked superiority in speed on the long straights of the Rheims circuit, but we drivers were not unduly worried, as we felt confident that we could still match them on a more twisty circuit where road holding and braking were more important; two weeks later, we were able to prove it.

.    .    .    .    .

Meanwhile the Ferrari team had a date at Rouen, for the Grand Prix on the Les Essarts circuit, where we had a fairly easy job, being opposed only by the Gordinis, which were chronically unreliable, and a number of independents. I took the lead, with Trintignant second, and as time went on we made a race of it, passing and re-passing each other. When I stopped for fuel, which we had to do as the race was of three hours' duration, Ugolini told me that Trintignant was to win. I was rather annoyed at this as I was the senior man and had had a bad season, with no successes other than the Supercortemaggiore sports-car race, while Trintignant had only recently joined the team. He was given a quicker fill-up than mine and went on ahead, so I put on a spurt for a few laps and caught up with him. As I went past I held up two fingers and pointed to myself to show that I was going to be second, and then held up one finger and pointed to him. He nodded his head and I went ahead.

I built up a bit of a lead and was beginning to have a struggle with my conscience about letting Trintignant overtake me again when there was a loud bang and another connecting rod came through the side of the engine; once again I had to take to an escape road, but this time I managed to stop without a lot of drama.

There was a lot of prize money and it was important to finish, so I thought I would try and get the car back on the course and push it to the finishing line. I turned it round and got it back onto the track, but I just did not have the strength to push it up the gradient which followed.

Meanwhile, I noticed that the maximum recording needle on my rev. counter stood at 7,600. Now we had been warned before the race that the engines were still rather fragile and Ugolini said we must on no account go over 7,200 r.p.m. I must have let the revs. rise too high in my anxiety to make a good getaway at the start, but I just could not face the row there would be if they saw this at the pits, so I borrowed a pair of pliers from a fireman and turned the needle back to 7,350, which seemed a more reasonable figure.

I then signalled to Trintignant, pointed to the back of my car and indicated that I wanted a push. Next time round he gently pushed me until I was clear of the hump and went on, but he damaged his clutch in the process and towards the end could hardly change gear, so that we nearly ruined two cars. Nor did it avail us anything, for although I got to the finish, I was disqualified for receiving assistance. To round it off, there was such a row when Ugolini saw my rev counter that I felt it could not have been worse if I had left it at 7,600. It was made quite clear to me that if I broke another engine at Aintree the next week-end there were no more available and I could consider my season at an end.

I then went back to England for the second time since my father's funeral, but by now no one seemed to be interested in the question of my military service. For the time being it had ceased to be news.

## Chapter Fifteen

## THE MERCEDES CHALLENGE

FOR THE British Grand Prix at Silverstone on July 17, there was an all-star turn-out to do battle with the Mercedes-Benz team for the second time. Fangio and Kling, on two of the streamlined Mercedes which had been used at Rheims, faced Gonzales, Trintignant and I on Ferraris, Ascari, Villoresi, Marimon and Mieres on Maseratis, Behra, Pilette and Bucci, another recruit from the Argentine, on Gordinis, several Connaughts and a number of independents, including Stirling Moss and Bira with their Maseratis.

During practice it was obvious that the Mercedes Silver Arrows were very difficult to handle on the fast swerves of the Silverstone circuit and although Fangio put up fastest lap in 1 min. 45 sec., at 100.35 m.p.h. unofficially beating Farina's record with the Ferrari Thin Wall Special, it looked very dangerous and was only done at a cost of a badly crumpled front wing through contact with one of the marker drums. The Maseratis did not arrive in time for official practice and so were relegated to the back two rows at the start.

Our Ferrari were the old type and after practice, Gonzales said to me: "Our axle ratio is too high for this circuit." We could just about hold our own on a dry track, but if it rained we would lack acceleration, and rain threatened on race day.

I saw no smiles among the drivers at the start, for we all knew it was going to be a tough struggle. There was some last-minute excitement when Villoresi's Maserati was found to be losing oil from a broken oil pipe and a spare car was substituted in the nick of time.

Kenneth Evans dropped the flag and Gonzales streaked away into the lead. For the first few laps I was second, followed by Fangio, Moss, Behra, Marimon and Kling, but at five laps, Fangio came past me and went in pursuit of Gonzales. Then Stirling closed up and came past. I took him again, but I simply could not hold him on acceleration; he drew ahead gradually, while I fought for every foot to stay with him. The rain became heavier, but if it was holding me back, it was affecting Fangio more and the sliding Mercedes was tossing marker drums into the air until both sides of its snout were crumpled.

There was pandemonium in the pits and I never saw so many pit signals. Neubauer was frantically trying to speed up his two Mercedes and getting no response. The two drivers, their faces blackened by a mixture of oil and dust from the brake linings, were having a rough time and Fangio seemed to be in trouble with his gearbox—the gear change worked the opposite way to normal and they eventually had to fit a complicated system of sliding guards to help drivers to engage gears in the correct sequence. At fifty-five laps, Stirling took Fangio; two laps later I lapped Kling and got past Fangio, overtaking the two Mercedes in quick succession. I was still working hard to keep Stirling in sight when ten laps from the end his Maserati broke a drive shaft— one more dose of the bad luck which haunted him that year. So Gonzales and I finished first and second, with Marimon third and Fangio fourth.

For the drivers it had been a grim, hectic struggle on a track which was sometimes wet, sometimes dry, and sometimes a little of each. But we had avenged the Rheims defeat and the twelve bottles of champagne which the Germans had brought to celebrate their victory remained unopened behind the pits.

. . . . .

The Mercedes-Benz équipe withdrew to Germany to start testing a new version of the Silver Arrow with exposed wheels and unstreamlined body on the Nurburgring in preparation for the Grand Prix of Europe on August 1, a race which they simply dare not lose, while we went down to Lisbon for the Sports Car Grand Prix of Portugal. The race was held on the $3\frac{1}{2}$-mile Monsanto circuit in the hills to the north of the city which has one straight of about $1\frac{1}{2}$ miles along a main road, followed by a continuous succession of corners and gradients, which keep the average speeds down.

Gonzales and I had two of the 750S 3-litre cars and the chief opposition came from the young American, Masten Gregory, in a 4.5-litre Ferrari. Despite our smaller engines, the terrific low-speed punch of the four-cylinder engines gave us better acceleration out of the slow corners and Gonzales and I went into the lead, until he spun, leaving me first, with Gregory second. However, Gonzales was determined to win and he broke the lap record at 85.8 m.p.h., to catch us both and finish 14 sec. ahead after 202 miles.

.    .    .    .    .

After another short visit home to give a little help at the garage, I went out to the Nurburgring for the premier event of the year, the Grand Prix of Europe.

We drivers stayed at the Sport Hotel, which forms part of the grandstand, and in the evening we used to go down into the cellar to play skittles. This time, we played after the first two days of practice and Marimon did wonderfully well, but he always pitched the ball instead of rolling it and he had his leg pulled quite a bit.

Saturday was the last day of practice, and I was going fast down that long twisting hill after the Kallenhard, when I glimpsed a hole in the hedge on the outside of a corner and two straight black skid marks leading up to it. I knew someone had gone over the edge, and at this particular point there would not be much hope of survival. I carried on to the pits and found everyone upset because Marimon was missing. I mentioned the hole in the hedge and the two black marks on the road. Gonzales jumped straight into the 3-litre sports car we used to put in extra practice and tore round the circuit to see what had happened, but when he got there Marimon was dead, killed instantly as his car somersaulted down the bank. This cast a great gloom over all the drivers, for he was very popular, but especially over the little Argentine contingent and Gonzales broke down completely. It was all the more sad, because his father had flown over from South America to see him drive in the big race of the year.

I think he probably died trying to approach the time put up by Stirling Moss, whose Maserati was third fastest in practice after Fangio's Mercedes-Benz and my Ferrari. He had questioned Stirling about the gears he used for various parts of the circuit and Stirling had said that he went down this hill in second, but Marimon thought he could gain a little time by snatching third gear before braking and changing down again for the next corner. The car was found in third gear after the crash. He had also had trouble with a sticking throttle and some people thought this might have been the cause, but I was told that there was no defect on the car afterwards.

Maserati decided to withdraw their cars as a mark of respect, but this only affected Villoresi's car in the end as other drivers started as independents. Mercedes-Benz had three new cars with square-cut un-streamlined bodies and exposed wheels for Fangio, Kling and pre-war ace Lang, and a streamlined one for Herrmann. Gonzales, Trintignant, Taruffi and I were on Ferraris, Behra, Frere, Bucci and Pilette had Gordinis, and Maseratis were driven by Moss, Mantovani, Mieres, Bira and Schell.

I made one of my bad starts and got caught behind some slower cars going round the South Curve, while Gonzales, Fangio, Moss and Kling went ahead. Stirling's engine broke up almost immediately and by the third lap I was fourth, behind Fangio, Gonzales and Lang. I was gaining on the Mercedes, when I felt the familiar shock as I approached a nasty right-hand turn. I immediately thought it was another engine failure which meant oil on the tyres and the car running amok. Gingerly I touched the brake pedal and the car slowed; thank heaven, it was transmission failure, and having got over the shock, I could hear the noise of the broken drive as the car clanked to a stop.

Walking back to the pits, I saw that Stirling was missing and I could see that Gonzales, terribly upset by Marimon's death, was dropping further and further back. I reported to the pits and asked could I leave, but Ugolini said: "Wait, we might want you to take over from Gonzales"; I replied: "If you do, do it now, because he is losing ground all the time," but Ugolini decided to wait until two-thirds distance, when the tank was topped up with fuel and we changed drivers. I passed Kling's ailing Mercedes to take second place, but by then could not challenge Fangio. However, with my car second and Trintignant third, the simple old-style Ferraris, developed at modest cost from the 2-litre cars of the previous formula, were not yet completely outclassed by the new technical wonders built at fabulous expense in Stuttgart.

· · · · ·

The fourth round of the battle was at Berne, where we assembled for the Swiss Grand Prix. Manzon, the French driver, was being given a trial in the Ferrari team, but during practice, the tricky behaviour of the Squalo on the wet course defeated him, and he crashed, smashing the car, but suffering no serious damage himself. That left Gonzales and I with the old-style cars which we much preferred and Maglioli driving a spare Squalo. Ascari and Villoresi were still waiting for their Lancias, and did not compete, so the main hope for Maserati was

Stirling Moss, but among the other Maseratis was the 250F owned by the Owen group, and driven by Ken Wharton, with Dunlop disc brakes and special wheels which were being tried out for the B.R.M. There were also a couple of Gordinis.

Mercedes brought three unstreamlined cars, with Fangio, Kling and Herrmann as drivers, but this time Fangio could not manage fastest practice lap, which went to the credit of Gonzales who was in terrific form once more. In the race, however, there was never any doubt about it; Fangio led from start to finish.

Although based on the old chassis, Gonzales's car was a new one with a high tail fairing; it was very smooth, very pleasant to drive and held the road much better than mine, but being then Number 1 driver of the team, he naturally had first choice of the available material. He started off at high speed, second to Fangio, but once again I made a poor start. I started to catch up and could see Gonzales and Moss ahead of me, but going up to a nasty right-hand corner on a damp surface in the woods, I braked, tried to turn and went straight on. By now I suppose I was a bit jumpy and immediately concluded that the worst had happened, the steering had broken. In a split second I caught sight of one of the front wheels—an advantage of the conventional type of single-seater—and saw that it was locked. I released the brakes and scraped round. It happened again several times and I dropped back, but as the brake bedded down the trouble disappeared and I passed both Gonzales and Stirling to get into second place. I was gaining on Fangio, too, and could see the agitation growing in the Mercedes pit, when the engine started misfiring and I smelt petrol. I stopped at the pits and found that another of their unsecured union nuts had come undone. Lampredi, the chief designer, who is normally an equable sort of person, flew into a towering rage to see the car stopped by such a trivial fault. I re-started, but soon afterwards the engine stopped and I managed to get the car to a standstill without any trouble. I took a look at the engine to make sure there was no escaping oil and no holes in the crankcase and then set off to walk back to the pits through the woods in the centre of the course. These woods are barred to the public during the race and the Swiss police use fierce Alsatian dogs to enforce the ban. One of them went for me, snarling and snapping, and it took the policeman in charge of it some time to calm it down. Life as a professional racing driver has lots of risks which have nothing to do with motor cars.

I got lost in the woods and it was about half an hour before I got back to the pits, where I got a cool reception. Speaking French, which we always did together because his English is about as good as my Italian, Lampredi said in effect: "Right, let's have it! What did you break?" I said I thought it was fuel-pump failure, but he looked at me with frank disbelief and said: "Come on, is it another rod through the side?" I persisted that it was the fuel pump, and afterwards he apologised, because he found that the fuel pump drive had sheared.

Again Fangio had won, again Gonzales had chased him home and this time they had lapped every other car on the course. The combination of Fangio and the new Mercedes was proving invincible, but there was obviously no one else in the Mercedes team who could do anything like as well.

. . . . . .

To strengthen the Italian teams for the Italian Grand Prix at Monza, Ascari joined Ferrari and Villoresi went to Maserati. Gonzales had one of the Squalos which had been modified, and was holding the road much better, while Ascari had one of the old-type cars with a Squalo engine, which had a different bore and stroke and different cylinder head from the engines we normally used. Trintignant and I had the old-type cars, but the rear tyre size had been increased from 6.50-16 to 7.00-16 and the axle ratio lowered to make up for it. This completely changed the handling characteristics for the worse. I protested about it, but they said using the smaller tyres would make it essential to stop for a wheel change before the end of the race. We just could not contemplate this, so I had to put up with it, but it gave me a very unhappy ride, and I took no important part in the early stages of the race.

For this circuit, Mercedes had gone back to the streamlined cars used at Rheims and Silverstone, but they seemed to be as difficult as ever to handle and Fangio made some large excursions onto the grass in his efforts to keep up with the Ferraris and Maseratis. Ascari and Gonzales soon took the lead from Fangio, then Fangio closed up again and Moss also passed Ascari, who missed a gear in his efforts to get back, sent the revs sky-high and broke a valve. When he came into the pit, Ascari was almost in tears, for he was convinced that on this circuit he could have beaten the Mercedes and subsequent events showed that he was probably right.

After 20 laps, I was only in sixth position, feeling my way round the corners behind Ascari, Fangio, Moss, Villoresi and Kling. Then Kling shot off the track at high speed with broken suspension. Villoresi retired with clutch failure, Gonzales dropped out when a valve dropped in and Moss took the lead. Peter Collins had worked into sixth place with the Vanwall, so we now had three British drivers in the first six and Stirling was steadily increasing his lead. But once again the fantastic Moss jinx, 1954 model, struck again. He stopped for oil, came past spraying me with it, suddenly realised what was happening and finished pushing the car to finish tenth. A broken pipe union on his oil tank had robbed him of what seemed a certain victory. So once again I finished second to Fangio with Gonzales, who had taken over Maglioli's car, in third place and Herrmann on the remaining Mercedes fourth.

. . . . . .

It was back to sports cars again for the R.A.C. Tourist Trophy race at Dundrod in Northern Ireland. We sent over two 750S 3-litre cars, while Lancia sent two of their open 3.3-litre cars with trailing-arm front suspension and inboard brakes at front and rear and two of the later 3.8-litre type, which still had V6 engines with four overhead camshafts, but had wishbone front suspension and all brakes mounted on the wheels. Jaguar sent one 3.4-litre D-type, and two experimental 2½-litre cars to take advantage of the handicap. All the big entry started together, but the smaller cars started with credit laps according to their engine size. We did not rate our chances very highly because of the handicap, the narrow roads and the presence of a lot of little cars going right down to D.B.-Panhards and Renaults.

Gonzales had never seen the course before, so Ugolini asked me to pilot him round for a lap. I started off with a slow lap and then speeded up a bit. Gonzales fell behind, so I drew in at the pit and Musso stopped his Maserati to say that Gonzales had crashed in braking for the right-hand turn at Tornagrough. I raced round and arrived just as he was being put on a stretcher. He had apparently lost control while braking, hit the bank and been thrown out. When I got there, he realised he had had an accident, but had no idea where he was, so I went with him to hospital in the ambulance.

On the way he said: "This is the end, Mike. No more racing!"

I had been through this stage so I said: "Don't worry, we all feel like that, but you'll change your mind in a couple of days."

It was quite a job manoeuvring his enormous bulk on to the table for the X-ray examination; he had a great bump on his shoulder, his knee was black and he was badly bruised. When it was done and he was put to bed, the doctor came and told me he had a dislocated shoulder, but no bones were broken. He added: "The funny thing is that there's hardly any fat on him at all. He's all muscle."

This misfortune was followed by the news that Maglioli's mother had died, so he had to return to Italy, leaving Trintignant to drive the remaining 750S with me.

After the next day's practice, I went to see Gonzales again and asked him if he was still determined to give up racing.

He answered: "Well, I might have a go in one or two."

To which I replied: "I thought so!"

There was a traffic jam of over fifty cars at the start and it took some time to sort it out. Ascari on a Lancia went into the lead, followed by Rolt (Jaguar) and myself. Tony Rolt kindly slowed, moved over and let me through, and then Ascari waved me on. Neither Ascari nor Fangio, who was also in the Lancia team, liked the circuit, which they found too narrow and tortuous and too much confined between its banks; most of the Lancias clouted the banks at some time or other, but every time I broke the lap record, Ascari responded and matched my time, until I got down to 4 min. 49 sec. for the 7.4-mile circuit, equal to 92.38 m.p.h., which stood as the new record. The Ferrari pit crew increased our lead by quick pit work while I stopped to hand over to Trintignant and Ascari's car was taken over by Villoresi.

When Ascari took over for the final spell, he had a narrow escape from serious injury, as the propeller shaft broke and tore through the centre tunnel within inches of his thigh. That left me to win the award for the greatest distance covered and complete the points required by Ferrari for the 1954 World Championship for Constructors, but I was quite unable to catch the little D.B.-Panhard of Loreau and Armagnac, which was still ahead on handicap and won the Tourist Trophy.

## CHAPTER SIXTEEN

## SPANISH RHAPSODY

FERRARI then gave me permission to drive other people's cars in two races at the end-of-season meeting at Goodwood. Joe Kelly had invited me to drive his privately owned 750S 3-litre Ferrari, and as I drove out to the start, I thought the back axle sounded noisy. The mechanics assured me: "They're all like that. We've only just put it together"—but I still did not like the sound of it. I had not practised with the car, so was on the third row at the start. I put in the fastest lap of the race in catching Masten Gregory's 4½-litre Ferrari and was chasing Roy Salvadori, who was going very fast in a C-type Jaguar, when there was a horrible crunch and the rear axle broke. The whole casing was split, so Joe sold the car to Jaguars, who stripped it down for technical examination.

This was also my first drive on the Vanwall, which Peter Collins had been driving in several events. He was driving the 4½-litre Thin Wall Special in the 10-lap Formula Libre event, so I took over the Vanwall. Peter went into the lead, pursued by Ken Wharton on the 16-cylinder supercharged B.R.M. and I could do nothing about that, but I had an excellent scrap with Stirling Moss on his Maserati, although the Vanwall engine at that time was only 2¼ litres against the Maserati's 2½. The car oversteered, so that I dared not go round corners as fast as I would have liked and the injection system produced a nasty flat spot, where the engine just rumbled away and took some time to build up its revs. The real power did not come in until about 4,500 r.p.m., but above that it was very fast indeed. I could catch Stirling on the straight and the disc brakes allowed me to gain a little on the approach to the corners, but as often happens, the cockpit didn't fit me and the gear lever was somewhere under my knee, where I had to fumble for it. On the last lap we were screaming round wheel to wheel and I hoped to take Stirling on the run from Woodcote to the chicane, but instead of second gear, I got third and I went over the line a fifth of a second behind him.

Despite this, I was impressed with the Vanwall's possibilities and when Tony Vandervell invited me to drive it the next week-end at the Aintree International Meeting I agreed. In the Daily Telegraph Trophy event, Stirling Moss led on the Maserati, with me second, harried for a time by Behra on the Gordini until Schell came up on his Maserati and took me on. The engine seemed to be fluffy over 7,000 r.p.m., and I suspected fuel starvation; I couldn't go any faster and Harry got past. On the last lap, as we approached Tatt's Corner, I thought I would try to nip past on the inside, but Harry was ready for this and pulled across to the right to block the way. First point to him, but this put him off the correct line for the corner, so I swung out, and as he slid wide, I went past on the apex of the corner and beat him to the finishing line.

In the second race, a brake locked at Cottage Corner and I went onto the grass, which so choked the oil cooler with dirt that the temperature started to rise and I had to retire.

．　　．　　．　　．　　．　　．

All this time Ferraris had been working hard to cure the faults of the Squalo, which had proved so disappointing, and we assembled at Monza to try a new version, with coil spring front suspension instead of the transverse leaf spring. It was improved out of all recognition and had become a very nice little car. Maglioli and I spent some time driving it round and then Gonzales, who was recovering after his Dundrod accident, said he would like to try it. He had only done a few laps when the de Dion axle tube broke just as he was going round the Curva Grande. We heard the engine noise die away and rushed round to find the car stopped after a hectic series of swerves with one back wheel at a very peculiar angle. It is extraordinary how things seem to break the moment you come back after recovering from an accident—just to remind you that Motor Racing Is Dangerous.

This car was repaired and sent out to Barcelona for me to drive in the Spanish Grand Prix, with one of the old type fitted with a Squalo engine for Trintignant.

The Pedralbes circuit at Barcelona is composed of broad avenues and wide streets and there are some very fast stretches, but it is also bumpy in parts. It measures 3.9 miles to the lap. The race had brought together the finest collection of cars seen in the whole season, for apart from the Ferrari, Maserati, Mercedes and Gordini teams and the solitary Vanwall, now fitted with an engine of the full 2½-litre size, Lancia had decided to bring out their long-awaited new cars, designed by Ing. Jano. They had V8 engines, with four overhead camshafts and four double-choke carburetters, in a very light chassis with remarkably slim independent front suspension which looked almost fragile. The rear axle was de Dion and transverse leaf springs were used for suspension. They seemed quite small beside the other cars and looked quite different because of the fairings between front and rear wheels, which carried fuel and oil tanks.

The Ferrari team had a setback quite early when Vuzzi, our chief engineer, got involved in a collision while driving our 3-litre sports car and hit a lamp post, suffering severe bruises and a cut face, which upset him rather badly.

On the last day of practice, Collins, cornering fast on the Vanwall, was caught out by the oversteer, slid into a sandbank and flipped over. A few minutes later Moss came in with the back end of his Maserati crumpled.

I laughed at the two of them, saying: "You simply shouldn't do that sort of thing."

I then went out to try and do a fast lap in the Squalo, lost it on a corner at the top of a hill and spun backwards into the straw bales, smashing up the tail end.

Just before this, Basil Cardew of the *Daily Express* had been spouting to Tony Vandervell about how good the three British drivers were, so when Tony heard about my slide, he sent Basil a telegram saying more or less:

*Your three British champions Moss Collins Hawthorn all crashed within 300 yards of each other Stop How much now for British champions.*

Moss's Maserati and my Ferrari could be repaired in time for the race, but the Vanwall chassis was bent so the car was a non-starter. The new Lancias proved very quick and Ascari made fastest lap in practice, which put him in the front row at the start with Fangio and I, but the mechanics seemed to be very busy changing engines and the cars were not yet reliable. It was rumoured that the bearings were giving trouble. On race day, Villoresi's car was only got ready a few minutes before the start and Ascari was starting with a light load of fuel with the idea of going for the lap record and setting a fast pace at the beginning, which he did. Schell had also started with a partly filled tank in the hope of breaking up some of the opposition before he had to stop for fuel and in the early stages I got involved in a struggle with him and Trintignant. I could slipstream the Maserati down the straight and use

...ing with Fangio in the Tourist Trophy Race, 1955. *Left:* Fangio, Mercedes 300 SLR. *Right:* Hawthorn, D-Type Jaguar. [*Klemantaski*

...gain in the Rheims Grand Prix, 1957. *Left:* Hawthorn, Ferrari. *Right:* Fangio, Maserati. [*Klemantaski*

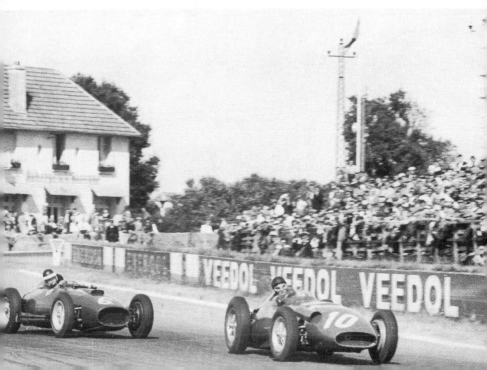

Driving Fon Portago's 3-litre Ferrari in the Nine Hour Race at Goodwood, 1955. We later retired with back-axle trouble.

Leading at the start with Tony Brooks second on the ill-fated B.R.M.s in the British Grand Prix, 1956.

him to pull me along. We could get round the corners faster than Schell could, but coming out of each corner he would accelerate away again just fast enough to prevent us getting past. It was most frustrating.

Villoresi had retired after only one lap with brake trouble; at nine laps I saw Ascari at the pits and so our little group was in the lead and the Mercedes challenge had not yet materialised, for Fangio was running fifth and Herrmann sixth behind Stirling Moss.

We were lapping at about 100 m.p.h. and trying a bit too hard. I spun at the beginning of the straight, to the despair of Meazza, our chief mechanic, who was standing there. I got away again and caught up with Schell and Trintignant, who were having a terrific scrap, changing the lead on every few laps.

On lap 22 I got into the lead, but Harry came back and something had to be done to shake him off. I saw my chance while coming round a left-hand bend, leading into a shortish straight which ended in a right-hand corner; I kept well to the left down the straight, which gave me the right approach to the right-hander and Harry came up on my right. We were both going as fast as we could and I decided to leave my braking until the last possible moment because, knowing Harry's volatile temperament, I expected he would try to hang on even longer. I crammed my brakes hard on just in time to take the corner, but sure enough, Harry kept going and the last I saw of him he was motoring at high speed straight into the straw bales. A short time later Trintignant dropped back, and stopped at the pits soon afterwards, and as Harry Schell had retired with a broken axle, I was out in front alone, pursued by Fangio, who had got past Moss when he stopped for adjustments to the Maserati.

The Squalo was going beautifully, while the Mercedes was giving trouble and Fangio was struggling on, covered in oil and black dust. We had a new problem when a dust storm blew up, which filled the air with dead leaves and flying newspapers. These lodged in the air intakes, and several people's engines overheated as a result, but my luck held. The pit signalled each lap to tell me what the gap was between Fangio and I, but towards the end the Mercedes began to trail a smoke-screen, and was beaten into second place by Musso's Maserati. So I won my second Grand Prix for Ferrari. Ugolini kissed me on both cheeks and I got a fantastic reception from the crowd.

It was a wonderful ending to the season, but for me the celebrations were clouded by the knowledge that I must soon go into hospital again.

Ever since I was seventeen, I had suffered intermittent pain in my back and I mentioned it to my doctor when I got back to England after recovering from the Syracuse burns, and he sent me to a specialist, who diagnosed kidney trouble and said I would have to have an operation at the end of the racing season.

When I went along for my deferred medical examination, about three months after my father's death, I took along some X-ray plates which showed the state of my kidneys, but the medical board simply said: "There's nothing we can do with these here; we must pass them on to Head Office."

I lost my temper and said: "No, but if it had been anyone else you would have thrown me out as soon as you had seen them, wouldn't you?"

They agreed, and added: "We would probably have rejected you on your burns alone, but you are a special case and we have had special instructions."

So the plates with the report on the rest of my disabilities were forwarded to a higher authority and eventually I heard I had been rejected as unfit.

Now it was time for the operation, and I moved into Guy's Hospital, where Mr. Kilpatrick performed the operation. I was five weeks in a nursing home after it and felt rather frail for some time afterwards.

The season had closed well after a bad start; I had won the Seaman Trophy again and was runner-up for the B.R.D.C. Gold Star, but I was not feeling strong and I had now seen how precarious a professional driver's life can be when he is paid solely out of starting money and prize money. I was reluctant to leave Ferrari, but I felt that I ought to give some attention to the garage which was my only source of regular income during the ups and downs of motor racing.

When Tony Vandervell invited me to sign a contract to drive the Vanwall, with a regular retainer as an added inducement, I was very tempted, for it would give me the chance to spend more time in England. Jaguar knew that Stirling Moss would no longer be available to them for sports-car racing, as he was joining Mercedes-Benz, so when they too offered me a retainer to sign with them for sports-car racing, I decided to make the break and throw in my lot with the two British constructors. The Vanwall was improving fast, Jaguar had more power up their sleeves for the D-type and I looked forward to a good season in 1955.

PART IV

TRIUMPH AND DISASTER

CHAPTER SEVENTEEN

## SEBRING AND SILVERSTONE

I SPENT the winter quietly recovering from the operation. It was a relief to feel that I only had a few miles to travel to Silverstone or an aerodrome to test cars instead of flying off to Modena or Monza at short notice, but I was genuinely sorry to leave Ferrari, for he had given me a chance to learn the terribly difficult and exacting job of the professional Grand Prix driver. With Ferrari I had learned to think calmly and methodically while driving on the high side of 150 m.p.h., I had learned to use some of the tricks with which the professional bluffs the opposition; and I had gained invaluable experience in coping with the hair-raising emergencies which are routine in racing, and even more in the testing which the public never sees. All this was priceless knowledge which the best of drivers only acquire at colossal cost in broken and damaged cars, usually accompanied by a lot of discomfort and a certain amount of personal suffering.

In allowing me to acquire this skill and experience, Ferrari had made a heavy investment and was naturally annoyed that I should decide to leave, but after all that had happened in 1954, I felt the need of a quiet spell which would allow me to get thoroughly fit again, while keeping an eye on the progress of the garage, which represents my major investment for the days when I can no longer drive in first-class racing. Yet the contracts I had just signed started a train of events which were to involve me in bitter controversies eclipsing all that had gone before and plunge me into the spotlight as one of the central figures in the biggest disaster in the history of motor racing.

. . . . . .

I missed the Argentine races and my first event of the year was the 12-hour International Grand Prix of Endurance at Sebring. Briggs Cunningham had entered a D-type Jaguar and he invited me to drive it with Phil Walters, one of the most experienced American sports-car drivers. The car had already seen a good deal of racing, so Len Hayden, one of the Jaguar mechanics, was sent over to prepare it for the race. I flew to New York and went on to Palm Beach for a few days while Len worked on the car.

The main opposition came from a large selection of Ferraris, including Kimberly's 4.9-litre V-12, several 3-litres and some smaller ones. They were private entries, but Chinetti, the New York representative for Ferrari, was there and Ugolini had come over from Italy to supervise the pit work.

There were 80 cars lined up for the Le Mans type start on one of the main runways and I got away first, building up a lead which we held throughout the race until the last spell, when Walters was driving. We had over a lap lead on the 3-litre Ferrari driven by Phil Hill and Carroll Shelby, but our cylinder head had warped during ten hours of hard driving, and Walters had to make several pit stops. He was using a lot of oil and water, and had to change the plugs which were fouling up. During one of these stops the Hill-Shelby Ferrari got ahead, but our pit was satisfied that Walters had passed them again and kept him comfortably ahead of the Ferrari. We were flagged as the winners. Then ensued one of the most remarkable scenes of confusion ever to be seen at the end of a major motor race.

Our pit control was not quite certain that the 12 hours were up when Walters crossed the line, so they sent him off to do a precautionary lap, during which he ran out of fuel, but it was later confirmed that he had been officially flagged anyway.

The Ferrari outfit were, however, convinced that the Hill-Shelby car had won. Their lap charts showed them as a lap ahead and they claimed they had slowed their man down towards the end. The loudspeakers announced that we were second and then changed it to first. Briggs Cunningham insisted that we had won, so the lap charts from the Jaguar and Ferrari pits were handed over and compared with those of the race officials, as a result of which the Jaguar was declared the winner. As usual, Briggs had everything organised on the grand scale and we had about 16 people in our race control and lap scoring organisation; on the other hand, it is very rarely that Ugolini makes a mistake. Personally I had lost track of the relative positions during Walters's pit stops, and could only accept the decision of the officials, whatever it was.

Although I had been at Sebring as a spectator the previous year, this was my first race there, and indeed my first race in the United States, and there were a number of things that rocked me after racing in Europe on well-established courses run by officials of long experience.

During the first few laps Redele, the French driver, hit an oil patch on his 1063 Renault saloon, which rolled over several times and threw him out on the track. I managed to dodge it, but Bob Said, who was running second on a Ferrari, came round the curve to find the track blocked by the upturned Renault, an ambulance with the doors open, a stretcher party and the prostrate Redele. At one moment it looked as if he was going straight up into the ambulance among the stretchers. He managed to swerve clear, but swiped the corner of the ambulance in passing and wrecked the Ferrari.

Soon afterwards some fuel spilled out of the tank of McAfee's Ferrari; it caught fire, and he drove for some time quite unaware that the car was burning merrily away at the back. Finally he stopped it about a mile past the pits and it began to burn really well, but when I went past no one seemed to be doing anything about it. Next time round I heard a frightful clanging noise and looked round to see a fire engine racing me. It was a great monster festooned with ladders and things, with characters in long-tailed helmets clinging on all over it, just like a scene from an old-time film comedy. I managed to keep clear of this lot and got on with the motor racing.

Sebring is an aerodrome circuit measuring 5.2 miles to the lap and there are a lot of sharp corners which are absolutely murder for the brakes. The course was lined with little conical markers studded with reflectors so that they could be seen at night, but in the course of the day these were knocked over or simply flattened and as darkness fell it became extremely difficult to see where the corners were. The drivers gradually evolved their own circuit, converting the sharp corners into gentle sweeps, which put the lap speeds up considerably. To stop this, some officials piled a load of new markers into a car and set off to re-mark the course, but they drove round in the opposite direction to the racing cars, so that we would find a car facing us with its headlamps on, and somewhere in the blackness beyond, these officials putting down markers to bring us back onto the old line. They must have been very brave men.

Incidents like this made one realise just how much the organisation of the sport in Europe—and the safety of both drivers and spectators—

depends on the great army of unpaid officials who give up their time to marshalling and scrutineering and all the other necessary jobs which make motor racing run smoothly.

In Europe there is a long motor-racing tradition and a great mass of experience which is passed on from one to another. The Americans started after the war with nothing but their enthusiasm and all the Atlantic Ocean separated them from the sources of guidance on how to run our kind of motor racing. They had to learn the hard way, but they have made enormous progress since then.

Financially, there is practically nothing to be made out of racing at Sebring. Sports-car racing in America is rather like pre-war motor racing in England; a sport for wealthy amateurs who can afford to ignore financial considerations. Members of the Sports Car Club of America must be amateurs; they may not accept payment for driving; and, if inadvertently confronted with filthy lucre in the form of prize money or bonuses, must hand it over to charity. At that time there were no cash prizes for the races. It was fine if you happened to own a bank, a meat factory or an oil well in Texas, but was hard on the impecunious character who hoped to scratch a living by driving. Briggs Cunningham paid all my expenses and I received a nice little spirit heater with a pan on top to make soufflés.

.    .    .    .    .    .

I left the Florida sunshine immediately after the race and came back to the English winter as I had to be available to test the Vanwall, but the car was not ready until some time afterwards. Its first appearance in England with the new 2½-litre engine was to be in the Easter Monday meeting at Goodwood in April, but it was not ready for testing until the Sunday before the meeting, when we took it down to Odiham aerodrome, where the C.O. had given us permission to do a test run. I found the injection system was still producing a large flat spot —or rather a complete depressed area—between 4,000 and 5,500 r.p.m. and although there was plenty of power above 5,500, the car was obviously not in a condition to perform well on the Goodwood circuit, so it was withdrawn and efforts were concentrated on getting it ready for the Monaco Grand Prix on May 22.

I kept my eye in with an excursion to Ibsley, the 2-mile airfield circuit near Bournemouth, where I ran my own Gran Turismo Lancia Aurelia in the closed-car handicap. Starting on scratch, Tommy

Sopwith (Sapphire) and I found ourselves handicapped out of the race, but I did get the prize for the fastest lap.

. . . . . .

At the Daily Express International Trophy meeting at Silverstone on May 7, I had a full day's driving in prospect with the Vanwall entered in the main event, a D-type Jaguar in the sports-car race and a Mark VII saloon in the production-car event.

There were no Continental works teams present, but Ken Wharton and I on the Vanwalls faced strong opposition from a number of privately owned Maseratis, including Stirling Moss's, the Owen Organisation's disc-braked car driven by Peter Collins and Syd Greene's car driven by Roy Salvadori.

This time there were no heats; it was a straight 60-lap event. Our cars had gone well in practice and I found myself on the front row at the start, having tied with Salvadori for fastest lap in 1 min. 48 sec. With us were Moss and Fairman on the new streamlined Connaught. However, I was in trouble early in the race with oil sweeping back over my visor owing to a fault in the oil supply to the valve gear. This had worried me during test driving and the gearbox had been checked for leakage. It was eventually found that oil was dripping from the engine into the undertray, from where it drained back and got onto the drive shafts, which flung it forward into the wind and by this roundabout means sprayed it all over my face. I struggled on for a time, but had to give up.

Ken Wharton had been into the pits early with a broken throttle linkage, which had been repaired with copper wire. He then got involved in a tremendous scrap with Salvadori and was clipping the grass, trying to squeeze past the Maserati at Copse Corner, when he found himself too close as Roy braked and hit one of the marker posts stuck in a barrel of concrete. Before the horrified spectators massed behind the earth barrier, the car leapt in the air, stood on its nose and slewed sideways. The broken rear axle gashed the fuel tank and in an instant the rear end of the car was a mass of flames. Ken, with his arms and neck burned, hurled himself from the cockpit, ran dazedly onto the track, then recovered himself and fell back to collapse on the grass verge.

While the ambulance rushed Ken off to hospital, ineffective efforts were made to quell the blaze with hand extinguishers. It seemed quite a time before the fire engine appeared and tackled the fire to the accompaniment of ironic cheers from the crowd, while Tony Vandervell raved at them from the opposite side of the track—but then, if your house were to catch fire, you would no doubt feel as if it were a deuce of a time before the fire engine arrived.

In the sports-car race, the D-type was leading fairly comfortably, about 10 seconds ahead of Parnell's Aston Martin, when there was a loud plopping noise from the engine and a lot of water came back into the cockpit. I stopped, found that a top water hose had burst, tried the engine and found it ran reasonably well, so carried on gingerly and finished fourth.

The Mark VII won the production-car event quite easily. It was great fun, because the big saloon had an exhaust note like a D-type and leaned over at a spectacular angle, but it cornered extremely fast.

I have always had a prejudice against driving a car with Number 1 on it, but all three of my cars that day were Number 1 and having run into trouble on two cars of the three, I found extra support for the superstition.

## CHAPTER EIGHTEEN

## THE DEATH OF ASCARI

THERE was no hope of rebuilding Ken's Vanwall in time for the Grand Prix of Europe at Monaco on May 22, even if another driver could have been found, so mine was prepared as a lone entry. I tested it at Silverstone before it was sent off to Monaco and found that I could keep out of the flat spot in acceleration if I kept the revs up. It went well and I put in a lap in 1 min. 46 sec., which was in the lap record region. I felt it would go even faster, but accelerating away from Copse Corner I heard a horrible clanging and I knew that a connecting rod had come thorough the side of the crankcase. We found that one of the gudgeon pins had apparently been assembled without a circlip to locate it, with the result that the pin had moved in the piston and had twisted the head off the connecting rod.

This was a hard blow, for it meant that the engine had to be taken out of the incinerated wreckage of Ken's car and rebuilt to go in mine and the car had to be despatched to Monaco with no spare engine. I followed it by air with other members of the Vandervell entourage in his de Havilland Dove.

As the premier event of 1955, the Monaco race attracted a full turn-out of the fastest cars and drivers such as had been seen only once before, at Barcelona.

Ferrari sent two Super Squalos developed from the type on which I had won at Barcelona, with coil spring front suspension and a fuel tank in the tail as well as at the sides, to give greater latitude in weight distribution. These were driven by Schell and Taruffi, while Farina and Trintignant remained faithful to the old-type cars. Lancias, making their second Grand Prix appearance, sent three cars, for Ascari, Villoresi and Chiron, while Mercedes had two new short-wheelbase cars with outboard front brakes for Fangio and Moss, with a medium-wheelbase one for Herrmann. Behra, Musso, Mieres and Perdisa, a bright new recruit, had 250F Maseratis, Manzon, Bayol and Pollet had Gordinis and my lone Vanwall completed the list.

The Monaco circuit, entirely in the streets of the town and only 1.9 miles long, is unique among the courses used for the classic international events in the continuous punishment it imposes on engines, transmissions and brakes, and the unremitting concentration and physical effort it requires from the drivers. In the course of 100 laps, we have to make 1,400–1,500 gear changes and apply the brakes about 1,000 times. It starts on the footpath on the sea front, goes along to a hairpin turn at the gasworks, doubles back along the promenade, then up a steep winding hill to an S-bend in the square between the Casino and the Hôtel de Paris, then sharply down a winding descent via another hairpin outside the railway station to the sea front again, plunging into a curving floodlit tunnel, before descending at full speed towards a chicane which leads onto the edge of the harbour, and so back via a sharp left-hand turn to the starting point. During practice, Fangio and Ascari both lapped in 1 min. 41.1 sec., chopping 5.4 sec. off the record lap time established by Caracciola on a supercharged 5.6-litre Mercedes in 1937. These performances by two different cars with $2\frac{1}{2}$-litre unblown engines giving less than half the power of pre-war cars dramatically demonstrated the advances in road-holding, steering and braking which have been made in the intervening years.

At this time the Vanwall had not achieved quite the same standard, particularly in steering and braking. The steering lock was limited, which made it difficult to get round the hairpin outside the railway station smoothly, and I had some trouble with the special type of ventilated disc-brake which Vanwall was using. They required a hard pressure on the pedal, but if one pressed too hard, they would lock and they frightened me once or twice by locking at the tricky, slippery chicane where the road sweeps onto the edge of the harbour. However, I managed a lap in 1 min. 45.6 sec., which gave me a place in the fourth row at the start.

On the first evening of practice, I was walking up the hill to the Casino with Mr. Kosmicki, our chief engineer, who had previously been with Nortons and was responsible for the basic resemblance which the Vanwall engine bore to four motor-cycle engines mounted in line. As we walked along discussing the behaviour of the other cars, we heard a Mercedes coming up behind us. The next moment there was a screech of tyres and a loud crash as Herrmann's car spun off the road and wedged itself under a heavy stone balustrade. Herrmann got away with a fractured hip, but as the main mass of the stonework finished up a few inches from his head, he could count himself lucky. Mercedes produced a spare car for the race which was given to the French driver Simon, to his surprise and joy, for the best he had been hoping for was a drive at Le Mans.

At the start of the race, as we all crowded into the first hairpin, Simon was baulked by someone else and put on his brakes. I was right behind, and ran into his tail, denting the nose of the Vanwall slightly, but doing no serious damage to the Mercedes. Damage of this kind is frequent at Monaco and soon Rosier came in with the whole tail of his car hanging loose.

I settled down in 10th or 11th position and the car was going well, but going past the Casino the engine cut completely and I found that one of the ball joints had come adrift in the throttle linkage. The split pin securing it had worn through as a result of continuous vibration and had fallen out. I put it together and being on a slope was able to re-start and return to the pits. Here an attempt was made to patch it up with copper wire, but having seen the Herrmann crash, I felt the Monaco circuit was the last place on which to have the throttle stick open, so the car was withdrawn.

Fangio seemed to be a certain winner, but at half distance his Mercedes stopped with a fault in the desmodromic valve gear, leaving Moss in the lead with Ascari second and trying hard to avoid being lapped. Then came one of the most dramatic incidents in motor-racing history. Moss came into the pits, the engine of his Mercedes trailing smoke, but before the pit crew had a chance to inform Ascari that he was now safely in the lead, he came into the chicane too fast, slid into the bollards and car and driver plunged into the harbour. Frogmen, waiting for just such an emergency, fished him out with nothing worse than shock and a cut nose, while Trintignant went on to win an unexpected victory.

We did not realise it at the time, but looking back one can see that this was a really historic motor race, which will long be remembered. Not only was it exciting because of the dramatic changes of fortune which marked its course; it also brought together a glittering collection of first-class cars and a company of great drivers which we were never again to see assembled together.

.    .    .    .

The next week-end the Supercortemaggiore race was being run at Monza and I had permission from Jaguars to drive a 3-litre 4-cylinder Ferrari with Maglioli. I drove up to Monza to try the car, but the track was deserted, so I wandered over to the bar, where I found Meazza, the Ferrari chief mechanic, obviously suffering from a severe shock. He just looked at me and murmured: "Ascari e morto."

I could not believe my ears, for when I left Monte Carlo I understood Ascari was safely tucked up in bed recovering from his dip in the harbour and now Meazza was telling me how he had been killed at Monza an hour before I arrived.

It seems he had insisted on leaving hospital almost at once and returned to Italy, where he went out to Monza as quickly as possible to immerse himself in the motor-racing atmosphere once again. He had been entered to drive a 3-litre Ferrari with Castellotti in the Supercortemaggiore event, but was not expected to practise on this particular day and had not brought his crash helmet with him—it was being repaired after the Monaco crash, which had torn the strap.

It was almost lunch time and he was chatting with several drivers before leaving for home, when on a sudden impulse he decided to do a lap in the Ferrari. He borrowed Castellotti's helmet and roared away. The little group on the terrace below the grandstand heard the note of the exhaust rising and falling and then, abruptly, it stopped. Warned by some premonition, they dashed for their cars and drove round, but when they found him, Ascari was dying. The car had slewed round into a long slide on the very fast Vialone Curve and had turned over, crushing him as it somersaulted off the track.

The crash seemed a complete mystery and all sorts of theories were advanced to account for it. Had he had a black-out, as a delayed-action effect from his Monaco accident, or had he missed a gear, changing into third where he should have been getting fifth? I believe the explanation is quite different. The tyres we wanted to use for these cars were 6.50–16, but they were not available at the time in the particular make we were using, and so 7.00–16 covers had been fitted. I had driven the car with these tyres on it and found it very nasty indeed when it came to the Vialone Curve, where there were a lot of little ripples in the road surface. I came to the conclusion that the rims were too narrow for these tyres and I had them taken off my car. Where Ascari crashed there were long, broad, black tyre marks, followed by marks of the wheel rims digging into the road, and it seemed to me that he probably changed into fifth speed just as he hit the ripples, the car started to slide, the tyres rolled under and the rims gouged into the road, causing it to somersault.

Barrel-chested with a plump round face, Ascari was easily spotted at any race track, and he was very popular with the other drivers. When he died, at the age of 37, he had been World Champion twice and was right at the peak of his capabilities. He was the fastest driver I ever saw; in my opinion, faster than Fangio at that time. But apart from his brilliant career as a driver, he found time to be a successful business man, with a charming wife and two small children; it was a tragic coincidence that his own father had been killed at almost exactly the same age, also leaving behind a small son.

The news caused great gloom in Italy, where Ascari was a national hero, and quite overshadowed the race that week-end.

The event began with a rolling start as usual and I at once got involved in a tremendous struggle with Behra who was driving a Maserati. There were the usual prizes for the leader of every lap and Behra could always get into the lead on the back stretch, but I could always overtake him coming out of the South Curve and cross the finishing line first, so he was taking the lead every lap, while I took the prize money. He obviously was not very pleased about it and dropped back after a time, working out another strategy.

When I came in and handed over to Maglioli, Behra kept going and built up quite a useful lead over us, before handing his car over to Musso. Behra took over again as soon as the regulations allowed and built the lead up to about a minute, until I went out again and pulled it back to about 50 seconds. I could not see any hope of catching him before the race ended, but three laps from the end I came into the finishing straight to see the crowd frantically waving me on and I spotted Behra disappearing into the distance. He had run out of petrol just before the last corner and had managed to coast into the pits, where they tossed some fuel into the tank and sent him away with a mere 20 seconds' lead. I pulled out all the stops and cut this down to 17 seconds, but Behra won. His car and ours had lapped all the other competitors, including the Perdisa-Mieres Maserati which came in third.

. . . . .

For the Belgian Grand Prix at Spa, one Vanwall had been prepared, the only British car entered. It started off quite well on the first day of practice, but suddenly started throwing a lot of water back at me and we found that the header tank, which in those days was behind the engine, against the bulkhead, had split, allowing water to be forced out under the pressure generated by the pump. I also found that oil was being thrown onto my visor again.

The second day I had only done a couple of laps, when the gearbox felt as if it was seizing; gear changing became extremely difficult, so we had to call it a day. On the third day we tried to start the car by pushing it in gear, but the clutch would not disengage properly and the gearbox stuck in neutral. I was rather puzzled about the clutch and made enquiries, from which I learned that Mr. Vandervell, who is a terrific enthusiast and an ex-racing driver himself, had been unable to resist taking the car out for a test run round the narrow streets of the town. We had a very high bottom gear to give us the range of performance we wanted on the hairpin of La Source and it would have been extremely difficult to drive in town streets without slipping the clutch. But one could not accuse the patron of doing in his own clutch simply on hearsay.

Lancia had announced their retirement from racing after Ascari's death, but they sent Castellotti as a "private" entry with full works support, which suggested that they might yet change their minds and he showed that the cars were now really in form, by making fastest practice lap, beating both Fangio and Moss on Mercedes. One day I was chatting with Giulio Ramponi when he remarked that the Vanwall was not going very well and he wondered if Mr. Vandervell would consider releasing me to join another team. He added: "Lancias are looking for a Number 1 driver and would like you to lead the team." As a result I had a long talk with Ing. Jano, their chief engineer, who confirmed that they would be happy to have me as team leader, so it was agreed that they would approach Mr. Vandervell about it.

I made a good getaway in the race, but it was the first time I had ever driven the car with full tanks, which loaded it down at the back; I found it rather frightening. The front end felt too light and it was difficult to steer it on the extremely fast curves of the Spa circuit. Then the oil started pouring out again and spraying over my visor. I kept going, wiping it off with my hand until gloves and jacket were soaked with it, but it seemed as though it was coming from the gearbox this time and there was obviously very little hope of survival if the gearbox seized at the speeds we were doing, so I drew in to the pits and retired.

We all admired the immense drive and effort Tony Vandervell had put into creating a British Grand Prix car, at enormous expense to himself, and it was very difficult for him to accept the fact that the car was still not ready for top-line international racing, but that was the hard truth and there was still a great deal to be done before it could reach the level of performance and reliability which has since been achieved.

Lancia had already approached him regarding the possibility of releasing me, which did not please him at all, but that night we agreed to part. I told Lancia I was free and they agreed to send a definite proposition to me at Le Mans. When I got there I received a message to say they had definitely withdrawn from all racing. I had resigned from one job and lost another.

Incidentally, I had an awkward moment when travelling flat out down the Masta straight towards Stavelot. There were two pigeons standing in the road and they rose much too slowly to get out of the way of a racing car travelling at about 150 m.p.h. I missed one, but the other went straight into the air intake and hit the radiator. This is one of the little-known risks of racing, for if a bird hits you in the face at high speed the consequences can be very unpleasant. It has been suggested that one of the worst crashes Caracciola ever had might have been caused by a bird hitting his face when he was travelling fast, nearly knocking him unconscious. The news of my incident with the pigeon was reported in the press and next time I got back to England I found a letter waiting for me, saying what a swine I was to go around killing birds. You have to keep a sense of proportion!

The race was won by Fangio, who led all the way and averaged over 118 m.p.h., making this the fastest road race ever run in Europe.

## CHAPTER NINETEEN

## LE MANS, 1955

TEAM managers, drivers, mechanics, timekeepers and marshals, pressmen and photographers, wives and girl friends and all the great army of colourful individualists who make up the motor-racing scene now converged on the French provincial city of Le Mans for the 24-hour Grand Prix d'Endurance, the big sports-car event of the year. For most drivers Le Mans is a stage on their upward progress and a class win or a good placing in the Performance Index handicap is an adequate reward for their first appearance, but I was in the thick of the competition for an outright win, driving a car which already had an established reputation in this event, for Jaguars had won in 1951 and 1953 and come in second in 1954.

We had a team of D-types, with increased power and improved streamlining, to be driven by Rolt and Hamilton, Beauman and Dewis, Stewart and I, and backed up by independents from America and Belgium. Ferrari, the winner in 1954, had a team of 4½-litre sixes driven by Castellotti and Marzotto, Maglioli and Hill, Trintignant and Schell, while Maserati had Mieres driving with Perdisa, and Musso with Valenzano. Aston Martins were driven by Collins and Frere, Salvadori and Walker, Brooks and Riseley-Prichard.

Mercedes-Benz had a team of the new 300 SLR two-seaters, which were already regarded with awe since Stirling Moss's win with Jenkinson in the Mille Miglia. Their drivers were a truly cosmopolitan bunch; Fangio from the Argentine was paired with Moss from England, Kling, the only German, with Simon (France) and finally the veteran Levegh had been given a Mercedes in recognition of his exploit in 1952 when he all but snatched victory from the Mercedes after driving his Talbot single-handed to within 75 minutes of the finish; he had as his co-driver John Fitch from the U.S.A.

The Germans knew that their chassis-mounted drum-brakes, although of enormous size, could not compete with the disc-brakes of the

Jaguars; they had already run into trouble with cracking of the drums and their cars were fitted with four buttons on the instrument panel which allowed the driver to squirt oil into any brake where the drum became defective to prevent it grabbing—a fairly desperate expedient in itself. To ease the load on the brakes, they had therefore devised a startling new air brake. A lever on the facia worked hydraulic jacks which lifted up the whole rear deck of the car, including the driver's head fairing, to present a great flat surface which quickly slowed the car from high speeds. Naturally it obstructed the driver's view through his driving mirror and the scrutineers insisted that windows must be made in the flaps before race day.

I was supposed to be driving with Jimmy Stewart, but he had been obliged to give up motor racing. He had damaged his elbow very badly in a crash in an Aston Martin in 1954 and had damaged it again when his Jaguar overturned at Nurburgring in 1955; he was warned that any further damage would probably result in the loss of the arm and he had to give up. Jaguars therefore brought Ivor Bueb in to drive with me. He had been tried out on D-types during a Jaguar test day at Silverstone some time before, after a brilliant career on single-seater five-hundreds, and he had proved both fast and safe. I had argued strongly in favour of Don Beauman, who was a friend of mine and in a sense a protégé, as my garage prepared his cars and I advised him on his racing. Beauman therefore got the job and Bueb was furious. Now we were driving together. It was a prickly situation, but Ivor is a straight-speaking, forthright motor trader, and so we soon established a businesslike relationship and got down to our racing programme.

I spent some time learning the circuit during the daylight practice period, and by the time Ivor's turn came it was evening, so he had to learn the circuit in the dark. Personally I do not think this is necessarily a disadvantage; one can concentrate more, because fewer distractions are visible, and one sees less of the potential dangers. Sometimes, when trying to reproduce my night-time speeds in daylight, I have been appalled to see how fast trees and other solid objects come rushing at the car and I came to the conclusion that darkness can help to keep your mind off the dangers if you have to go really fast.

Two incidents in practice stuck in my mind, as they spotlighted the peculiar hazards of the Sarthe circuit. One night I was coming very fast to the turn on the top of the brow before the descent to the White

CHALLENGE ME THE RACE

House and someone waved a yellow flag at me to indicate that there was danger on the other side. As I zoomed over the top, I spotted a Gordini, half on the road and half up the bank, with great lumps of earth scattered around and petrol and oil spreading over the road. It turned out to be Bayol's car, and we soon heard he had been taken to hospital with serious head injuries. In fact he has done very little racing since.

The second incident was at the pits when Stirling Moss was waved out for a practice run just as a D.B. was coming in. The little car cannoned off the Mercedes and struck two people standing at the pits, one of them being Jean Behra, who suffered injuries to the head and legs which prevented him driving in the race.

This was not the first incident of the kind and drivers with previous experience of Le Mans regarded the stretch past the pits as the most dangerous part of the course. Cars were hurtling past at close to maximum speed, with their drivers straining to spot pit signals, while on their right other cars pulled in to the pits or drew away again with no effective control beyond the good sense and alertness of the drivers. Many people regarded a bad pile-up at this point as a distinct possibility, but I think most of them thought in terms of a multiple collision, with cars slamming into the earth retaining wall or the pits. In short, it was a potential danger to the drivers, and a driver who goes around complaining of the dangers too often is liable to be told sooner or later that he has chosen the wrong profession. That is, incidentally, one of the reasons why U.P.P.I., the recently-formed union of professional drivers, can perform a useful function in presenting an agreed viewpoint where a circuit or a method of running a race seems to present unreasonable hazards.

A strange thing happened to our car in practice and I never heard the reason for it. As I was driving fast down the Mulsanne straight there was suddenly an awful bang just like an explosion. I slowed, checked the oil pressure and temperature and the water temperature, but everything seemed in order, so I carried on. I did a couple more laps and it happened again; I reported to the pits and the plugs were changed.

Ivor then went out and it happened to him, giving him a terrible fright, as it was his first time on the circuit and his first race with the Jaguar. The engine seemed to be running perfectly, but it was taken out and a spare engine put in the night before the race. It had only been run in briefly on the test bed and I was told to take it easy during the first few hours of the race. What a forlorn hope! Few engines have known such a hectic running-in period as this one was to have.

Race day was perfect, calm, warm and sunny, and a hush descended over the packed enclosures as the drivers stood, each in his little painted circle, facing the line of shining cars parked in echelon along the line of the pits, while the seconds ticked away to four o'clock. Then Count Maggi, one of the organisers of the Mille Miglia, dropped the flag, we sprinted across to our cars, jumped in, started up and surged forward, swerving, weaving and jockeying for position in a thunder of exhausts, raising a great cloud of dust as we accelerated away under the Dunlop bridge down to the Esses.

Castellotti tore away in the big Ferrari as if he were driving in a 3-hour Grand Prix instead of a 24-hour endurance test, and as we screamed past the pits at the end of the first lap he was leading me by about 300 yards. Fangio had made a bad start, getting the gear lever stuck up his trouser leg as he tried to emulate Stirling Moss's trick of jumping in without opening the door, and he had to make his way through a pack of slower cars, but I soon got signals from the pit to say that he was catching me; I opened up and started closing on Castellotti. So much for running-in the engine! We were lapping at 117–118 m.p.h., and at the end of the first hour I was five seconds behind Castellotti, with Fangio practically breathing down my neck.

From then on a terrific battle developed as the three of us swapped places, each one sizing up the others to see how he could snatch a slight advantage. I was highly elated when I found that the Jaguar could pass both the Mercedes and the Ferrari on the straight and even if they used my slipstream the others could not get past again. During practice, Norman Dewis, Jaguar's chief tester, who was driving in the race, reported that he had touched 6,100 r.p.m. in top on the straight which calculations showed was equivalent to about 190 m.p.h. and I was reaching 5,800–5,900 which would be between 180 and 185 m.p.h. Duelling with the Mercedes and the Ferrari at these speeds, while continually passing groups of slower cars which were also passing and re-passing each other, all within the width of a normal French main road, demanded fantastic concentration and this looked like going on for hours.

Fangio was working away with the air brake, which was flapping up and down, making the Mercedes look like a great fish rising at flies, and with its aid he could leave his braking just about as late as I could on the disc-braked Jaguar.

When we went round a slow corner like Mulsanne, the Jaguar could hold the Mercedes on acceleration in first or second gears. When Fangio got into the third speed of his five-speed gearbox he could draw ahead, but once I got into top on my four-speed box I could gain on him. The Ferrari's brakes were not as good as ours and their behaviour on corners was not all it might have been; but on acceleration Castellotti just left us both standing, laying incredible long black tracks of molten rubber on the road as he roared away.

On fast corners, the Mercedes, with its independent rear suspension, was distinctly better than the Jaguar. On slow corners, there was not much difference, but on a medium-fast sweep like the White House, where one is doing over 100 m.p.h., Fangio could gain quite a lot.

Gradually we left Castellotti behind and Fangio built up a lead of about 100 yards. I suppose at this stage I was momentarily mesmerised by the legend of Mercedes superiority. Here was this squat silver projectile, handled by the world's best driver, with its fuel injection and desmodromic valve gear, its complicated suspension and its out-of-this-world air brake. It seemed natural that it should eventually take the lead. Then I came to my senses and thought: "Damn it, why should a German car beat a British car?" As there was no one in sight but me to stop it, I got down to it and caught up with him again.

From then on, we battled wheel to wheel for lap after lap in an all-out struggle which put even our famous Rheims encounter in the shade. I had one bad moment going through the Esses, when the tail came round and the car started sliding for the barricades. I thought: "Whoops! This is it!" whipped the wheel over to the right, over-corrected slightly and just managed to catch it as the tail swung out to the left at the exit from the second bend. It is a second-gear corner, and I probably was not doing more than 65 m.p.h., but it felt very dangerous sliding within inches of those high wattle and earth banks where so many cars have come to grief.

Another time, going under the Dunlop bridge, I found myself going rather too fast, tried to brake, spotted Fangio in my mirror and had to stay on the wrong line. I got onto some loose sand and felt the tail sliding out; Fangio seized the chance to nip past and I managed to sort it out.

At this stage I was driving flat out all the way and had absolutely nothing in reserve. I was wondering what Fangio had up his sleeve and I asked him afterwards, but he said he just could not have gone any faster. Fangio took the lead for three laps, but I took him again with a lap in 4 min. 6.6 sec., for the 8.36 miles at an average of 122.39 m.p.h. which remained unbeaten and stood as a new record. At the end of the second hour, there was less than a second between us after nearly 250 miles of motoring and we had lapped everyone except Castellotti, Maglioli, Kling and Levegh.

I had by now built up a small lead, but it was soon time to come in for fuel and a change of drivers. I had been receiving the signals from the pit which started three laps before we were due to come in and I knew that this time round I was due to stop. I overtook Kling's Mercedes just before the Indianapolis turn, and Levegh's car just after the White House where the straight run up to pits begins.

The only car now in front of me was Macklin's Austin-Healey and as I came up alongside I worked out whether there was room to pass him and then pull in to the pits. In my view there was, so I kept on and then as the pits drew nearer I put up my hand, put the brakes on and pulled in. I was nearly there, when out of the corner of my eye I saw something flying through the air. It was Levegh's Mercedes which went cartwheeling over the safety barrier, bounced once and disintegrated with the force of an exploding bomb. Simultaneously Macklin's Austin-Healey came past spinning round backwards, then slewed across in front of me towards the pits.

It was all over in a second or two, but it remain fixed in my mind like a slow-motion film. There were three people standing in front of the pit right in the path of the crippled green car; a gendarme, a photographer and an official. I could see the car was going to hit them, and they could see it, but they stood there frozen with horror and the car mowed them down. Then it bounced off, spun round again and finished up a crumpled wreck on the opposite side of the track, where Lance Macklin, miraculously unhurt, jumped out and ran for cover, while a tyre spun lazily in the middle of the road.

Dazed by what I had seen, I had let my Jaguar roll on past our pit and as reversing is forbidden I stopped it and ran back to see if "Lofty" England agreed to my doing another lap before coming in. He sent me off to do the extra lap and, sick with horror, I went over the sequence of events in my mind. What had happened behind me? And what had happened to the spectators?

Driving mechanically, I only wanted to get out of the car and get away from the track. But as I swept round towards the White House, I thought my eyes were playing tricks, for there was a wrecked car, blazing, with a great pillar of black oily smoke rising into the sky. This could not be the Mercedes, it was too early. Then what else? Only later I heard that in those few tragic moments Dick Jacobs had also crashed in one of the new M.G.A.s and had been injured, but not desperately.

Back at the pits, the track was littered with debris. The mangled wreckage of the Mercedes, minus engine and front suspension, lay blazing on top of the earth barrier and beyond it, mercifully hidden from us by the dense cloud of smoke, rescuers were already moving the dead and injured from the public enclosure. I only wanted to get away from it and blot out the scene from my mind. I staggered from the pit saying that I was finished with racing and was not going to get into the car again. I suppose I was near to hysteria as a result of the shock, coming on top of the concentrated nerve strain of the previous two hours I was led away by Duncan Hamilton and his wife Angela who took me to their caravan, sat me down and put a drink in my hand while Duncan talked to me like a father, trying to calm me down.

When he had seen all the team cars refuelled, Lofty England came over to see how I was and I again said that I was not going to drive again, but Lofty said quite firmly: "Oh yes you are! You're going to go out there and finish the race. It's the only thing you can possibly do!"

During those terrible hours he was a tower of strength. While people went back and forth consulting precedents and debating about what should be done, Lofty saw the situation quite clearly and simply. Nothing he could say or do would alter the consequences of the accident in the slightest degree. He had come to Le Mans to win a motor race and so long as the race kept going, it was his job to win it.

Some of the Ferrari mechanics came in and some of the Aston Martin people, all telling me that it was not really my fault, and gradually I pieced together what had gone on behind me from that fateful moment when I put on the brakes to stop at the pit.

As I swung in, Macklin pulled out, blocking the path of Levegh, who was coming up on the outside at around 150 m.p.h. Levegh just had time to put up his hand as a warning to Fangio, who was behind him, then tried to squeeze through between the Austin-Healey and the protecting barrier. He struck the barrier, crashed into the back of the Austin-Healey and then leapt into the air. The car mowed down the spectators in a small club enclosure and then hurtled on to crash in flames on top of the earth barrier, while the engine and front suspension, torn away by the force of the impact, cut deep swathes through the closely-packed ranks of the spectators in the main enclosure. It was quite clearly the worst accident any of us had ever known, but even then we had no conception of its true gravity.

All this time Ivor was out on the course doing a wonderful job hanging onto the Mercedes, which was now being driven by Stirling Moss. He had been through an ordeal calculated to shatter the nerve of most people. As he stood there on the pit counter, waiting to take over from me and keyed up at the prospect of taking over the leading car in his first Le Mans race—and, indeed, his first big road race on a fast car—he saw the accident and all that followed during the interminable five minutes while I was sent off to do another lap. Yet he was driving beautifully, holding second place and keeping the Mercedes lead down to reasonable proportions so that we could counterattack later.

Towards ten o'clock I took over again and kept on until after midnight. It was easier in the dark; the world was reduced to the blur of road in the light of the headlamps, brightened by the stabs of red from the tail lamps of slower cars and punctuated once every four minutes and twenty seconds or so by the sudden rush up the bright alleyway between the floodlit pits and grandstands. But I remember very little of the rest of the race.

Soon after 1.30 a.m. I heard two cars revving their engines at the Mercedes pit and thought this was strange, because they would never have arranged to have both cars in at the same time. Then we heard that they had been withdrawn from the race on instructions from the directors in Stuttgart, which had been delayed because of the jam at the Le Mans switchboard, where thousands of people were trying to make calls simultaneously. After that there was no serious challenge to the Jaguars, but we had our own troubles. Beauman's car slid into the sandbank at Arnage and he slaved away for some time digging it out. He was just preparing to re-start when Colin Chapman's Lotus arrived at speed and pushed him back in again. Soon afterwards the Rolt-

Hamilton car stopped because the gearbox had run dry and seized up, so our box was topped up with oil at the earliest opportunity.

All the traditional gaiety of the Le Mans scene had been drained away, the familiar dance music on the loud-speakers had been silenced and on Sunday the rain came down in torrents to add to the gloom. I remember stopping to borrow a pullover because I was cold. And so the hours dragged on until 4 p.m., when the Jaguar crossed the line to win at 107 m.p.h., breaking the record set up by Rolt and Hamilton in 1953, while Collins and Frere brought their Aston Martin in a good second.

The atmosphere was somehow tense and expectant, for we all sensed that the end of the race was only the beginning of something far bigger. It was as though we were at the point where a great rock had been hurled into a pond, sending out waves of shock and horror and indignation which would later flow back, bringing consequences which no one could foresee.

As the special editions of the newspapers began to arrive it was obvious that public opinion was going to turn against motor racing in a way which had not been known since the Paris-Madrid race of 1903 was stopped at Bordeaux after leaving a trail of victims and wrecked cars across France.

But public opinion is something which is aroused and moulded by people far away in newspaper offices and radio studios, by politicians and "informed sources". The tens of thousands of spectators at Le Mans showed no anger; only a staggering fatalism. The accident might have been as remote as an earthquake in Chile to the thousands lining the circuit, for they stayed on to the end, despite the cold and driving rain. As soon as the dead and injured had been removed and the frightful evidence of carnage cleared away as far as possible, the spectators crowded back against the rails three and four deep, pressing right up to the burnt-out wreck of the Mercedes and trampling the newspapers with their screaming headlines about the disaster into the mud which only a short while before had been tinged with the blood of the dead and dying.

After the race I had to make a statement to the police and next morning I had an interview with a number of French officials in company with Lofty England. Le Mans was plunged into mourning, and people spoke in hushed voices of the mounting toll of dead and injured.

All possible evidence was collected by an official commission of enquiry, and after examining it for months they decided that no one person could be held responsible.

We can see now that the stage was set for tragedy, for the performance of the cars, increasing each year, had outstripped the existing safety measures on this and a number of other circuits. We drivers knew the dangers which could send cars shuttling back and forth between the safety barriers as they had done before, and as Macklin's car did on this occasion, but I doubt if anyone thought in terms of a car flying through the air, disintegrating like a bomb in the public enclosure to project eighty people into eternity and maim a hundred more.

When I passed Macklin, I was travelling about 25 m.p.h. faster than he was and I decided I had ample time to get ahead before braking for the pits. I certainly had disc brakes which could pull me up very quickly, but so had he. But when a faster car passes you it is almost automatic to glance in your mirror to see if there is another one coming. Now during the briefest possible glance in the driving mirror, Macklin's car would have travelled 80 to 100 feet. And if he happened to miss my signal and found me braking unexpectedly, he would travel another 50 feet before the brain could get a message to the foot to put the brakes on.

What we do know is that Macklin, taken by surprise, for some reason, pulled over to the left and from that moment Levegh's plight was desperate.

The Mercedes would travel about 70 feet while his brain was registering the emergency. We know that he then put his hand out, for Fangio says he owes his own life to this last gesture by Levegh, but while he made this gesture he would have travelled another 250 feet. The footbrake would not slow him down very fast from about 150 m.p.h. and there was no time to get the air brake into action; and so he careered helplessly into the Austin-Healey and the earth barrier.

Some of this is mere conjecture, but it does serve to illustrate the main point: that at modern racing speeds, on a fast circuit like Le Mans, the car travels so far while the brain is registering an emergency and organising counter measures through the hands and feet of the driver, that a minor incident can set up a chain reaction which leads to a major disaster—unless the course is designed with adequate safety factors.

There was a great controversy over the fact that the race had been allowed to continue after the accident, but even Charles Faroux, the veteran clerk of the course, could find no precedent in all his long experience for the situation which confronted him. He did recall that when a crashing jet plane had mown down the spectators at the British air display at Farnborough three years earlier, the show had gone on, but a more immediate reason for continuing was the fear that, if the details of the accident were announced at once and all the hundreds of thousands of spectators were turned loose by stopping the race, the work of evacuating the dead and injured would be rendered difficult if not impossible. Once the race had been allowed to continue during that period he and his associates felt it was best to let it run its course.

The fierceness of the conflagration when the wreck of the Mercedes caught fire started all sorts of wild rumours. Some people maintained that the car had actually exploded and there was dark talk of a secret tank filled with some explosive fuel. Others alleged that the magnesium alloy started burning at once and could not be put out. This greatly worried the Daimler-Benz directors, who flew pressmen from all over Europe to Stuttgart to demonstrate that magnesium is slow to ignite and, once ignited, can be put out by normal extinguishers. However, they went so far in their anxiety to set the record straight that one of the journalists present was moved to ask whether this was a defence of Mercedes or a trial of Hawthorn.

One ray of brightness among the desolation was the action of the insurers—largely British—who promptly accepted liability and paid out about half a million pounds which, if it could not mitigate the sorrow of the bereaved or the suffering of the injured, at least protected them from subsequent hardship.

The consequences for motor sport were far-reaching and we have not heard the last of them, for whenever a serious accident occurs, like de Portago's crash in the Mille Miglia of 1957, memories of Le Mans are aroused afresh to inflame new agitation against motor racing.

The immediate result was that all motoring events on public roads, races and rallies alike, were banned in France until further notice and many classic races, including the French, German, Swiss and Spanish Grand Prix, were cancelled as authorities re-examined safety measures and found them wanting. At Le Mans itself the race authorities, with extraordinary courage, put in hand a far-reaching reconstruction of the course in the accident area, moving the pits back, providing a slip road in front of them and increasing the distance separating the spectators from the track.

Oddly enough in England, where there has always been a strong body of opinion hostile to motor racing, there were probably fewer repercussions from Le Mans than anywhere else. British tracks, being small, do not permit very high speeds and as they are used exclusively for motor racing they already have properly designed permanent protection for spectators which is more effective than anything that can be arranged on a public road closed for the occasion.

## Chapter Twenty

## THE TOURIST TROPHY

THE DUTCH had only a couple of days in which to decide what to do about their Grand Prix which was due to be held among the sandhills at Zandvoort the weekend after Le Mans. In spite of the rising storm, they calmly reviewed their safety arrangements and decided to go ahead. Mercedes had issued a rather huffy statement to the effect that they would only take part in further races if "more and sufficient" precautions were taken on the course and sufficient supervision and discipline of drivers assured; to the surprise of many people they decided to settle for the Dutch safety measures and sent three cars, a short-chassis one for Fangio, and two medium-wheelbase models for Moss and Kling.

Following the Lancia retirement, Ferrari got in touch with me at Le Mans just before the race and invited me to drive for him again. I was naturally delighted that he was prepared to take me back and found myself teamed up with Trintignant and Castellotti, who had also just joined Ferrari. Musso, Mieres and Behra had Maseratis and there were some Gordinis and independents.

Having made the best Ferrari practice lap, I found myself in the second row at the start with Musso, behind the three Mercedes. Fangio and Moss led the race from start to finish, although challenged for a time by Musso, who was in excellent form. It was the first time I had driven the Super Squalo which had been developed from the car I drove at Barcelona and I could not do much with it on this circuit. It suffered from extreme understeer and even with the steering on full lock it seemed to keep on going straight ahead for an awfully long time on corners. It was quite fast, but mine kept sticking gear. I stopped at the pits twice and they could find nothing wrong with it, which made me look rather foolish, but the third time I arrive with the gear well and truly jammed. There was nothing to be done with it, so I kept going and finished seventh.

I had a clear month before my next race, the British Grand Prix at Aintree, so I went home to Farnham, but once again fate struck and carried off Don Beauman, one of my best friends.

He was killed when his 2-litre Connaught crashed just after setting up fastest lap of the day in the Leinster Trophy race at Wicklow. Don started racing in 1953 on my 1½-litre Riley, which he bought from us, and he graduated to the Connaught in 1954. He was progressing well and was sometimes brilliant, but occasionally he made mistakes, for no obvious reason, which I think was more a flaw of temperament than of driving ability. The news was one more blow in a year which was turning out to be a sad one for me personally and for everyone connected with motor racing.

For the British Grand Prix, Ferrari reverted to the old-style cars which simply were not fast enough—even the privately entered Maseratis could get away from us and the Mercedes took the first four places, Stirling Moss winning half a second ahead of Fangio. The weather was fantastic for Aintree, sunny and extremely hot, and I began to feel the effects, so I handed over to Castellotti, who brought the car in sixth, behind Musso.

I had a bad race in the sports-car event too, as the Jaguar's rigid rear axle produced wheelspin on the slow Aintree corners and the Aston Martins with their de Dion axles left us. I came to the conclusion that Aintree is not a circuit I like very much. For me, most of the corners are too slow and the one after the pits is rather unpleasant, with that great brick wall on the outside. The one part I enjoy is the Melling Crossing, which is really interesting.

The relative merits of the D-type Jaguar and the DB3S Aston Martin often form a subject for discussion and I had a talk with Peter Collins about it. At Le Mans, the Jaguar wins repeatedly because its greater power gives it a higher maximum speed along the straight, but at Aintree and on the Nurburgring, and on many other difficult circuits where road holding is at a premium, the Aston runs away from it. Yet at Silverstone the Jaguars have always been able to win, except when they ran into mechanical trouble. Why should this be? Peter's view was that the Aston liked very fast corners and very slow corners, but did not show any great superiority on those in between; it is these medium-speed corners which predominate at Silverstone.

. . . . .

Stirling Moss had gone abroad and did not expect to be back in time to drive his Maserati in the International Trophy event on the twisty little London track at the Crystal Palace, so I agreed to drive it. I won the event and made fastest lap, after duelling with Roy Salvadori on the Gilby Engineering Maserati in the heat, and with Harry Schell on the Vanwall, which made a slow start, in the final. It was ironical that the car should give me a victory on my first attempt at driving a Maserati after all the bitter disappointments it had caused Stirling, particularly as he had arrived back in time to drive, but he had sportingly let me carry on.

Jaguar had decided not to compete officially in the Goodwood Nine Hours race, although a car was later found for the Rolt-Hamilton entry, so I arranged to drive a 3-litre Ferrari with de Portago. On paper it should have won, but after the first few laps I found it difficult to get the gears in and then difficult to get them out. It took a long time to adjust the linkage and we lost about seven laps. We managed to work up into fourth place, but the back axle broke. The car was magnificent while it lasted and I always think the 3-litre was one of the best sports cars ever built.

The Ferrari pit crew were right off form and drove the officials frantic because they had to block the loop road into the pits completely every time they changed a wheel. John Bolster wrote in *Autosport*:

"Compared with all this efficiency, the crazy gang in the Ferrari pits provided some light relief. . . . For some odd reason, the racing jacks had to be used from the side of the chassis, which meant man-oeuvring the vehicle into a position at right angles to the pit. The whole comic opera, of which Harry Schell was undoubtedly the prima donna, was performed in three languages. Yet, it was altogether rather a tragedy, for under proper management these cars might have won the race."

The race was won by Aston Martin for the third time in succession, but was marred by another fatal accident, when Mike Keen was killed in a Cooper-Bristol which somersaulted and caught fire at St. Mary's after leading its class.

On the Monday after the race I had some more tragic news; after eleven days of unconsciousness, Julian Crossley had died as a result of a crash in a motor-cycle race at Dundrod. Julian and I had known each other for about nine years and we had done a lot of flying and motor-cycling together. When I first heard the news of his accident, I had flown out to Belfast the following day as his mother was too ill and upset to make the journey. I stayed two or three days and then flew home when his mother was fit enough to go over. Isabel Baird, the widow of Bobby Baird, who was killed at Snetterton in 1953, was very kind and put her house at Mrs. Crossley's disposal while she was out there.

.        .        .        .        .        .

The duel between Ferrari and Aston Martin was renewed in the *Daily Herald* International Trophy event at Oulton Park the following week, with the same result. Reg Parnell on the only works-entered DB3S beat me by 32.6 seconds after 221 miles. This race taught me a lesson about tyres. I had made fastest lap in practice by a margin of nearly two seconds, but we did not have enough tyres with us after wearing out a large number in the Goodwood race. One of our Pirellis was part worn and the expert doubted if it would last the race. We therefore put Pirellis on the front, and Dunlops on the back. Reg Parnell told me afterwards that when he saw what was happening he was delighted, because he knew I would have trouble holding the car; and he was right, the back end slid all over the place. We should have fitted Dunlops all round or carried on to see how long the Pirellis would last. Reg got into the lead at the start and I never saw him again. Later, Peter Collins came up in another Aston to challenge me for second place, but I managed to hold him off, although it was quite a struggle, because by this time one of the shock absorbers had failed and the car was pattering its way across the road coming out of the corners.

.        .        .        .        .

During this time some interesting things were happening in Italy. Following consultation between Lancia, Ferrari, Fiat and other interested parties, the whole of the Lancia racing material, including nine V8 Formula-1 cars, their transporters, spare parts, drawings and technical data, were handed over to Ferrari and Fiat guaranteed him a subsidy to enable him to run them for the next five years.

The combined effects of an ambitious building programme and very heavy expenditure on the racing department had created difficulties for Lancia and this arrangement allowed their very advanced cars to go on running for the benefit of Italian engineering prestige, even if no longer under Lancia management, and left Lancia free to re-establish their financial position.

At the same time, workmen were busy at Monza completing the new oval high-speed track with banked turns, which was to be combined with the existing road circuit to give a total lap distance of 6.2 miles for the Italian Grand Prix in September. The work was only completed about three weeks before the race and, apart from the new problems posed for drivers, constructors and tyre manufacturers by the continuous high speeds which could be maintained, the banking was very bumpy in parts and imposed a severe strain on the chassis, to say nothing of the driver.

The original intention was to operate the Lancias and Ferraris as separate teams, but during practice the Lancias ran into tyre trouble. Farina threw two treads; one of them went while he was doing well over 150 m.p.h. on the banking, throwing him into a spin during which he hit the safety fence, and he was very lucky to get away with it. Lancia were using tyres which were not very suitable for these new conditions, so the team was withdrawn and a spare Super Squalo was found for Castellotti.

I was driving a Super Squalo and did not like the new track at all. I told both Farina and Villoresi that they could have my car if they wanted a drive, but there were no takers, so I was stuck with it. Yet once the race started, I enjoyed it very much, and was very disappointed when I had to retire.

Mercedes carried out a series of experiments with various types of droop-snoot on a short-chassis streamliner, then sent for normal streamliners for Fangio and Moss, giving normal and short non-streamlined cars to Kling and Taruffi. The works Maseratis were using five-speed gearboxes; Peter Collins was driving in the team for the first time, and Behra had a new streamlined car with partly-enclosed wheels, which proved slightly faster than the other Maseratis in practice. The new 8-cylinder Gordini, with its curious parallel-action suspension by leading and trailing arms, was also appearing for the first time.

Up to this time I had had no experience of throwing tyre treads, but as it was obviously a possibility in this race I asked some of the Dunlop people what were the symptoms. They told me that I might feel no more than a slight vibration, but that when it started I would have only a few seconds in which to slow the car down before the tyre burst and things really started happening.

The four Mercedes set a very high speed, pursued by Castellotti, but as the race went on Moss and Kling were eliminated by gearbox failures. I had worked my way into fifth place behind Castellotti and Behra and had high hopes of finishing fourth.

The two surviving Mercedes lapped me, but by belting round the banking absolutely flat out I got past Taruffi again and was gaining slightly on Fangio, when the car started to vibrate. I shut off and waited for the bang of the bursting tyre, but nothing happened, so I called in at the pit. They could find nothing wrong with the tyres and it happened twice more before they spotted that the brackets holding the gearbox had snapped, allowing the whole gearbox and differential assembly to float about.

Fangio won at an average speed of 128.5 m.p.h., making this the fastest race run on a road circuit since the war and Stirling Moss put in a lap at 134 m.p.h. to set up the first record for the new circuit. That was the last race in which the brilliant W. 196R Mercedes-Benz single-seaters appeared, but we still had the 300 SLR sports models to contend with in the Tourist Trophy race at Dundrod.

    .      .      .      .      .

This was a tremendously exciting race, but one which added heavily to the 1955 casualty list. With Desmond Titterington as co-driver, I had a single D-type Jaguar against the Mercedes team of three and the Aston Martin team which had won at Goodwood. Stirling Moss shot into the lead at the start with me on the Jaguar second but we had only done two laps when a column of smoke appeared beyond Deer's Leap. The yellow flags were out as we hurtled down the hill and as we breasted the final hump wrecked cars were strewn around and the road ahead was obliterated by a mass of flame and smoke. There was no hope of stopping; Moss disappeared into it and I followed, praying that we should not hit anything. Miraculously we got through. But as we came round again, lap after lap, we could see the wrecks of seven cars involved in this terrible multiple pile-up.

Piecing the story together afterwards, it seemed that du Barry's 300 SL Mercedes was being closely followed by Wharton's Frazer-Nash over the hump, when Jim Mayers swept past them both. In a flash his Cooper-Climax struck the bank, bounced into some concrete posts and broke into pieces, spraying burning petrol over the road. Mayers was killed at once, and Bill Smith, following him through, hit the wreckage, receiving fatal injuries. His Connaught caught fire to add to the confusion. Ken Wharton's Frazer-Nash crashed as he strove to avoid the spinning cars and burned out, but he and Kretschmann, whose Porsche skated through somehow, got away with fairly minor burns. The road now seemed completely blocked and Macklin, Russell and Jopp all crashed their cars to avoid sliding into the inferno.

Stirling was steadily pulling away and Fangio who had lost time at the start came up from behind and passed me. This was too much, so I took him again with a lap at 94.61 m.p.h. which set up a new record, beating even Farina's figure with the supercharged 1½-litre 158 Alfa Romeo.

It looked as if Fangio and I were all set for one of our gruelling struggles, but driving right to the limit I found that I could get away from him and built up a useful lead before refuelling and handing over to Titterington. The Mercedes pit work was far slower than usual and by the time Fangio and Moss had refuelled and handed over to Kling and Fitch, the Jaguar was nicely in the lead, Moss's advantage being cancelled out while the mechanics cut away body panels which had been shattered by a burst tyre.

It was raining heavily now, and Titterington was gaining steadily, but when Stirling took over from Fitch he started cutting down the lead. I got back into the Jaguar and pulled out all the stops to keep ahead of him, but it just could not be done. I could hold my own over most of the circuit and even gain a little on the fastest bits, but the Mercedes could definitely get through the tight corners faster; I lost ground through one group between the hairpin, and at a second group between Rushyhill and Leathemstown. On these stretches especially in the wet, a rigid rear axle was at a disadvantage.

We seemed certain of a good second place, but as I went round one of the corners just before the pits on the lap before the last, I felt something go in the engine. I put the clutch out and freewheeled round the next corner, but the car suddenly whipped round sideways and spun on its own oil. The crankshaft had broken and cracked the sump. It was a bitter disappointment with the finish almost in sight.

But there was still more bad news, for I had seen the upturned wreck of R. L. Mainwaring's Elva burning at the roadside and I learned at the pits that he had been burned to death in the crash. Mainwaring and I had been to school together and he was developing into quite a good driver, but he had apparently followed someone else too fast through an S-bend and lost control. I had known Jim Mayers ever since my

Riley days and had been talking to young Bill Smith, a very promising newcomer, only the night before the race. Three drivers gone in one race. Everyone was very subdued that night, for motor racing seemed to be haunted by disaster.

.    .    .    .    .

The last event of the season for me was the *Daily Dispatch* International Gold Cup race at Oulton. Ferrari had sent over two of the V8 Lancias for Castellotti and me and a normal model for de Portago. Works Mascratis were entered for Moss, Musso and Gould, while Salvadori had the usual privately owned one. Collins was giving the new 4-cylinder B.R.M. its first public outing, Schell and Trintignant had Vanwalls and there were a lot of Connaughts and Cooper-Bristols. We used practice as an opportunity to experiment with tyres on the Lancias. We tried them with the normal Engleberts first and then I went out with a set of the new R3 Dunlops; these really transformed the car and enabled me to put up the fastest practice lap. With these tyres and a light load of fuel I was very impressed with the car's behaviour. For race day, however, we had to revert to the normal tyres which did not suit this particular circuit so well. Ing. Jano, the designer of the car, made some adjustments to the shock absorbers, and made the car quite reasonable to handle, but when the tanks were filled it became quite difficult to hold.

Castellotti and I got away first, but Stirling came past and neither of us could hold him. Musso and Collins also passed us, but the Maserati lost its gears and the B.R.M. lost its oil pressure, so I got an unexpected second place.

.    .    .    .    .

It had been a tragic mixed-up season. I had had some sports-car successes and the B.R.D.C. awarded me the John Cobb Memorial Trophy, but I had not won a single point towards the World Championship. Three of my closest friends and several acquaintances had been snatched away in accidents and I had been caught up in the greatest disaster in the history of motor racing.

I was grateful for the understanding shown by the Editors of the *Motor Year Book, 1956*, who wrote in their summary of the season:

"Overshadowed, perhaps, but not overlooked were two outstanding performances by Mike Hawthorn, whose fortunes have not flowed much in his favour during the season. We rank among the greatest motor-racing exploits his win at record speed in the Le Mans 24-Hour Race, ably if quietly backed by his co-driver Ivor Bueb, a star of the 500 c.c. racing firmament, who did exactly what was asked of him in keeping the Jaguar where it was wanted while Hawthorn rested. In that race velocities were fantastic. During the opening stages Hawthorn raced wheel to wheel with Fangio's Mercedes, beat him and broke the lap record at over 122 m.p.h. Then came the appalling disaster, after which not only had Hawthorn to regain lost distance but must have been worried psychologically by the Levegh tragedy. In spite of these things he grimly held the Jaguar in the battle, and when the Mercedes tardily withdrew, continued to beat every other car in the race and to win at over 107 m.p.h. His other feat, in our opinion, was his drive in the Tourist Trophy where he fought a lone Jaguar entry against the complete Mercedes team, passed them, fell back, regained lost ground, lapped Fangio and was a certain 'second' just before the end when the over-stressed car failed."

All the same, I fervently hoped that 1956 would have something better in store.

PART V

CHEQUERED

CHAPTER TWENTY-ONE

## TEETHING TROUBLES

AT THE end of the 1955 season, Enzo Ferrari invited me to go down and discuss the question of driving for him during 1956. I was very anxious to do so, but Jaguars had already told me that they wanted me to drive for them in sports-car races, and I therefore suggested to Ferrari that I drive for him in Grand Prix races and in any sports-car events where Jaguars were not entered. As the Jaguar programme was quite a limited one, covering perhaps six races, this would still leave me many opportunities of driving Ferraris, but he was not prepared to consider it and I was not prepared to quit Jaguars, so we had to part. Later, of course, Ferrari consented to share Peter Collins with Aston Martin in the way he had refused to consider with me.

After a conference with Sir William Lyons, Mr. Heynes, technical director, and Lofty England, I signed up to lead the Jaguar team. Soon afterwards negotiations also began with Stirling Moss, who had been freed by the retirement of Mercedes-Benz from racing, but he was not prepared to run as No. 2 to me. I agreed to run with Stirling as joint team-leader, but the thing finally fell through on details.

After failing to agree on terms with Ferrari, I had had a chat with Omer Orsi regarding the possibility of driving Maseratis in Grand Prix events and he was interested, but I had agreed to try the B.R.M. first. I tried it on a wet day and found it very frightening indeed. It snaked at high speed and one had to hold it very firmly to keep it going in a straight line. On the other hand it was extremely fast and obviously had plenty of power. I still wanted to drive British if possible and Mr. Owen offered me an excellent contract, with a retainer plus 50 per cent of all prize money, starting money and component bonuses, so I accepted.

We then started testing at Silverstone, but ran into a lot of trouble with the oil pump which caused it to lose its oil pressure after a few laps. Valves were stretching and valve springs were breaking, causing a lot of delays, but during this time a big improvement was made in the steering. The car would hold a straight line quite well at speed but was still rather twitchy on corners and this characteristic remained with it for a long time. The tail would go if one tried to accelerate too early, and would whip back the other way if one eased off.

It was obvious that the car was not going to be ready for the Argentine races, so I suggested they send out the Maserati which Peter Collins had driven the previous year. This was a 1954 model with 1955 modifications, plus disc brakes and Dunlop wheels. It was rather prone to oversteer with a full tank and switch to understeer as the fuel was consumed, but it was quite a nice little car.

The Argentine expedition was agreed, but as time was short the car had to be sent by air which cost about £1,500 each way. I flew out with Basil Putt, who had just joined as team manager after doing the same job for Connaught, and Reg Williams, who used to be Bira's mechanic and was going to look after our car. It was a tourist flight in an elderly Constellation which rattled and rolled; there were no hot meals—only coffee, cocoa and thick sandwiches—and we decided it was a thing to avoid if possible.

Ferrari, like a boy with a new constructional toy, was trying out all the models in the book at one and the same time. His Argentine collection included examples of the standard V8 Lancia and the old-style 4-cylinder Ferrari, the Lancia with new tail tank and smaller side tanks in the fairings between the wheels, the Super Squalo with the Ferrari 4-cylinder engine and the same with the Lancia V8 engine. The only thing he did not have was a Lancia with a Ferrari engine. The Maseratis were as at Monza, with five-speed gearboxes.

At the start Gonzales and Menditeguy led with Maseratis and Fangio ran third on a modified Lancia with fuel tank in the tail. The Owen Maserati was outclassed, but I had a private dice with Peter Collins in a Ferrari with a Lancia engine, which did not seem to handle too well and was not very fast. Fangio stopped with his engine misfiring and took over Musso's Lancia. Castellotti dropped out, Piotti braked sharply in a corner and was rammed by Collins, and Moss broke a valve, leaving me very happy to get third place behind Fangio and Behra.

But once again the Argentine Grand Prix ended in protests. Once again Fangio was involved, and again it was Ugolini, now managing for Maserati instead of Ferrari, who was the accuser. Fangio had spun off and had been pushed to re-start by a number of people, including photographers. Ugolini demanded that he be disqualified for receiving outside assistance, but the protest was rejected and later the F.I.A. confirmed the decision, with the extraordinary dictum that everyone on the circuit wearing a badge is an official and *ipso facto* entitled to assist competitors. Yet it is not difficult to think of other people who have been disqualified since in similar circumstances.

Fangio himself is a splendid sportsman who plays fair and observes the rules, but it seems that when he gets out to Argentina he becomes the victim of over-enthusiastic helpers to whom all's fair as long as their national hero wins.

The whole circus then moved on to Mendoza, a pleasant little city which is a centre of a large wine-growing area in the foothills of the Andes. We flew the 600 miles or so in a well-worn D.C.4 and during the flight someone remarked that there was a lot of oil streaming back over the wing on his side; then someone else swore he could see petrol leaking, so we all trooped over to have a look. Immediately, somebody else announced that the same thing was happening at the other side, so we all rushed across to see. Goodness knows what the pilot thought when he found the plane being buffeted about by the passengers, but he got us there safely.

It was very hot and dry—so hot that the start of the race had to be put back for a time—and the altitude created carburation problems, but Maserati helped us out with some alternative jets. The circuit, about $2\frac{1}{2}$ miles long, is in the scrub just outside the city; it has a tar-macadam surface and twists a good deal, with several fast bends, but the surface was then rather rough.

During the race I found that my steering was becoming rather vague on the bumpy surface; the car was lurching from side to side, and would sometimes leap across the road when going into corners; I pulled in and we found that the bracket which holds the steering column to the dash had fractured. It was patched up and I finished ninth. The race was another victory for Fangio, with Stirling Moss on a Maserati second.

We owed a lot to Jackie Greene, son of the late Eric Greene, who provided some of his boys to help in the pit, but we did not get very highly organised in the time available. No complete lap score was kept, so our people did what so many other people do—nipped along to the Maserati pit and asked Ugolini.

Among the drivers Ugolini is looked upon as a wizard who has everything under control and it is quite a normal thing to find drivers working for his biggest competitors going along to consult him about their practice times, because they know he will have timed them all and will produce the figures accurate to within a tenth of a second long before the official times are announced. They say he can time every car in a race with one stopwatch and he has a capacity for unruffled concentration which enables him to keep track of everything that is happening to his own and his rivals' cars so that he can react at once as the situation develops. He is certainly the greatest timekeeper I have ever seen in action.

In the B.R.M. outfit we were additionally handicapped by lack of equipment. After years of racing there was no proper signalling gear, only a much-used blackboard on which the new signs got mixed up with the traces of the old ones.

When I got back to England we started a programme of brake testing on the B.R.M. to try out disc brakes provided by Girling, Lockheed and Dunlop. We finally chose the Girling, but the single rear brake presented a continuing problem, as the pads wore rapidly and it would start giving trouble about halfway through a Grand Prix event.

. . . . . .

The tests concluded, I left for Sebring, where three works Jaguars painted in the American colours of blue and white, had been entered by Briggs Cunningham. Titterington and myself had one car, Bueb and Hamilton another, and Briggs drove the third with John Gordon Benett. The British drivers of the team, with Colin Chapman and Bryan Turle, flew out via New York, where we spent an amusing evening, but it snowed during the night and next day there were no planes leaving for Palm Beach. We settled down to a game of poker.

Suddenly the phone rang. I answered it and Lofty England said we had half an hour to make a train for Washington where we could pick up a plane. I broke the news and made a dive for the kitty.

Everybody got something except Duncan Hamilton who sat there bellowing: "You can't stop now. I've got four aces!"

I have noticed since that it is always Duncan's luck to be stuck with the best hand ever, when the game breaks up.

We flew to Miami and then on to Palm Beach, where Briggs

provided us with cars. I got a Cadillac convertible with power-assisted steering which was very fast but terrifying to drive.

Our D-type with fuel injection went extremely well in the race, leading the Moss-Collins Aston Martin and the Fangio-Castellotti 3.5-litre Ferrari for the first four hours. The Aston Martin dropped out with engine trouble and it looked as if we might win, but we ran into trouble with the disc brakes, the pads of which wore out, allowing the fluid to escape; we were left with no alternative but to withdraw.

Fangio and Castellotti won, exceeding 1,000 miles in the twelve hours for the first time; Musso and Schell on another 3.5 Ferrari were second; and a D-type Jaguar driven by Indianapolis winner Bob Sweikert with Jack Ensley came in third.

·　　·　　·　　·　　·

The Easter Meeting at Goodwood opened the season for the B.R.M. and we had two cars, one for me and one for Tony Brooks, who had joined us following his runaway win on the Connaught at Syracuse at the end of 1955. There was a good entry for the Richmond Trophy event, including three Syracuse Connaughts, Moss and Rosier on Maseratis and the 8-cylinder Gordini. Brooks's car had not been ready in time for practice so he was in the back row, but my car made a beautiful getaway and I led for 1½ laps before being overwhelmed by Archie Scott-Brown on a Connaught and Stirling Moss who were fighting a wheel-to-wheel battle which only ended when the Connaught disappeared in a cloud of smoke and dust with a broken crankshaft.

I was still second, but the car was becoming a bit difficult to hold and suddenly, while I was doing over 100 m.p.h. near Fordwater, it started to slide. Correction had no effect and the car spun round in the road while I held on tight. Then I felt it hit the earth as it left the track and I knew it was going to overturn. I must get out. I let go of everything just as it pitched into the air and I felt myself being thrown out. There was a split second of panic as my ankle jammed between the seat and the chassis. The car was cartwheeling over—quite slowly it seemed—and I knew I must break free before it landed again or I should be finished. Suddenly there was a feeling of utter relief. I had broken free and was alone in mid-air. It was quiet and I seemed to be floating in space, defying the law of gravity. Then came the bone-jarring shock as I hit the ground. I got my breath back after a few moments, but there was a sharp pain in my ankle as I tried to stand. I sat there rather dazed, trying to figure out what had happened.

The car was some distance away badly crumpled, with its wheels in the air. But there were only three wheels. One of the front wheels had been torn off as it landed after the first somersault.

When the car was stripped down it was found that one of the rear universal joints had seized owing to a fault in the rubber cover which had allowed the oil to escape. I was certainly lucky for I was the only survivor in three crashes that day. Young A. F. Dennis, a newcomer driving Duncan Hamilton's D-type Jaguar, got first gear instead of third when approaching Woodcote; the wheels locked and the car slid into the infield where it overturned and he was killed. A. P. O. Rogers was also killed when his car overturned at St. Mary's. He had overturned a car at the same spot the previous season, and had miraculously survived a bad crash at the Melling Crossing at Aintree.

I had entered a works D-type Jaguar at this meeting, and Mr. Heynes the technical director, had provided an experimental car with fuel injection and a de Dion rear axle but for some reason which I could not fathom it did not suit Goodwood and I could not get round nearly as fast as the Ecurie Ecosse cars. It oversteered and I could only lap in about 1 min. 39 sec.

·   ·   ·   ·   ·

While we were in the United States, Ivor Bueb had invited me to drive his Lotus-Climax in the British Empire Trophy race at Oulton Park, while he drove his Climax-engined Cooper. Unfortunately Ivor crashed the Cooper at Druids early in the race. I had a good tussle with Chapman, Salvadori and Moss in a Lotus and two Coopers, to finish third in the heat, but I could not do better than fourth in the final, which was won by Stirling after a stirring struggle with Colin.

My engine seemed to be lacking power and we found later that it had needles of two different sizes in the carburetters.

·   ·   ·   ·   ·

Soon afterwards I flew up to Bourne to demonstrate the B.R.M. to the O.R.M.A., the supporters' club. They were given an explanation of what had happened at Goodwood, the bits from my car were laid out for inspection and they were assured that the trouble had been rectified, but this later proved to be an optimistic assumption. We certainly had no more trouble with the universal joints that day, but the rear suspension came loose while Flockhart was doing a few laps.

Photographs taken at this time show that I was sitting half out of the car like a man in a hip bath and I was trying to persuade Peter Berthon to produce a car with a longer wheelbase, not only so that I could sit in it, but also because I thought a little extra weight and a slightly longer wheelbase would improve the stability.

The car in which I crashed at Goodwood had not been completely destroyed. Front suspension and body were badly damaged but the chassis frame was checked in the jig and found to be practically free from distortion. It was rebuilt in preparation for the Aintree meeting and we went to Silverstone to try it. I did a few laps in Brooks's car first and then went out in mine. I had only done a few laps, and was just coming into the straight before the pits when things happened so quickly that I literally did not know what hit me. The bonnet had come off, hit me in the face, smashed my visor and almost knocked me unconscious. Dazed and groggy I somehow managed to stop the car, although I nearly lost consciousness.

I was taken to a doctor in Towcester who proposed to stitch up the wound on my face. I said: "No you don't," and after a bit of discussion he agreed that he would have preferred to do without the stitches if it had been his face, so he stuck some plaster on it and I went back to the track. It turned out that the bonnet was not the one belonging to my car; it had been put on by mistake and did not fit properly. My luck was in, because if it had come round at a different angle it could have taken my head off. I did a few more laps but I was now feeling off form so I went home.

.    .    .    .    .    .

The Aintree "200" was a revival of a race which the old J.C.C. used to run at Brooklands and produced a field of fifteen cars. The Vanwalls were not ready, but there were three British Grand Prix cars in the front row at the start; Scott-Brown's Syracuse Connaught, my B.R.M. and Titterington's streamlined Connaught. Behind us were Moss and Salvadori on Maseratis, Brooks on the other B.R.M. and more Connaughts and Maseratis. Our times were below those of 1955 and the best I could do in practice was a lap in 2 min. 4 sec. against the record of 2 min. The B.R.M.s were very fast and the brakes were powerful, but they were still not very happy in the corners.

I made a good start, but left my braking rather late at one corner and was so busy concentrating on holding the car straight that I did not have time to change down. By the time I had got the lower gear in, Archie Scott-Brown had whipped past. I managed to get past him again on the straight and concluded he was probably trying to save his engine in view of the Goodwood blow-up. However, he was pressing me hard when I tried to brake going into Cottage Corner. But there *were* no brakes; not only that, there was no pedal! I stamped my foot down again, thinking I must have missed the pedal, but all I succeeded in doing was catching my foot against the accelerator and I went careering off the road onto the open grassland.

I was in a towering fury as I motored slowly back to the pits and I did not spare anyone's feelings. We found that the clevis pin connecting the pedal to the brake gear had dropped out; apparently because it had no split pin to hold it.

At that moment Raymond Mays, the director of the B.R.M. organisation came up and said: "It's a funny thing; I was saying to my mother this morning: 'Mike has had two bad crashes, one when the car turned over at Goodwood and one when the bonnet flew off in his face. There's usually a third, and I hope it isn't going to be a bad one.'"

Archie's engine had blown up again in the meantime and Brooks was leading on the second B.R.M., but he had to slow down because the pads on the rear disc brake had worn away and Stirling won.

I had some small consolation from a win with the Lotus in the 2-litre sports-car race.

.    .    .    .    .

Despite all our troubles I still had great faith in the B.R.M. as I was convinced that its defects were curable in a few months of concentrated development work and I persuaded Mr. Owen to enter one car for me in the International Trophy race at the *Daily Express* Silverstone meeting while two others were being got ready for Monaco the following week-end.

There was quite an impressive entry, with Ferrari-Lancias for Fangio and Collins, the Vanwalls with their new chassis for Moss and Schell, the Connaughts and various others. Moss and Schell lapped in 1 min. 42 sec. in practice; Fangio and I did 1 min. 43 sec. which beat all previous Silverstone records.

At the start, Fangio went into Copse ahead of me, but as I came out of the corner in third gear I pulled out, put my foot down and just

Dicing with Colin Chapman, both in Lotuses, at Goodwood in 1956. Eventually we both spun and collided. *[Benjafield*

My first time out in a Maserati—and Stirling's at that—Crystal Palace, 1955. *[Klemantaski*

Why Klemantaski was not run down by my Cooper-Bristol we shall never know. [*Kleme*

Struggling with the B.R.M. in the British Grand Prix, 1956. The car later developed an oil leak and I retired.

left him on acceleration. It shook me almost as much as it did him. The performance was absolutely terrific and I drew away, putting in one lap in 1 min. 43 sec. to set up an official record at 102.3 m.p.h., which was equalled but not beaten by the Vanwalls. Moss came past the Lancia and moved into second place, but I was managing to hold my lead. I was debating how long I could stick it, however, for this was not my car; the seat did not fit me and the mechanics had not been able to do anything about it; I was in increasing pain from the cramped driving position. However, the problem was solved on the thirteenth lap. The engine cut and my race was over.

The sudden stoppage was due to the breakage of an old-pattern timing wheel which had been excessively drilled for lightness. It was known to be weak, but there had been none of the correct pattern available when the engine was being built up and so it had to be used.

The remarkable thing was that the car had showed performance equal to anything else on the track although I was holding the engine down to 8,000 r.p.m., compared with the 9,000 r.p.m. limit permitted at Goodwood. The lower limit was imposed because a slightly heavier type of valve was being used. The lighter ones had been breaking up and the revs were cut down to prevent the heavier ones stretching.

．　　　．　　　．　　　．　　　．

I had two drives for Jaguar, in the big sports-car event and the production-car race, but my luck was out all day. For the sports-car race I had a D-type Jaguar with fuel injection and an ordinary rear axle, while Titterington had a car with a de Dion axle. At Silverstone the de Dion gave a smoother ride and cut out the wheelspin on corners which the cars with the ordinary axle experienced even with a ZF differential. The de Dion weighed more, which tends to be a handicap at Silverstone, but on balance I preferred it. However, Titterington said he could not do as well with the rigid axle as with the de Dion, so I took the old type.

After the usual Le Mans start Moss and Salvadori on Aston Martins led Titterington and myself, but as we went past the pits at the end of the first lap the three of us rushed past Stirling. We were tightly bunched at Stowe and as we approached Club Corner Titterington was inside Salvadori. The Aston Martin started moving over to the right to take the corner, and I could see that Titterington was having to move further in towards the edge of the track; I knew he was never going to get round the corner so I slowed and glancing in my mirror saw that Stirling was doing the same thing. In a flash Titterington spun in the middle of the track and I just managed to pull to the left and go round behind him, followed by Stirling. As we accelerated away I heard a terrific crunch and glancing back saw a D-type bonnet rise in the air while cars slid in all directions. Collins's Aston had rammed the Jaguar fair and square, Sanderson's D-type had climbed backwards onto the earth bank, Parnell's Aston was in the ditch and Wharton's Ferrari had spun. Yet no one was hurt.

Salvadori had by now got a lead of a few seconds and I set up a new sports-car record with a lap in 1 min. 47 sec. (98.48 m.p.h.) trying to catch him. But the steering started to stick and the car began weaving about in an alarming way; a ball joint was seizing up and I had to retire.

I had made fastest practice lap for the production-car race with one of the new 2.4 Jaguars and hoped this one at least was in the bag. Duncan Hamilton had a similar car and Ivor Bueb a Mark VII. But on the second lap the oil pressure slumped and I was out with a broken valve spring. Ivor took the lead, chased by Duncan, but in between them, to everyone's surprise, came Ken Wharton driving with terrific verve in an Austin A90 with Weber carburetters, racing head and lower, stiffer suspension.

## CHAPTER TWENTY-TWO

## FLYING LICENCE

AFTER getting my initial flying tuition in the Argentine, I had obtained a pilot's licence and was using my own Fairchild Argus to fly to meetings whenever possible. I therefore thought it would be a good idea to fly out to the Monaco race, taking a friend of mine, Neil McNab, with me, but it was my first attempt at flying to France and we did not break any speed records. We left from Fair Oaks one afternoon and after clearing customs landed at Le Touquet because of the heavy cloud. We were told that it was clearer about seven miles on, so we took off and made for Abbeville. As this town proved elusive we decided to make for Beauvais and after flying round for a while we spotted a rather large town with a tall tower in the middle and realised we were over Paris.

We landed at Toussus le Noble, got a taxi into Paris, which cost about £3, and stayed the night with some friends. It was a late night as sometimes happens in Paris and we were late getting up next morning. Feeling somewhat jaded, we eventually got airborne, but it was a hot day with a lot of bumps, which magnified themselves in our heads, so we abandoned hope of reaching Nice that night and settled for Lyon.

We knew that private aircraft were not allowed to land at Nice after 10 a.m. and therefore had to start soon after six o'clock next morning, which caused a bit of gloom at the little café where we put up for the night, but we made it and for a minor prince's ransom we were able to persuade a taxi driver to take us from Nice to Monte Carlo.

Next day I practised on the circuit with the B.R.M. and it went very well, except for a slight delay in picking up after the Station hairpin, where the four-speed gearbox was at a disadvantage. But suddenly the engine went woolly and we had to have the head off. It was valve trouble again.

The B.R.M. has two valves per cylinder and they are exceptionally large—about 2¼ in. in diameter. To save weight the ones we were using were hollow, with a disc like a penny welded into the head to seal the aperture. In some cases the welds had parted and the disc had dropped out; in others the welds held but the disc split and curled up. When the discs dropped, they naturally broke the pistons.

More valves were flown out, but the same thing happened again. We could have patched up the engines sufficiently to start in the race and collect the starting money, a dodge which is sometimes practised in motor racing, but Raymond Mays acted with exemplary integrity. He told the organisers frankly that the cars could not last the distance, withdrew them from the race and paid me what I would have received as my share of the starting money.

This gave me a chance to see the race as a spectator and I found it extremely exciting watching the other chaps earn their keep.

The return flight to England was rather better organised. We left Nice at 8 a.m., refuelled at Lyon and Le Touquet and got back to England after eleven hours, which made quite a tiring day.

．　　　．　　　．　　　．　　　．

The next week-end I enjoyed a long tussle with Colin Chapman at Goodwood. We were each driving a Lotus-Climax and ran wheel to wheel for a large part of the race until we both spun in close formation. Colin went on to win, but I had to stop for a moment to pull a bent wing away from the wheel and came second.

．　　　．　　　．　　　．　　　．

The 1,000 kilometre sports-car race at the Nurburgring was the fourth round of the 1956 World Championship and all the fastest sports cars were there. We had two D-type Jaguars for Titterington and me, Hamilton and Frere. Ferrari had 4-cylinder 3½-litre cars for Fangio-Castellotti and de Portago-Gendebien, and 12-cylinder models of the same size for Trintignant-Musso and Hill-Wharton. Behra-Moss and Schell-Taruffi formed the crews for 300S 6-cylinder Maseratis, Collins-Brooks and Walker-Salvadori were paired off to drive DB3S Aston Martins. There were also some very fast Porsche, A.W.E. and Alfa-Romeo Giulietta entries.

Nurburgring with its twisty corners and bumpy surface does not suit the Jaguar very well but we were making quite good times until Paul Frere slid straight over the edge and down into a deep valley, hitting various shrubs and trees, and ended up with the car nearly on its side against a tree stump. He got out unhurt but the chassis was bent. Norman Dewis rushed another car out from the works, a considerable feat of driving in itself, but the car did not arrive in time for practice and was relegated to the end of the starting line.

I got into the lead round the South Curve but Moss and Fangio passed me during the first lap. On the second lap Musso also moved up and was close behind me as we went round the South Curve; as I reached the end of the straight at the back of the pits I glanced in my mirror again and he had disappeared. I found out later that he had touched me—so lightly that I had not felt anything—as we came off the curve and had spun into the ditch, where the car turned over on top of him. He was soaked in fuel as he crawled out and was very lucky to escape with only an injured arm.

After another few laps I came very fast up over the slight bump that leads to the wide straight past the pits and saw a small Porsche in front which was well over to the left. I kept on my course and passed him on the right. Soon afterwards I saw a black flag being waved, but there seemed to be nothing wrong with the car and I could not think of anything I had done wrong, so I kept going.

Next time round there was another Porsche on the left and again I kept straight on and passed him on the right. The black flag was out again when I came round again so I pulled in to the pits where Lofty England said: "You must keep to the left. The officials are complaining about you passing on the right."

I went off again, but round the back of the circuit I soon came up behind another Porsche, which was well over on the left, just as I was coming up very fast into a left-hand corner. Because of all this waving of black flags I hung back and did not go past him on the right. Immediately following this there was a right-hand bend and as the Porsche was still on the left I prepared to take it normally when he suddenly spotted me in his mirror and pulled right over to the right. I could not stop and hit him from behind, fortunately doing nothing worse than denting the body panels.

But this was not the end of my troubles. Towards the end of my spell at the wheel, I started feeling dizzy. Petrol was swilling about in the bottom of the car and the fumes were being trapped under my visor, where they were getting up my nose and into my eyes. I pulled in to the pits and staggered out of the car feeling all in.

Our main fuel tank was a flexible aircraft-type bag in the rear, but we also had an auxiliary 2-gallon metal tank in the passenger's seat. One of the rivets had sprung, allowing a thin jet of fuel to spray into the cockpit. The mechanics plugged the leak with a rubber grommet and sent Titterington on his way, but the German officials, who really seemed to be giving us special attention, demanded that the car be called in again so that they could satisfy themselves that the repair was effective. Lofty, as team manager, refused and there was another long argument.

We had been lying fourth until this happened, but the last pit stop dropped us to ninth place. Titterington was trying hard to make up lost time, but on the last lap of the race a half shaft broke and all our efforts were brought to naught. First place went to a Maserati driven in turn by Taruffi, Schell, Moss and Behra, beating the Fangio-Castellotti Ferrari after a very close struggle which became really exciting towards the end.

The Germans made a big fuss about the incidents in which I had been involved and all the hostility which had been latent since Le Mans boiled up. Some sectors of the German press turned on me, but when a radio reporter asked Huschke von Hanstein, Porsche's competition manager, for his views on the incidents, he said frankly that if the Porsche drivers were on the left they were in the wrong and there was nothing else I could have done.

This question of passing is a difficult one and it was natural that it should be very much in peoples' minds at that time. In Grand Prix racing and in some sports-car racing, especially on British circuits, it is quite usual to pass on the inside if one is certain that it is safe to do so and knowing this, drivers keep a look-out accordingly. If the German authorities want to stick firmly to the rule of overtaking on the outside only—that is on the left on a clockwise circuit—which they are perfectly entitled to do, they have got to teach their drivers to keep to the right and get them into the habit of using their driving mirrors.

·     ·     ·     ·     ·

The B.R.M.s were not going to be ready for the Belgian Grand Prix at Spa and I was therefore free to seek another mount. I talked to Ugolini about it at the Nurburgring and he said he would let me know if a Maserati could be made available. When I got back to England I received a telegram from him saying that a car was being sent to Spa for me, but it was followed by another to say that it had not been possible to come to an arrangement about starting money, so the matter seemed to be dropped. I then sent a telegram to Ferrari who said he would be very pleased to provide me with a car.

Just before I left another wire arrived from Ugolini saying: "Waiting for you with your car at Spa." Things were now in a fine muddle, so when I arrived at Spa I saw Ugolini and explained that when I received his wire about the difficulties over starting money I had arranged to drive for Ferrari. I also explained the situation to Sculati, Ferrari's manager, who quite understood and said: "Drive which you like." As I had approached Maserati first I took their car and tried it out. Unfortunately, Sculati told me that evening, Ferrari was furious and had threatened to withdraw all his cars if I drove a Maserati; I felt the only possible thing to do was withdraw from the race.

The event provided Peter Collins with his first major Grand Prix win and Paul Frere, also on a Ferrari, was a brilliant second, after very little experience with the car. Stirling Moss set up a new lap record and came third with Perdisa on a Maserati, and the Vanwall driven by Harry Schell was fourth, so Britain was not badly represented.

· · · · · ·

This year's Supercortemaggiore race was limited to sports cars up to 2-litres and I felt we might put up quite a good show with a 1,500 c.c. Lotus-Climax, so I entered Bueb's car and got Duncan Hamilton to come as co-driver. Some furious work went on to get it ready in time. We had fitted long-range fuel tanks and hoped to get through on two stops at 3-hour intervals, but we found that the oil consumption was likely to be rather high, so had to instal an oil cooler and an extra oil tank. Brit Pearce finally got it away on the lorry and we followed by air. Before going to Monza for practice I took it down the Autostrada for a test run, with Duncan and Brit following me in the lorry. They went by when I stopped for petrol and soon afterwards black smoke started pouring out of the bonnet and flames came writhing out of the carburetter air duct. I stopped, grabbed the fire extinguisher and squirted like mad. This put the flames out and I then found that one of the pipes to the oil radiator had burst and the escaping oil had caught fire. We therefore by-passed the radiator and went on to Monza, but as I drove into the park there was a horrible grinding noise and the gearbox fell to pieces.

There was no hope of getting a new gearbox in time so I approached Sculati and Amorotti to see if there was a chance of driving a Ferrari in the race and it seemed our luck was in. I was given the chance of driving with Peter Collins and Duncan was paired off with Phil Hill. Unfortunately Sighinolfi, the chief tester, crashed Fangio's car on the way to the track, so the Hill car was taken for Fangio and Duncan was left without a drive.

It was quite an eventful race. Moss and Farina were to drive a special 1,500 Maserati with 2-litre engine, but Farina overturned it and was removed with a broken collar-bone. Once again the Supercorte-maggiore had proved an unlucky race for him.

Collins took the lead from the start and Moss retired almost at once with a broken propeller shaft. Then Perdisa came in to refuel expecting to hand his Maserati to Taruffi. Moss was put in instead, which caused a lot of excitement as apparently no one had remembered to inform Taruffi of the change of plans and he was furious. Taking over after the refuelling stop I managed to hold our lead at about a minute ahead of the Fangio-Castellotti car, with Moss third. Then Stirling moved into second place and our pit control, having miscalculated the amount of fuel we needed, brought me in for an unscheduled stop to take on some more. By the time this was done our lead had been cut to about 23 seconds and with Stirling trying his hardest to exploit the situation, Peter had to go all out to achieve his win.

· · · · ·

B.R.M., still busy on engine development, had decided to miss the French Grand Prix at Rheims, leaving me free to accept an invitation from Tony Vandervell to drive the Vanwall. The usual 12-hour sport-car race had been divided into two events, one for 1,500 c.c. cars and one for the larger cars but this cut down the time between the latter and the Grand Prix and as I was driving a Jaguar in the big sports-car event it was going to be difficult to get some rest between the two.

An agreeable feature of the practice period was the offer of 100 bottles of champagne to the first driver to do a lap at 200 kilometres an hour (124 m.p.h.). When this was announced there was a concerted rush for the cars and Harry Schell got the first Vanwall away, but failed to make the required time by a mere tenth of a second. I then had a go and after a few laps one of the mechanics stood out in the road waving a bottle of champagne to show that I had won the prize.

On the second day of practice, Colin Chapman followed me round. He had taken a large part in the design of the 1956 Vanwall chassis and was being given his first chance to drive one.

We were going down to the Thillois turn at the end of the long straight and I was just about to take the corner when there was a terrific crash at the back of the car. My head flew back and hit the headrest and my car was shunted down the escape road. I looked back just in time to see Colin's Vanwall, with its bonnet flying in the air, plough onto the grass, hit a small concrete post and then bounce into a big one. I ran back and was relieved to find that he was all right, but the car was a sorry sight. The body was crumpled, the chassis bent and the radiator smashed, but I noticed that nothing on the steering had broken, which suggested that it was solidly made.

Evidently his offside front brake had locked on as he was coming up behind me and when he took his foot off the pedal the brake had stayed on, pulling him into the back of my car. Poor Colin was terribly upset, especially as this was his first time out on the car, and he went through a bad time as we walked back to the pits together but Tony Vandervell took it wonderfully. He just shrugged, said: "That's motor racing" and got busy organising the repairs. Colin's car was *hors de combat* but his tank was put onto mine, which after minor repairs to the chassis frame was ready to race again.

The Lotus, fitted with a new gearbox, was driven by Ivor Bueb and Mackay Frazer in the 1,500 c.c. sports-car event, but they had no luck as the new gearbox gave trouble and then a connecting rod broke, wrecking the engine. The centre main bearing had failed, allowing the crankshaft to whip and straining the big-end bolts, which finally parted. The crankshaft was salvaged, which was a little bit of luck, as they were hard to get, but it was an expensive blow-up.

The race for the big sports cars started at midnight on Saturday and finished at midday on Sunday, which left drivers little time for rest before the Grand Prix which was scheduled to begin at 4 p.m. on Sunday. It was arranged therefore that I would hand over to Paul Frere for the last part of the race while I went into Rheims to get some rest.

During the first part of the race Ivor Bueb and I took the lead. He drives extremely well in the dark and we kept ourselves amused. His car had fuel injection and mine had carburetters and I was surprised to find that on this circuit the fuel injection was a distinct advantage.

He could gain about 70 yards from me on acceleration away from corners and his maximum speed was as good as mine or better, so that I had to drive really hard round the corners to keep up with him. Rain on Sunday morning added to the difficulties, but when Paul Frere took over my car for the last spell we were in the lead, and Lofty gave the drivers the signal to hold those positions.

I set out for Rheims to sleep, but there was a complicated one-way traffic system in operation and despite my protests I was forced to drive about 25 miles by a roundabout route to get to my hotel.

By the time I got there I could not sleep and when I returned to the circuit I was right off form. My condition did not improve when I said to Lofty: "We won, didn't we?" and he replied: "No. You came in second."

It was apparently a long story but watchers had seen Duncan Hamilton forging ahead at the wheel of the Bueb car to leave Paul behind regardless of pit signals, and soon after the end of the race he ceased to be a member of the Jaguar team.

For the Grand Prix Fangio, Castellotti and Collins with Ferrari-Lancias were on the front row, Schell (Vanwall) was next and I was in the third row with Behra and Moss on Maseratis. The rest of the field was made up of Ferraris, Maseratis, Gordinis and the solitary Bugatti with transverse 8-cylinder engine behind the driver, which was making its long-awaited first appearance with Trintignant at the wheel.

I made a good getaway and got into fourth place behind the Ferraris but I felt drowsy and was making little mistakes which can lead to big trouble on that very fast circuit. I had said that if Harry Schell's car ran into trouble I would hand over to him, and therefore when I saw him standing at the pit I pulled in and thankfully gave him my car.

Harry then set off on an epic pursuit of the three Ferraris, which caused consternation in their pit, for they had thought he was a lap behind and it was some time before it dawned on them that he was really fighting for the lead. Out went the "Faster" signals, but Harry was right in amongst them, passing Castellotti and Collins to go in pursuit of Fangio. He actually got up alongside the World Champion but the strain was too much and he had to stop for adjustments to the fuel pump control linkage, which dropped him to tenth place.

The Vanwall was still not sufficiently reliable to complete a full-length Grand Prix at racing speeds without adjustment, but it had obviously made enormous progress. This run served notice that before much longer it would be a serious challenger to the top Continental teams. The new chassis had made an enormous difference and it handled very well, although the front end still seemed rather light, especially when the tank was full. The one feature I did not like was the disc brakes, which still required heavy pressure and were rather prone to lock, as Colin Chapman had discovered.

CHAPTER TWENTY-THREE

BRITISH GRAND PRIX

THE B.R.M.s were ready for the British Grand Prix at Silverstone on July 14 with three cars, driven by Brooks, Flockhart and I, but we faced some formidable opposition. Stirling got his Maserati round in 1 min. 41 sec. in practice, which gave him pole position at the start, accompanied in the front row by Fangio (Ferrari), myself and Collins (Ferrari). Behind us were Schell and Gonzales on Vanwalls and Salvadori (Maserati), with Castellotti (Ferrari), Brooks (B.R.M.), Scott-Brown and Titterington (both Connaughts) in the third row. Altogether there were twenty-eight starters: eleven of which were British cars.

My B.R.M. and Brooks's got away to a terrific start and I was soon well in the lead, shadowed by Tony. They were going beautifully and were certainly the fastest cars in the race, clocking 137 m.p.h. down the straight to Stowe. This went on for 15 laps with Moss and Salvadori on Maseratis and Collins and Fangio on Ferrari-Lancias grouped behind us.

Then I began to feel uneasy about the back end. There was a very slight change in behaviour which seemed to be getting worse. Moss came past, while Salvadori and Fangio closed up behind me—Collins was out already with loss of oil pressure. By now I was convinced that a drive-shaft oil seal had failed again, so I pulled in to the pit. At first glance the mechanics reported that all was in order but I refused to continue without a closer inspection and they then found that the oil seal had failed and another universal-joint seizure was imminent.

Flockhart's B.R.M. had been withdrawn early from the race with valve trouble, so only Brooks was left, and soon he stopped out on the circuit with a broken throttle rod. He managed to get the car back to the pit, where a new rod was fitted and he re-started, but a few minutes later there was an ominous column of flame and smoke from Abbey Curve and Brooks failed to appear. The throttle had apparently stuck open for a moment as he went through this difficult curve and the car slid wildly, somersaulted, landed upside down and caught fire. Brooks was extremely lucky to be thrown out before it landed and escaped with a broken jaw and fractured ankle.

So once again the B.R.M. effort was finished after a brilliant start. The Vanwalls were in trouble, too; Gonzales, flown over specially from South America, had broken a half-shaft on the starting line and the other two were eliminated by choked fuel lines. Fangio won, with Collins second on a car he had taken over from de Portago; Behra was third and Fairman fourth on a Connaught which had run reliably and steadily to finish as the highest-placed British car.

I knew exactly how Brooks felt in the emergency which faced him because it had already happened to me in the course of a practice run at Silverstone at exactly the same place. I lifted my foot slightly and the car went on at full speed. I could not remember which way the ignition switch worked, so I just banged it upwards praying that this was the correct way. It was, luckily, so that I was able to cut the engine before things got out of hand.

When I stopped at the pits the throttle seemed to be working perfectly and the whole thing was a bit of a mystery. Lofty England, who was there supervising some Jaguar tests, suggested that it might be due to a little spring which sometimes breaks in the Weber carburetters. It seems Jaguars had taken their springs out because of this, but they were all right. We finally discovered that one of the screws holding a throttle butterfly had dropped out, allowing the butterfly to slip and jam momentarily. A small thing, but after a time such things begin to sap the driver's confidence, because he finds himself wondering what is going to happen next.

. . . . .

After the unhappy Silverstone experience, the B.R.M.s were withdrawn for further development and Ron Flockhart bore the brunt of the somewhat eventful test-driving during the ensuing months. Silverstone was in fact my last drive for B.R.M. and I was released to drive for Ferrari in the German Grand Prix on the Nurburgring. But this precipitated another international incident.

The insurance company acting for the Automobilclub von Deutschland refused to insure me for the race.

Dean Delamont of the R.A.C. therefore suggested that we should try to get Ferrari to arrange the cover provided the A.v.D. would pay the premium; failing this the R.A.C. would approach its own insurers. The insurance was eventually arranged through Ferrari, but on reflection I decided that I was not prepared to drive in Germany under these conditions and withdrew from the race.

· · · · ·

Before this storm blew up, the racing spotlight focused on Le Mans, where we found the circuit very much changed since the previous year's tragic happenings. At a cost of 340 million francs the pits had been moved back and reconstructed in impressive new two-storey form, the road had been widened and lowered, a service road inserted between track and public enclosure, the curve under the Dunlop Bridge modified, the track resurfaced, protection for spectators generally over-hauled and a new signalling station installed at Mulsanne in telephonic communication with the pits so that drivers no longer had to strain their eyes to see signals as they drove past the pits.

The rules of the race were profoundly altered too and in their anxiety to set a new standard in safety the organisers had placed restrictions on the competing cars which automatically excluded the event from the 1956 World Championship. Engines of prototypes were limited to 2,500 c.c. and all vehicles were treated as prototypes if the manufacturers could not show that 100 examples had been built.

We were favourably placed as Jaguars had in fact built a series of 100 D-types, but it came as a surprise to many people to see two of the DB3S Aston Martins accepted as cars which also existed in a series of a hundred. There was also a solitary Mercedes 300 SL, but all other makes had engines below 2,500 c.c. A greater minimum width for bodies and insistence on an effective passenger seat and a door on the passenger's side helped to eliminate freaks, but less popular with drivers was the compulsory full-width windscreen, 7.9 in. high; they feared it would be difficult to see over it and impossible to see through it, at least in heavy rain.

Ivor Bueb and I had agreed to drive together again and the odds were strongly in our favour, but it looked too good to me. I am not normally a pessimist, but I felt something was bound to go wrong at the last moment and the practice period did nothing to cheer me up. Titterington spun his car off the road into a narrow space between two trees without damaging it and I had two incidents.

The compulsory interval between refuelling had been increased as an additional measure to keep speeds down and mixture strengths had been cut to reduce fuel consumption. At the same time axle ratios had been raised, which reduced revs., but also cut down acceleration.

I was doing a few practice laps when the engine faltered and smoke poured out. We took the bonnet off and started the engine again. There was a terrific bang. The lid flew off the oil tank, the whole thing split and buckled and smoke poured out everywhere. Further examination showed that the weak mixture had burned a hole in a piston, and when the engine was started a second time the mixture had fired in the crankcase. It was the end of that engine and the spare was installed. In fact the Jaguars had quite a good margin with either carburetters or fuel injection, and even when the mixture strength was adjusted to avoid further piston trouble we had no difficulty in averaging 12 m.p.g. at racing speeds.

My next moment came when I was going down to Mulsanne at about 140 m.p.h. Suddenly there was another tremendous bang and the whole car started to vibrate and shake. Thanks to my briefing at Monza I knew that a tyre had thrown a tread and I managed to get the car safely onto the grass at the roadside. Lofty then decided to try out all the tyres to see if any more would throw treads and some did. Ivor was the guinea-pig for a lot of these investigations.

Just before the start it began to drizzle and as we swung out in the mass start I felt a shock as though another car had hit me; then it came again and again. The tyres were alternately gripping and slipping on the slippery road surface. It was very treacherous indeed and we all felt our way down through the Esses, round Tertre Rouge and out onto the long straight.

Braking gingerly for Mulsanne I heard a hooter blowing and saw Stirling in the Aston Martin weaving up on the inside as though he was out of control, so I waved him on, not turning into the corner, and he craftily nipped round the corner into the lead. The Jaguar's extra acceleration enabled me to get past again and third time round I was horrified to see two of our team cars wrecked at the roadside. Two laps gone and mine was the only works Jaguar left in the race!

It had all started when Paul Frere's D-type spun in the Esses on the second lap and clouted the barricades front and rear. Fairman, braking hard behind him, had also spun and had been rammed by de Portago's Ferrari before he could get away again.

But fate had not finished with us. On the fourth lap my engine started misfiring and I began a long frustrating series of pit stops while plugs and coil were changed, fuel injection dismantled and every conceivable source of trouble checked without result.

Eventually the trouble was traced to a fault in the brazing of a nipple on one injector pipe, but by then all hope of winning had vanished. I thought the only thing to do now was to try for fastest lap, so I went out and motored the Jaguar as hard as it would go until I got a sign to show I had succeeded and came in.

As I handed over to Ivor I said: "Well, at least we've made a little money. We should share £500 for the fastest lap!"

Then somebody said: "But there's no prize for the fastest lap this year."

And there wasn't.

It was a shattering ending after everything had seemed to be so much in our favour, but happily the day was saved for Jaguar by the well-deserved victory of Flockhart and Sanderson in the privately entered car of the Ecurie Ecosse.

* * * * *

Unlike Stirling Moss and Peter Collins, I have never done any racing in Formula 3 five-hundreds but I got my first taste of the ruthless catch-as-catch-can driving style which it generates when I went down to Brands Hatch to drive Ivor's Lotus while he drove his Cooper.

I was at a disadvantage because the only engine we could find to replace the 1,500 Climax was a 1,260 c.c. unit of the type produced for racing under the 1,300 c.c. limit in the United States. However, it was raining hard on the day, which helped because this unit could be taken about 800 r.p.m. higher than the single-camshaft 1,500 unit, and so one could hold on longer in the gears, an advantage in the wet.

The circuit struck me as bumpy and the driving tactics were startling. People were barging about in all directions and nudging me until I began to wonder if it was motor racing or Autocross. Anyway, I won the heat. In the final it started all over again and I was being hustled from all sides, so I retaliated and shunted somebody off the course; it turned out to be Ivor, who had lent me the car, and he gave me a very old-fashioned look afterwards.

* * * * *

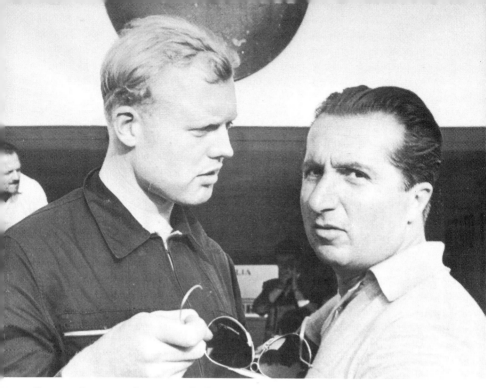

Talking with Ascari who was, I think, an even faster driver than Fangio. [*Hulton Library*

...io (Maserati) passing the two wrecked Ferraris of Peter Collins and myself at the ...aco Grand Prix, 1957. It was here that Ascari went into the harbour two years before. [*Klemantaski*

My Ferrari leading Stirling in the experimental 2½-litre D-type Jaguar at Dundrod, 1954.

Driving the fuel-injection D-type Jaguar at Le Mans, 1956. [*Klemantas*

Jaguars were not doing the Swedish Sports Car Grand Prix, so Ferrari offered me a 3½-litre to share with Peter Collins and Duncan was also offered a drive. The Rabelov circuit, a main-road loop of just over four miles near Kristiansand, was used, and although the surface had been given some treatment it was still bumpy by current standards and rather narrow. Ferrari and Maserati turned up in force and we had the choice of 4-cylinder or 12-cylinder Ferraris, all of 3½-litres. Peter Collins particularly liked one of the 12-cylinders but I decided to share a four with de Portago.

It was a bad day for Maserati as all their cars retired—Behra's after a fire during refuelling—and the various D-types, including the Ecurie Ecosse Le Mans winner, were eliminated by minor accidents; Ferrari had it all their own way.

Peter Collins was out ahead and our car was going quite well when I found that the brakes were failing as I approached a right-hand corner at the edge of a cornfield. I disappeared down the bank into the field with the standing corn up above my head and I had to stand up in the car to see over the corn so that I could navigate my way back to the road. De Portago then took over for a while and later, as people were being switched from one car to another with the utmost freedom, Duncan asked if he could try ours. Portago warned him that the brakes were very feeble but he proceeded to lap quite fast and we finished third.

As I got in to drive away, Duncan said: "No brakes at all, boy!" I thought he meant that the brakes were still very poor, but when I touched the pedal it banged down on the floor. The mechanics had a look and found that a back brake pipe had broken. The car had two master-cylinders, so we had been racing with front brakes only and now these were completely worn out. Yet Duncan had been motoring really fast.

It would be idle to pretend that racing drivers are always the perfect guests from the hotelier's point of view, and that night the hotels' magnificent fire precautions, consisting of highly polished devices like stirrup pumps in gleaming copper-bound tubs, proved an irresistible temptation. A hosepipe battle developed in which a good deal of water fell wide of the primary objectives. At breakfast next morning one of the race officials appeared and obviously had a problem on his mind.

It was obvious what the problem was, so after an exchange of pleasantries we said: "Well, how much is it?" He was immensely relieved and said: "Thank you, gentlemen! If you wouldn't mind leaving a little something at the desk when you go, the bill will be sent later." We did and a mutually acceptable figure was ultimately agreed upon.

．　　　．　　　．　　　．　　　．

The season came to an abrupt end for me at the *Daily Herald* Trophy meeting at Oulton Park on a day which was incredibly wet, even for England; so much so that fire pumps and brooms had to be pressed into service to clear flood water from the circuit and the races had to be curtailed because of the time lost. I was driving the Lotus again in the *Sporting Life* Trophy event for 1,500 c.c. sports cars, the chief opposition being Stirling Moss and Salvadori on Cooper Climax two-seaters. Stirling and I set to from the start, but he drew away and then Salvadori came past. I went past again at Knicker Brook, but got onto some mud washed onto the circuit by the floods and slid. The Lotus went straight up the bank towards a tree and I shall never forget seeing that tree coming up. On the track, one is not particularly conscious of the speed at which things flash past, but when you are heading out of control straight for some solid object, it is a different matter.

The car bounced off the bank and flipped over in mid-air. I remember seeing the green mass of the tree and then the grass beneath me and I knew that it was going to be terribly difficult to get clear before the car landed. I struggled convulsively and then must have been knocked out for I remember no more until I heard someone moaning and groaning I wondered who it might be, until it dawned on me that I was the person making all the fuss. Spectators rushed up and one started trying to comfort me, saying over and over: "It's all right, Mike, you're all right." "How the devil does he know?" I asked myself.

It all seemed to happen much more quickly than the B.R.M. inversion at Goodwood. I had very little time to think what to do and I was very lucky to have been thrown clear. Salvadori had an awful moment as the Lotus somersaulted right in front of him and the car actually struck his crash helmet as he passed underneath it flying through the air. As I came out I tore the door away completely with my hip, sprained an ankle and wrist, bruised my ribs and hurt my back, which kept me out of action long enough to miss the rest of the season's racing. I had had some lucky escapes from some hair-raising predicaments, but otherwise it had not been a memorable year.

PART VI

FERRARI AGAIN

## CHAPTER TWENTY-FOUR

## DRIVING FOR CUNNINGHAM

WHEN I heard that Fangio had signed with Maserati for the 1957 season I sent Ferrari a telegram saying: "I am interested if you are," to which he replied saying that he was interested and would provide me with a car for the Argentine *Temporada*. Just before Christmas I went out to fix the details, flying to Milan and going on to Modena by train. There was the usual wait before Ferrari was able to see me and show me the contract, but I found that the terms were more favourable than before and there was only one item which caused some discussion. I wanted to be free to drive for Jaguar at Sebring and this was eventually accepted because during the interval since our previous failure to agree on this point Jaguar had several times helped Ferrari by releasing me to drive for him.

We then adjourned to the Modena Autodrome to see Castellotti testing the latest 3½-litre V-12 sports car, and afterwards moved over to Maranello where I saw the chassis and frame of the V-6 1⅓-litre Formula 2 car. Ferrari claimed that the engine was producing nearly 190 b.h.p., or over 125 b.h.p. per litre, which was really phenomenal, and said that Vittorio Stanguellini, one of his neighbours in Modena, who knows a great deal about extracting power from small engines, had maintained that it could not possibly produce more than 160 horsepower. He had furthermore bet Ferrari that for every horse-power he could produce over 160, Stanguellini would buy him a dinner for five people. When I saw him, Ferrari was looking forward to eating well and cheaply for some time to come.

In view of the fact that Peter Collins, Castellotti and I would all be going out to win points for the World Championship, which was naturally the target we were all aiming at, Ferrari decided that he would not nominate anyone as Number 1 driver until we had run three World Championship events. The man who had scored the most points would then become Number 1, which implied the right to have the choice of the cars and to take over other people's cars if his own gave trouble during a race.

In January I flew to Rome, stayed the night and travelled on with Sculati, the team manager, and Luigi Musso to Milan, where we met the rest of our team and the Maserati team. There were de Portago, Bonnier, Castellotti, Perdisa and the two teams' mechanics. Harry Schell joined us at Lisbon and we had only been airborne again a few minutes when someone suggested playing poker; de Portago, Musso, Perdisa and myself formed a foursome playing for stakes up to £10, which I thought rather heavy. When I had lost £50 I gave my place to Bonnier and those boys really began playing. By the time we reached Buenos Aires, Musso had lost heavily and Bonnier was also in the red, so the prospective proceeds from their trip were condemned in advance.

We arrived on a Sunday night and practice did not begin until the following Wednesday, but we needed the time to get acclimatised to the oppressive, humid heat which kept the thermometer at around 100 deg. F.

The cars were developed from the V-8 Lancia which I had not driven since the Gold Cup meeting at Oulton Park in 1955 and I noticed a great difference. Normally they had equal-length wishbones at the front but Collins had had trouble with wheels lifting on corners and a new system with wishbones of unequal length was fitted to his car and Castellotti's. They also had oil coolers mounted externally at the front and wrap-round windscreens, which I considered a disadvantage in the heat.

I had the usual trouble finding enough space in mine so the mechanics lowered the floor, made some wells for my feet besides fitting my favourite type of four-spoked wheel, but I was still very cramped. There was no more space to be had as one sits with back hard against the gearbox and the engine is right up against the bulkhead at the front.

Handling was generally quite good, but the car understeered badly on sharp corners; if I got the tail sliding under power to help it round and then lifted my foot to control it, the rear came back rather viciously and tried to whip round the other way. Yet on fast corners it drifted nicely with all four wheels. The amount of fuel in the tail tank had been reduced and more was carried in the side tanks than in 1956. But the most unwelcome surprise was the discovery that the car lacked power. The inlet ports had been redesigned to give a straighter flow, which changed the angle of the carburetters and brought the intake bells on the two banks so close together that they had to be merged together at their edges. This arrangement had shown good results on the test bed and Ferrari had assured me it gave them an extra 15 b.h.p., but the horses had escaped in the course of installation in the car. After experiencing the surge of power from the B.R.M. in its periods of robust health this was very disappointing and Peter said the cars were definitely not as good as they had been in 1956.

We could not get down to the Maseratis' lap times and only Castellotti got a place in the front row, with Moss, Fangio and Behra. I was in the second row with Musso and Collins. All the entries were Ferraris or Maseratis, including some privately owned machines. The start was something of a farce because the flag had been entrusted to an individual who might have been politically prominent but had no conception of how to start a motor race. The idea was that he would drop a yellow flag and then bring up the national flag to give the actual starting signal. He was walking about until the half-minute signal and people put their gears in earlier than usual, which was not good for the clutches. He then dropped the yellow flag but could not bring up the national flag because he was treading on it. All this time engine temperatures were shooting sky-high and the start, when it came, was an extremely ragged one.

To our surprise we found that the Maseratis were little if any faster than us in the race and Castellotti took the lead followed by Behra, Fangio and myself. I learned afterwards that the Maserati team had changed their fuel and I concluded they might have been using nitro-methane to obtain good practice times and a favourable starting position. Collins passed Fangio and went after Castellotti, but soon retired with clutch failure, and Musso dropped out with the same trouble.

I then tried hard to catch the leaders and got within about six seconds of Fangio, who was now ahead of Behra, when Gonzales pulled out from the pits and got in front of me. He was soon holding me up, but apparently did not spot me in his mirror. I used the time-honoured method of waving my fist at him and the crowd took it up, waving their fists too, whenever he came round, but no one showed him a blue flag; they do not seem to understand what they are for. This did not last long, for my clutch too started to slip, so that I had to retire and the Ferrari challenge finally faded out when Castellotti lost a wheel, which luckily flew over the heads of the crowd without hitting anyone.

Fangio won his fourth successive victory in this race with Behra second. Stirling Moss lost a lot of time while a broken throttle rod was being repaired, but had the satisfaction of making fastest lap. I was quite pleased, because I had proved to myself that I could still gain on Fangio after being out of Grand Prix racing for a good many months. Gonzales was very upset when I told him he had been baulking me; he had not seen me and he gave me the impression that he had lost his enthusiasm for motor racing.

•    •    •    •    •

The Grand Prix was held as usual on the Autodrome, which, with its wide grass verges and general freedom from obstructions, is a safe circuit, but for the 1,000 km. sports-car event the organisers had reverted to the Costanera road circuit on the sea front which includes a stretch of two-way traffic down a terribly fast boulevard; the cars ran down this in both directions at 170 m.p.h. with nothing but an occasional straw bale between them.

They had also stretched wires between the trees to keep the crowd back, just at the ideal height to cut off the driver's head if a car got out of control.

After the Ferrari team had complained that it was too dangerous, an island was introduced, which slowed people down slightly; but Fangio was still lapping at 106 m.p.h. on the 4½-litre V8 Maserati. There were several accidents in practice; a 4.9-litre Ferrari was crashed twice, being written off the second time, and Ron Flockhart hit a lamp-post with one of the Ecurie Ecosse Jaguars.

Our twin-camshaft 3½-litre V12 was very fast and cornered well, but I found steering and braking required a lot of effort. I was acutely uncomfortable because the car was built as usual to the dimensions of the smaller type of Italian. My knees were up alongside the steering wheel in such an awkward position that after a few laps my leg began quivering whenever I pressed the brake pedal.

I was driving with Peter Collins and we had a newcomer to the team in the person of the young American driver, Masten Gregory, who was driving his own single-camshaft 3½-litre, which proved faster than the twin-camshaft cars and eventually won the race after being handled in turn by Gregory, Castellotti and Musso.

Stirling demonstrated the fantastic acceleration of the V8 4½-litre Maserati at the start by getting away so fast that he thought he had jumped the flag and he went on gaining about five seconds a lap on his nearest pursuers. Our race was over very soon, for Peter retired with a seized engine after three laps. The Maserati axle failed soon after Stirling had handed over to Fangio, so Ugolini then installed Stirling in a 3-litre six, which had already been driven by Behra and Menditeguy, and he proceeded to give a magnificent demonstration, making fastest lap of the day as he went in pursuit of the Gregory Ferrari and a surviving twin-cam model which de Portago was driving. He was gaining on the latter, but it looked as thought de Portago could just keep ahead when for some reason a decision was made to change drivers. Castellotti was installed in place of de Portago and, with the time lost in the change-over, Moss went into second place. There was a lot of friction between de Portago and the team manager as a result and next day de Portago flew back to Europe.

Time between the races passed very pleasantly with sailing, swimming, water ski-ing, barbecues and the occasional official reception. We taught "Wilky" Wilkinson of the Ecurie Ecosse water ski-ing and he made it after swallowing a large part of the river. Buenos Aires stands on a river off which are a number of rivulets which form convenient anchorages for various yacht clubs and I gave myself a bad fright through over-estimating my powers of seamanship while returning from a party late one stormy night in a borrowed cabin cruiser.

After that I went back to flying and took von Trips up in a Piper Cub to get some ciné pictures. He wanted to shoot some scenes of the river and the yachts, so I took him down low and was just thinking that this would be an awful place to have to make a forced landing, when the engine cut. Below us was nothing but water and semi-jungle; not a possible landing place for miles. I was just debating the chances of survival in a ditching when I glanced down and saw that the throttle had shut. The machine had dual control and von Trips had caught his elbow against the lever as he leaned out of the window with his camera.

On previous visits personal transport had been rather a problem as there were no hire cars and we had to rely on taxis or the cars of our friends, but this time we were able to hire Fiat 1100 saloons and Peter got hold of one of the little Autoar pick-ups made by the outfit which was founded by Piero Dusio of Cisitalia fame.

For the Buenos Aires Grand Prix, which was run in two heats, we returned to the Autodrome on a terribly hot day with the temperature running up to 104 deg. F. in the shade. Amorotti had told me to try to hold the water temperature at about 90 deg. C. and the oil at 110 deg. but temperatures started getting out of hand while the same starter did his act with the flags once more; some of us began to feel dazed by the furnace heat in the cockpits.

I made a bad start, changing from first gear into fourth instead of second—it was a five-speed box and the two were close together—and by this time the water temperature was nearly 115 deg. F. while the oil was off the clock. The engine felt very rough, but by holding it down to 7,000 r.p.m. I got the temperatures under control. I lost a lot of ground in the process but hoped to save my engine for the second heat. I caught Peter, who had a leaking fuel pipe, and Stirling, who was suffering from the heat and a locking brake, and finished fourth. Fangio, who is used to these oven-like conditions, came in first, but I was one of those who had to be helped out of the car.

I did not think I could possibly last through the second heat, but I got someone to drill a lot of holes in my crash helmet, went and stood under a shower for about twenty minutes, swallowed some salt tablets and put on a light sleeveless pullover. Musso had fallen ill with the stomach trouble which was to keep him out of racing for some time to come, so Peter took his car and Masten Gregory moved into Peter's car. I again made the silly gear change mistake and so did Peter and some of the others. This let Gregory get in front of us and although it was his first race on a Grand Prix car he drove as if he had been handling them for years, throwing it into the corners, correcting it calmly when it started to slide and holding it in a drift. After a while I passed him and when Castellotti spun I took the lead, but I was so exhausted by the heat that I slowed down and was passed by Fangio, Behra and Peter Collins. I would gladly have signed an undertaking never to go motor racing again and at the end of the race was practically prostrate. Yet Peter was as lively as a cricket.

I said: "That was a pretty good effort, Pete."

"Yes," he replied. "Weren't those pills wonderful?"

"What pills?" said I, and then I learned that while I had been monopolising the shower a doctor had been round distributing heart pills which had made everyone but me more or less immune to the heat.

I flew back via Nassau where I stayed a few days with some friends enjoying the life of the islands in the sun—terribly expensive, but no income-tax to pay—and checked on the plans for a future motor-racing circuit when the aerodrome track previously used ceases to be available. Petrol was only 2s. 6d. a gallon but there is a speed limit of 30 m.p.h. on all roads. I was very soon reminded of this by a coloured speed-cop who let me off with a caution when he found I was a visitor.

Returning via Rome, I looked in at Maranello again and saw the V-6 Formula 2 engine on the test bed producing 186 horsepower at 9,300 r.p.m. All the 2½-litre Formula 2 single-seaters were being fitted with the coil spring front suspension which gives a greater range of deflection, better ride and better handling than the transverse-leaf spring arrangement. Experiments were being made with a new independent rear suspension and one of the 4-cylinder 2½-litre engines was about to go on test with fuel injection.

I reported on the defects in the cars which the Argentine season had brought to light and the question of Syracuse cropped up. Having crashed and been burned there twice in two races I felt this was an unlucky race for me and Ferrari was very understanding about it, so I was omitted from the team for that event.

A few weeks after returning from the Argentine, I was watching the television one evening when the commentator announced the tragic news that Castellotti had been killed testing a Grand Prix Ferrari on the Autodrome at Modena. He was a fast driver and his epic win in the 1956 Mille Miglia will always be remembered. His presence in the Ferrari team was sadly missed.

•       •       •       •       •       •

In March it was time to fly the Atlantic again en route for Sebring where I was once again to drive a Jaguar entered by Briggs Cunningham's Company. There were only four of us this time: Lofty England and I, with Ivor Bueb and Harold Hodgkinson, the Dunlop disc-brake expert. As the 1956 event had shown up a defect in the brakes which cost us the race, a modified type with quick-change pads had been evolved. These had been fitted on the front of the other Cunningham cars, but ours had them on all four wheels.

We flew out in a DC7, a fast aeroplane but one which gives me the impression of being cramped because one cannot get up and walk about. The fat old Stratocruiser is still my favourite aircraft for long distances. Its spiral staircase and its bar on the lower deck give the passengers the opportunity to walk about and chat and get a change of scene which passes the time much more agreeably than sitting glued to one's seat for hours on end in the slim modern projectiles.

This time I took the chance of going up inside the Statue of Liberty in New York which I had always thought must be a fascinating chunk of structural engineering. The lift only reaches the feet of the figure; after that you climb a staircase, and I found it more exhausting than a motor race, but at last we were up there looking out from the dizzy height of the windows set in the old lady's spiked crown, which like the rest of the statue is made from copper plates laboriously riveted together and supported on an intricate web of steel girders.

As usual, Briggs met us at Palm Beach and provided transport in the shape of a new Cadillac. This was a 1957 model with a host of new buttons to press and the steering, road-holding and brakes all seemed to be a big improvement over those of the 1956 car. Briggs proposed to lead the way in his 2.4-litre Jaguar and said we would not be going very fast—the speed limit is 60 m.p.h.—but before long we were drifting along at 70 on a very small throttle opening and the inevitable speed-cop came screaming past. There was a smell of burning so I announced: "The car is on fire", which produced a slight diversion until we found that it came from hot paint on the new engine. I next produced my British driving licence which caused a certain amount of head scratching and finally we were allowed to go after a short lecture on the dangers of driving fast. Said the cop, looking at my car: "Take it easy with these things, son. I know them. They roll dead easy."

We checked in at Harder Hall where we always stay and then went to look at the cars. To compete with the enormous American engines, Briggs had been boring out the Jaguar cylinder block to 3.8 litres and had got a big increase in performance on his D-type but the factory engineers were not happy about it as it made the cylinder walls rather thin. Briggs therefore sent one of his bored-out engines to Coventry where it gave 306 b.h.p., but after it had been doing this for a while the cylinder walls cracked. However, this kind of horsepower was obviously useful for Sebring, so a special cylinder casting was evolved with modified water passages and two engines were built, one being installed in the 1956 Le Mans car, which steered better than any other Jaguar I have ever driven. This was the car we were going to drive in the race.

Briggs had meanwhile installed one of his own bored-out engines in the small light Cunningham car which originally had an Offenhauser engine and he took this out to warm it up before letting me try it. He was away a long time. More cracked cylinder walls. So we were left with three 3.8-litre Jaguars, only two of which had the fully modified works engines.

We also had a look at the new Chevrolet Corvette SS sports-racing prototype with which Zora Duntov was prominently connected. He had spent a year or so with Allard learning the ways of European sports-car constructors and the techniques of European racing and was now deeply involved in Chevrolet's efforts to beat the Europeans at their own game. The prototype had a tubular chassis and neat de Dion axle layout. Although it looked heavy they said it weighed only 2,000 lb. and had 300 b.h.p. One feature I did not like was the layout of the exhaust pipes which twisted and curved sharply upwards and downwards to get round the chassis tubes. When I encountered it in the race it was going very well until stopped by mechanical trouble. It cornered better than the Jaguar and had better acceleration until we got into third gear when I could gain a little. Maximum speeds were probably about equal.

Some of the features of current American production cars may appear atrocious to us, but up to now they have suited the American buyer and have sold in millions. Recently soaring imports of European cars have caused the American manufacturers to think again. There is no sign yet of any major change in policy, but they would very soon be able to take us on at our own game if they decided it was commercially expedient to do so.

I was not as happy with our car as I had been at Le Mans as the Sebring circuit is more bumpy. The brakes were tending to lock when braking from high speeds, as the ratio between front and rear brakes was not ideal, but there was nothing we could do to alter it. We also had some difficulties with the fuel pump for the injection system, ours being the only car without carburetters. However, I got round in 3 min. 28 sec. against 3 min. 25 sec. by the best Ferrari and 3 min. 26 sec. by the Maserati V-8. At night the headlamps did not give me the light where I needed it so I ran with them dipped and managed to get round within two seconds of the daylight times.

On race day Ivor and I slept late to get all the rest we could, but got caught in a solid traffic jam $1\frac{1}{2}$ miles from the circuit. We looked like missing the start, so took to the fields and road verges where we went ploughing along, with irate drivers blowing their horns at us because they thought we were jumping the queue.

I took the first driving spell at the start and managed to get into the car quite quickly after the usual sprint across the track, but when I pressed the starter button nothing happened and by the time I had coaxed the engine into life I was stuck behind all the little cars. I managed to work my way up into fifth place behind Behra, Collins, Moss and another Ferrari, and handed over to Ivor after two hours, by which time our rear tyres were worn out by the constant spinning and juddering on the rough surface. The thing that surprised us was the performance of the V-8 Maserati driven by Fangio who ran for three hours before coming in to take on fuel, tyres and a new driver. However, few people expected the Maserati to last longer than six to nine hours and Stirling had changed over to a 3-litre Maserati which he was driving with Schell.

We changed over at two-hour intervals, holding a good position, and at half-distance we changed pads on all four brakes, put on new wheels, took on 30 galls. of fuel and topped up oil and water in six minutes. We had not caught the V-8 Maserati but were still hopeful when I took over to drive for the last four hours.

I was going well in second place at the eleventh hour, when things started to go wrong. I had noticed at the last tyre change that there was a slight escape of hydraulic fluid from the offside rear brake and now the brakes began to feel spongy. At one point the pedal went straight down to the floor and I had to pump hard to find some pressure to get round the corner. At the pits we found the reservoir was empty and as the leak was obviously quite bad we had to cut off the rear brakes and run on front brakes only. I set off again but now ran into trouble with the engine, which would cut out altogether for fifty yards or so and then pick up again. Topping up the fuel tank improved matters and I set off for the last hour, just three minutes in front of Stirling with the 3-litre Maserati and hoping to stay ahead with only my front brakes working. When I braked I lost the feel of the steering and could not go into the corners properly, so I had to brake earlier and was losing 10–13 seconds a lap. Stirling caught me, to take second place behind Fangio and built up a lead of about three-quarters of a lap. I began to worry about Masten Gregory who was then running fourth. The engine was missing again and five laps from the end as I came round a sharp corner there was an alarming crunch from the rear. I hoped at first it was a flying stone, but as I accelerated up the straight I heard the back axle whining and knew that it was unlikely to last much longer. For the last two laps I just crawled round, but with half a lap to go I saw headlamps coming up behind me. Was it Gregory? I could not tell and I had to decide whether to risk all in a sprint to hold third place or crawl in for a safe fourth. I decided to risk it, put my foot down and stayed ahead to the finishing line. The headlamps were Fangio's and not Gregory's, but the gamble had come off and we were third behind Fangio and Moss.

The pinion bearing oil-seal had failed and the back axle was dry. The brake fluid had escaped through heat being transferred into one of the piston seals which had just crumbled away and put the rear brakes out of action. The cause of the intermittent misfiring remained a mystery, but it was thought that heat radiated from the brakes might have affected the pump which is situated in the bottom of the fuel tank.

Sebring remains the toughest test in the world for brakes. The Ferraris were using extremely hard linings which helped to prevent fade, but required such high pedal pressures that they gave the drivers' legs a terrible time.

This time there were cash prizes: 2,000 dollars for first place, 1,000 for second and 500 for third. As usual, the Americans were not permitted to soil their hands with the stuff and we were only able to participate by virtue of the fact that the car had been entered by a company and not by a private individual.

While in Florida I tried one of the rare XK SS Jaguars and liked it very much. The only drawback was the shrouding of the exhaust pipe which made the passenger's seat very hot, a fault which should be easily curable. Interest in it was enormous and orders were flowing in.

## Chapter Twenty-five

## TRIPLE CRASH

THE NAPLES Grand Prix on April 28 was interesting because the new V-6 Formula 2 Ferrari was being tried out for the first time. Luigi Musso, Peter Collins and I were in a team. I had driven down with Peter from Milan to Modena and we went on to Naples in his vast Mercury station wagon with his wife, Louise. Originally only Musso and I were to run, Musso driving the Formula 2 car—which looked so like a Formula 1 machine that it was difficult to tell the difference until you saw them together—and myself on the Formula 1 car; but at the last moment Ferrari decided to send out another F.1 car for Peter. My car was the side-tank model, still with the normal de Dion type back axle, but Peter's car had independent rear suspension. We had tried it before and it had not been very good, but they were giving it another trial.

It was the first time I had raced at Naples and I just could not do anything at all with the car; it was all over the road and felt terrible. The circuit is a twisting $2\frac{1}{2}$ mile run through parkland in the hills of Posillipo, overlooking the bay of Naples, and is unusual in being run anti-clockwise. When I got my lap times, I thought I must be losing my touch as I was way behind the other cars by about 7 seconds and I was quite worried. Peter was doing best in practice, in the F.1 car, and Musso was going very well only slightly slower. I came into the pits and told the mechanics the car was handling badly, so they had a look at it, adjusted the shock absorbers and I went out again, but it was just the same. I came in again and said: "It feels as though the shock absorbers are solid."

Peter then took it out and did a couple of laps and came in and said it was almost uncontrollable.

The car was wheeled away for inspection and I had a go in Peter's car, with the independent rear suspension, but Peter and I differ in height by four or five inches and I had to sit well and truly wedged into the car with my knees jammed under the steering wheel. I could not go fast at all and I really could not tell whether the car was better than mine or not.

Next day the mechanics told me the off-side drive shaft had seized on its splines and as this was a very bumpy course it made it very difficult to control the car. They fixed that for me and as soon as I started on the second day's practice I found a big difference. Peter had got down to lapping in 2 min. 8 sec. and after a few laps I also got down to 2 min. 8 sec., which was close to Ascari's record of 2 min. 7.7 sec. Now that record of Ascari's was rather an amazing one; it had stood since 1953 when he set it up on a Formula 2 2-litre 4-cylinder Ferrari and it was not beaten by the 2½-litre cars in 1954 or 1956. How he got it round in that time in the 2-litre I simply do not know. Peter and I got best lap times on the second day and Musso with the 1½-litre got down to 2 min. 9.2 sec., only 1.2 sec. slower than our time with the 2½-litre cars, which is pretty fantastic.

Road conditions were good and the weather was very hot for the race. I was first on the grid, with Peter next and Musso, to complete the front row. There were no works Maseratis entered but Horace Gould was just behind me in his privately owned Maserati and just before the start of the race, when I was standing on the starting line, he said: "Don't you try to hem me in at the start because I will slip through straight between you."

Knowing Horace, I quite believed him and, sure enough, when the flag dropped he shot away like a rocket in front of everybody with Peter second and myself third, but we passed him on the twisty downhill bit at the back and got away. Peter and I discussed this race beforehand and we realised it was no use racing our heads off to risk blowing the cars up because there was not much opposition. The main threat came from Stuart Lewis-Evans in one of the works Connaughts, but we eventually lapped him and were not terribly worried.

Before the race Peter and I had arranged we would put on a bit of a show for the crowd and he said: "I'm happy if we go over the line side by side; if you have the lead, you win and I will come in second, because I won at Syracuse."

I thought this was a very fair thing to say and we took it in turns to take the lead and were pushing each other fairly hard when I suddenly realised that a spray of something or other was coming into my face.

I thought at first it was water, but when I got a drop in my eye, I realised it was fuel, for it was stinging like the devil. I thought: "Oh Lord! Something has broken." It got worse and worse until it was streaming out of the bonnet louvres, so I pulled into the pits and they whipped the bonnet off and found that the pipe leading from the fuel pipe to the fuel pressure gauge had cracked. They cut the pipe off altogether then banged up the end and turned it over to stop the fuel coming out. This cut off my fuel pressure gauge, but this was of no real importance, for we only use it when we start up to make sure the fuel pumps are working.

The pit stop lasted 2 min. 35 sec. and I lost over a lap. Peter was now over a lap ahead, everyone else had gone past and I was quite a way behind. I rather enjoyed this, as it gave me something to fight for. I now had to start motor racing. The car was going very well indeed and I was knocking the lap time further and further down, beating Ascari's record repeatedly until I got down to 2 min. 5.6 sec. which made a new record and was not beaten that day.

When I set off again after a pit stop six cars had passed me. I repassed them all fairly easily—except Peter, of course. I got past him but he still had a lap in hand and there were Musso and Lewis-Evans in second and third places who had to be passed again. Only a few laps from the end a front hub split on the Connaught at a point where two loops of the track come close together and Lewis-Evans had a narrow escape from ploughing through the straw bales into cars coming the other way, so that put him out. I caught up with Musso on one of the last laps and got very close to him, but I nearly overdid it on one of the corners; the car nearly spun round and went up on the footpath. I managed to hold it and I caught Musso about half a lap from the end. I nipped past him and pipped him on the finishing line just when he was hoping he would make it for second place.

It was quite an exciting race from the spectators' point of view, with someone driving really hard to work his way up from the back. I might have won if there had been more laps to go and if Peter had let me get close enough, for he was not driving flat out.

My car had a specially lengthened chassis frame; the wheelbase was the same, but the engine was mounted further forward to give me more leg room, which is what I always need in these Italian cars, as they are always built for small people.

I thought Naples was a wonderfully attractive city, which lives up to what they say about it in the touring guide books, but the sea front has a rather odd odour which probably has something to do with the town drains. After Naples we stuck to de Dion axles and never used the swing axles again. Peter said that on small corners the swing axle was an improvement, but when it came to the fast corners it got a little dicey and while following him in the early stages of the race I did notice that it seemed to be rather a handful for him on one or two occasions.

.   .   .   .   .

Ferrari said he might want me to drive in the Mille Miglia and he might not; he asked me what I thought. I said I would rather not and I went home to England. I had been up to London on the day of the race and while driving home I switched on the radio for the B.B.C. news, to learn that Collins had led the race almost to the finish, when his back axle broke up, leaving Taruffi to win with another Ferrari. The announcer then said that there had been a fatal accident in which de Portago, Nelson and a large number of spectators had been killed.

It was a great shock coming like that as I knew "Fon" quite well and I liked him immensely. He was a wonderful all-round sportsman and would have a go at anything. He did not seem to know the meaning of fear, although he himself maintained that he did get frightened and enjoyed the sensation. He was a good steeplechase jockey and an outstanding performer on the Cresta run. The first accounts said that a tyre had burst whilst travelling at 160 m.p.h. causing the car to swerve across the road into a bunch of spectators. It then somersaulted back across the road, end over end, to finish in a ditch, but so far as I know the actual cause of this accident, which happened on a straight stretch of road, has never been established. Fon started driving in 1953–4 and was coming on very well. He was one of the fastest sports-car drivers and he was in the top twelve drivers of the world, but was still a little wild. I drove his car at Oulton Park once; we shared a drive together in the Goodwood Nine Hours of 1955 and also shared a car in Sweden in 1956. He was a wonderful chap, both as a co-driver and a companion, and the whole Ferrari team was deeply affected by his death.

The disaster stirred up anew all the feeling against motor racing which had been gradually subsiding since Le Mans and all road racing in Italy was banned. Other races elsewhere were stopped, too. For Ferrari, it was a heavy blow, as his team cars were impounded for examination and suspicions were aroused about a mechanical defect having caused the accident. No report was issued to say whether the examination had confirmed this or not.

· · · · ·

My next race was at Monaco which was the second in the World Championship series. Our team here was Collins, Trintignant, von Trips and myself. We were all to drive Formula 1 cars, but a Formula 2 car was sent along for use in practice to see how it behaved on this short tortuous circuit. Musso was not racing as he had contracted severe stomach trouble, and was ill for some weeks, while Behra had crashed and broken his arm during practice for the Mille Miglia, and thus was unable to race for Maserati.

There were no social events before this race and we did not meet Prince Rainier or Princess Grace, but they drove round the course for one lap before the start. Maseratis had Fangio, Schell, Menditeguy, the latter with one of the 12-cylinder cars which were being tried out at intervals, but proved disappointing. B.R.M. had Flockhart and Salvadori; Vanwalls had Moss and Brooks; and Lewis-Evans and Bueb were driving Connaughts.

I left Modena with Trintignant and he drove me up in his Renault Dauphine. The road from Genoa to Monaco is very difficult and twisty but these Renaults are fantastic little motor cars and he drove it flat out the whole time. Knowing that I am a very nervous passenger, he did the usual trick, waiting until I was just dozing off and then suddenly putting the brakes hard on, which scared the daylight out of me, as I thought we were just about to hit something. I did wake up once to see the back of a large truck looming in front of my face, but that was the only time we ever seemed to be in any real danger of hitting anything.

The Ferrari team missed the first day's practice because we could not get the cars ready in time, but I heard that Stirling had crashed at the chicane on the harbour's edge and had bent the chassis on the Vanwall. He had the same accident on race day. While waiting for our Ferrari to arrive Peter Collins tried out John Cooper's Formula 2 car Cooper-Climax, but when Ferrari heard about this he was furious as he did not like him risking his neck in somebody else's motor car. At this time Ferrari was more than usually temperamental as he had been so much upset by the Mille Miglia crash. We had three of the new Ferraris without sponsors, but Trintignant's car had one of the old-type Lancia bodies with sponsors on the outside. We had to get up at 5 a.m. for practice which upset everybody, including the local inhabitants who were awakened at dawn by the blasting from the racing cars' exhausts. I was not terribly happy with my car; the steering seemed to be very undergeared so that I had to work like mad to get it round the corners and I was not going very quickly. I had only driven on the circuit once before, in the B.R.M., but we did not run in the race.

Mile for mile more gear changes are needed in this circuit than on any other and the axle ratio should be on the high side, not on the low side as many people think. We had five-speed gearboxes using first only to start and the other four for racing. After my first practice on the Friday I got the mechanics to change the steering and during Saturday's practice it was a lot better, but I still was not satisfied with the performance of the car. Although we tried various carburetter jets and choke sizes, I could not get down to any reasonable lap time, so I asked Peter to take it out to see how it compared with his car. He did a few laps and then disappeared and I saw some people running on the other side of the harbour. Peter had gone through the chicane and had slid out, hitting one of the big bollards on the edge of the harbour. He very narrowly escaped driving right into the harbour and completely wrote off the front end of my car, so that we could not possibly race it. It was the long-chassis car and so I had to race in another car, a big side-tank model. I did much better with this, knocking about two seconds off my previous times, so Peter did me a good turn. The engine was better and the car had the normal short chassis which seemed much more suitable for that circuit and I decided to use it in the race,

Moss made the best practice time, with Peter second, Fangio third. Brooks fourth and myself fifth, so we took up the first two rows on the starting grid. Race day was very hot and there was quite a lot of excitement just before the race because Moss could not get his Vanwall going and it only started at the last moment. As we had a low back axle ratio I thought I would start in second instead of using first gear which I thought might give me too much wheelspin. However, when I let the clutch in I realized second was too high and I made a rather poor start.

I was lying sixth or seventh and on the first two laps tussling with Menditeguy with a Maserati; its performance was poor and, coming out of hairpin corners, it just would not pick up properly, so I got past him and also took Harry Schell's Maserati; the order then was

Moss, Collins, Fangio, Brooks and then myself. I decided that the thing to do in this race was to keep as near to Fangio as I could and I was going to try and overtake Brooks and then stay on Fangio's tail to watch developments. Moss and Collins were already having a terrific scrap out in front and with a long, difficult race in prospect Fangio was sitting back to give them a chance to blow themselves up.

On the third lap I came out of the tunnel and was diving down to the chicane at about 120 m.p.h. on the fastest stretch of the course when I saw a Vanwall go straight through the barrier where the escape road should have been, scattering poles and sandbags in all directions. We all slammed on our brakes and I saw Fangio go through the chicane safely. Brooks was just in front of me and as we arrived at the tricky left and right swerve I saw that there were some telegraph poles lying across the road. I thought we could go straight over them but Brooks, taken by surprise, slowed right down and almost stopped.

I swung the wheel hard to the left, trying to miss him, but my right front wheel struck his left rear wheel and my wheel, complete with brake drum, was sheared clean off. I caught a glimpse of it soaring high into the air as I careered on out of control at about 50 m.p.h. straight for Peter Collins's car which was lying wrecked on the edge of the harbour. He was standing up in the car but ducked down as he saw me coming. I hit the pole barricade running along the edge of the quay and the car rode up high, then crashed down on top of Peter's car, where my wrecked front suspension missed his head by inches. Peter leapt out, running like a deer across the road and I followed, while the tail end cars went whizzing by.

I was so relieved to find no one was hurt that I burst out laughing, but it was no laughing matter; three cars written off and three drivers —all British—out of the race in the first few minutes. The Vanwall had splashed a lot of fuel containing nitro-methane over Stirling's back and it was burning the skin, so the medical men cleaned this off and then bound up Peter's leg, which was rather badly grazed. I was the only one to get away without a scratch.

Apparently Stirling swooping down to the chicane at high speed had braked hard, leaving long black marks on the road from locked wheels. He found he could not possibly get through the chicane safely and, rather then risk diving into the harbour, had decided to take to the escape road despite the great barrier which had foolishly been placed across it. Peter, plunged suddenly into a confusion of flying telegraph poles and sandbags, tried to get through the chicane but hit the barrier on the quayside and only Fangio, running third, managed to nip through to take the lead. After that Fangio set his own pace, and won easily, chased valiantly by Brooks in the surviving Vanwall.

When we got back to the pit, Peter was obviously not able to drive any more, but I was asked to take over von Trips's Ferrari. I was quite willing, but knew it would be too small for me. The mechanics were ready to rip out knee supports and do everything they could to give me more space, but it seemed to me that they would lose so much time that it was better to let von Trips continue. However, Sculati insisted on trying so Trips was called in and I did a few laps. It was hopeless. My knees were wedged under the steering wheel and I had to keep releasing my grip on the wheel to miss my knees on the corners, so I handed the car back to Trips. Later the engine blew up, covering his rear tyres with oil just as he was nearing the top of the climb to the Casino. The car spun and crashed into the stone balustrade just as Herrmann's Mercedes had done at the same spot two years earlier. And, once again, the driver escaped—this time without a scratch— while the car remained among the shattered stonework poised precariously on the edge of a thirty-foot drop.

Menditeguy also crashed, losing control of his Maserati at the chicane and hitting a lamp post only a few yards from the piled-up wrecks of our two Ferraris.

For Ferrari it had been a disastrous day, with three cars worth in the aggregate fifteen to twenty thousand pounds completely destroyed. Rumours soon began circulating to the effect that he had again decided to retire.

It was not only the loss of the Grand Prix that was involved. His sports cars had been impounded after the Mille Miglia disaster in which de Portago had been killed only the previous week-end and he had refused to run his cars in any other Italian event until the Italian authorities had cleared the cars of any responsibility for the crash.

However, when Peter and I rang him from Monte Carlo he was full of fighting spirit. "You are unhurt, that is the main thing," he said. "We have more chassis frames and we are starting to build new cars immediately."

. . . . .

It was after the Monte Carlo race that the drivers met together to form the U.P.P.I.—the International Union of Professional Drivers.

The idea was that the drivers would be able to present an agreed point of view to race organisers and sporting authorities, particularly on questions of safety, instead of presenting individual viewpoints which carry less weight. The incident of the chicane illustrated the need perfectly. Here was the most difficult point on the course, a tight S-bend following the fastest stretch of the circuit, where drivers risked plunging into the harbour if they got out of control. There was a perfectly sited escape road which could have saved the situation for any driver whose brakes failed or whose engine broke up or who merely misjudged the approach, yet this road was sealed off by a heavy barrier which could be guaranteed to smash any car hitting it and would most likely injure the driver unless he was very lucky.

The Union ran into a lot of criticism because it opposed the 500-mile race against the American Indianapolis cars at Monza. When the race passed off without any serious incident it was held to be proof that the Union was wrong.

But what really happened? The Americans would not run on the road circuit because the American cars have only two-speed gearboxes, are designed to take left-hand bends only and have brakes which are not intended for continuous use. The race was therefore run entirely on the banked speed track, but in the opposite direction to normal, to ensure that all the curves were left-hand ones to suit the American cars with their offset engines. The Americans had developed special tyres for this race to avoid the risk of treads flying off, but there was no sign that any European manufacturer was prepared to do so.

Despite the gallant effort of the Ecurie Ecosse Jaguars, the American cars were never seriously challenged, yet they broke their steering and exhaust systems, split oil and fuel tanks, cracked their chassis, and were only kept going by energetic repair work during the two compulsory rest periods. Had they been seriously challenged—which, incidentally, would have meant more cars on the track to add to the danger—the inherent hazards of the situation might well have been forcibly demonstrated. At a time when the speeds reached by racing cars were causing considerable public disquiet, it seemed to be asking for trouble to stage a demonstration by freaks circulating continuously at 170 m.p.h.

Those at all events were my views. The point of view of the Union might have been better expressed than it was, but it was a new venture and got involved in this controversy before it was fully organised.

## CHAPTER TWENTY-SIX

## LAP RECORD

AFTER the Monaco race I spent a pleasant day with Peter and his wife Louise on Sir James Scott Douglas's yacht, afterwards going down to Modena to see Ferrari and on to Nurburgring for the 1,000 km. sports-car race, which was the third round in the World Championship for sports cars.

Moss and Fangio on the big 4½-litre V8 Maseratis made best times in practice and next fastest, to everyone's surprise, was Tony Brooks in the DBR 1/300 Aston Martin prototype. The engine was roughly the same as before, but this car had an entirely new chassis and Tony was making the most of it. I came fourth on the list in the 4.1-litre Ferrari, which I was driving with Trintignant. Moss and Fangio were paired together and Schell was driving with Herrmann, all on 4½-litre Maseratis. Brooks and Cunningham-Reid were driving the Aston Martin and the second works Ferrari was being driven by Collins and Gendebien, the new Belgian champion.

I leapt in at the usual Le Mans start, pressed the button, revved up, put in a gear and let in the clutch; then I realised that it was the engine of the car next to me which had started. Mine would not fire and in all the din of the start the mechanics could not hear me when I tried to draw their attention, so I just sat there churning away. Stirling Moss was in the same predicament and we were almost the last to leave.

In the course of the next few laps I passed about forty small cars but I knew that Stirling was still well ahead, until suddenly I came round a corner and saw the Maserati at the side of the road with a rear wheel missing and deep skid marks and grooves gouged in the road surface leading up to it. There was no time to see if the Maserati had been rolled over or not and I was very worried about Stirling until I saw next lap that the car was intact except for the missing wheel. The wheel had come off as Stirling was travelling quite fast and he did very well to get the car safely to a standstill.

Schell's car was then called in and Stirling was put into it. This kind of mobile musical chairs is played more systematically by Maserati than anyone else. The regulations for 1958 discourage it in Grand Prix racing, as a man can only gain championship points on the car in which he starts the race; but it is still permitted in sports-car racing and I think it is wrong. A race is run by a combination of car and driver—or two drivers in long-distance events—and I feel the original crew should stay with the car throughout the event. In this case Maserati gained no advantage, for the second V8 soon broke and by half distance the Aston Martin was leading. The Ferraris were handling beautifully on the difficult Eifel circuit, but the brakes were not sufficiently powerful to allow us to offer an all-out challenge to the disc-braked Aston Martin and we finished second and third behind it.

.　　.　　.　　.　　.

Having returned to England after the race, I decided to fly out to Le Mans in my Argus with a friend of mine, Pat Massey Dawson, who is a keen pilot. We were just about to take off when I was called back to take a telephone call. It was Ivor Bueb, whose car had run a big end en route for the coast, and he wondered could I give him a lift to Le Mans. Ivor is no lightweight, but by draining twenty gallons of fuel out of the tank I thought we could manage to carry him and we waited for him to arrive. By the time we were all on board with our luggage we must have been near to the weight limit for the Argus, but we staggered off and promptly got lost in the mist.

We finally headed down the coast and decided to stay the night at Deauville. It was getting late and when we landed the aerodrome was closed up and deserted, except for one small boy, who was persuaded to open the hangar for us and lead us to his home where we were able to telephone for a taxi. We completed the trip next morning. So far I have not missed a race, or even practice, as a result of flying delays, but the planned flight schedules often have to be scrapped because of the weather.

As the limitation of engine size for prototype cars had found no general support, the Automobile Club de l'Ouest dropped it for the 1957 24-Hours. This allowed the event to be included in the World Championship series once more, but opened the race to the over-powered "monsters" which had been so much criticised since 1955. Many people felt that the lessons of 1955 had not been learned and there was much disquiet when it was reported that Maserati were going to run a 4½-litre V8 with streamlined coupé body designed by Frank Costin, the aerodynamics expert whose low-drag body designs have made an important contribution to the success of the Lotus.

A maximum speed of about 200 m.p.h. was forecast but what people did not know was that three weeks before the race the Maserati was still a bare chassis without engine or transmission in a shed at Zagato's works and although Zagato worked valiantly day and night when he finally got some instructions, it was quite impossible for him to interpret Costin's ideas properly in the time allowed. When it arrived at Le Mans the car was unfinished, uncomfortable and appreciably slower than the open one.

Stirling Moss was to drive it with Harry Schell, while Behra and Simon took the open one. Fangio made fastest practice lap in 3 min. 58.1 sec. which caused many shivers of apprehension over the speeds that would be reached during the race, but he decided not to drive in the event. He no longer likes sports-car racing, has already announced that he will not drive again in the Mille Miglia and will not drive at Le Mans again if he can avoid it.

In the Ferrari team we had four cars; two 4-litre models for Collins and Hill, myself and Musso, a 3.8-litre for Lewis-Evans and Severi, and a 3.1-litre V12 for Trintignant and Gendebien, the prototype of a production model for 1958. There were no Jaguar works entries but the Ecurie Ecosse had a 3.8-litre for Flockhart and Bueb as well as a 3.4-litre for Sanderson and Lawrence. Duncan Hamilton was driving his own 3.8-litre with Masten Gregory, the consistently successful Belgian Jaguar entry was being handled by Rousselle and Frere and there was another driven by the Frenchmen Jean Lucas and Jean Marie. Aston Martins, always strong challengers but chronically unlucky at Le Mans, had Brooks and Cunningham-Reid in one car, the White-heads, Peter and Graham, in another and Salvadori with Leston in a third.

Our Ferraris had been fitted with a new type of piston for the race and this proved our undoing. Peter's car began smoking in practice and it was found that the piston rings had seized up on one bank of cylinders, so six of the old-type pistons were installed on that side of the engine.

At the start, Peter made a magnificent getaway and put up a new record for the standing lap, but his engine soon began laying a smoke screen and he was out of the race within a few minutes. My engine was rather slow in picking up, and Stirling passed me in his great Maserati coupé. I thought that he would just leave me and accelerate steadily out of sight, but as my engine picked up I accelerated past him in third gear. I remember looking in at him through his little side windows and he certainly looked surprised at being overtaken so easily.

He did not catch me again; from the second lap I was in the lead and in six laps I had gained about twenty seconds on the Maserati. Behra in the open V8 passed Stirling and started chasing me, but his car started giving trouble before he could catch me. My car was going beautifully, but suddenly it started vibrating and when I stopped at the pit we found that the left front tyre had thrown a lump off its tread. It was changed fairly quickly but when the mechanics came to put the old wheel back as the regulations stipulated, they could not get it in and they lost a lot of time struggling with it. I then set out to make up lost time and put in a lap in 3 min. 58.7 sec. at an average of 126.2 m.p.h. which was a new lap record.

Stirling was in trouble with a broken oil pipe on the Maserati coupé and when I handed over to Musso after refuelling, we were second, but with Behra, Gendebien, Bueb, Brooks, Masten Gregory and Salvadori all closely spaced in the leading group. Soon afterwards both the big Maseratis broke their axles, but we had our own troubles. Just as I was getting ready to take over again, Musso came in with smoke pouring from the engine; the pistons had failed and we were out of the race. Before long the Trintignant-Gendebien car also stopped with ruined pistons and the only Ferrari then left in the race was the one driven by Lewis-Evans and Severi. It was finally brought into fifth place after a valiant struggle; at one time the brake shoes were changed because the first set were worn out.

It is sometimes alleged that the drivers of the Italian cars start the Le Mans race as if it were a 3-hour Grand Prix and wear their cars out before midnight. This certainly was not true of the Ferrari team in 1957. The piston trouble which haunted us was a technical defect and we were warned before the race that if we used our brakes hard they would not last the race. Even when I set up the new lap record I was not using the brakes hard. At Mulsanne I started braking well before the 500-metre warning mark, putting them on and taking them off, putting them on and taking them off, to avoid too fierce a heat input in one rush. But even using them in this way the brakes would not have lasted the distance and when it becomes necessary to fit new brake shoes in the course of a race you cannot hope to win.

Frankly, I feel that it is now useless to try to win the Le Mans race with ordinary drum brakes as they just will not stand the strain. And although the new lap record stood to the credit of my 4.1-litre Ferrari at the end of the race, I am sure I could have got round faster on the 3.8-litre Jaguar purely by virtue of its better braking. The modified circuit is much faster than the old one, yet I only managed to knock about eight seconds off the best time I achieved with a 3.4-litre Jaguar in 1955—4 min. 6.4 sec. The only point where the rigid rear axle of the Jaguar restricts the speed on the Le Mans circuit is at the White House and the time saved by the disc brakes more than offsets it.

Naturally Ferrari and I have had many discussions on this subject but he has not yet seen eye to eye with the makers of disc brakes and his cars remain at a disadvantage in this one event.

· · · · ·

After Le Mans I bought a new aeroplane, a Percival Vega Gull with Gipsy Six II engine, and used it to fly out to Rouen where the 1957 French Grand Prix was being held on the Les Essarts circuit.

The Ferraris were in trouble again and for some reason were running badly. I tried the car with the extended chassis frame built specially for me, but it lacked power and I switched to another one, which was not much better. Fangio made fastest practice lap on his Maserati, 2 min. 21.5 sec. for the 1.97 miles, but the best I could do was 2 min. 27 sec., which put me in the third row at the start.

Stirling Moss was going to drive the Vanwall, but had to go to hospital with sinus trouble, and Tony Brooks was still out of action as a result of the leg injuries he received when his Aston Martin turned over at Tertre Rouge during the Le Mans race. The Vanwalls were therefore driven by Salvadori and Lewis-Evans and the B.R.M.s were in the hands of Flockhart and Mackay Fraser, who was having his first drive on a Formula 1 machine.

Musso, Behra, Collins and Fangio shot away at the start and, with my engine spluttering and banging as I tried to accelerate away from the corners, I was having quite a job to keep up with the B.R.M.s.

Mackay Fraser was driving particularly well and we were having a scrap which also involved Menditeguy and Salvadori. Salvadori gradually drew ahead but spun on a corner, dropping a little oil on the road as he went. I got round the corner with Flockhart on my tail and glanced in my mirror to see a great cloud of dust. Flockhart had spun on the oil, crashed and overturned; he was very lucky to escape serious injury. Fangio was leading, lapping consistently at over 100 m.p.h., and Musso was second. Fangio lapped me and I tried to stay with him for a few laps, but it was hopeless. The Vanwalls fell out and I came in fourth.

After the race I dropped in at Deauville where there was an air rally and I was faced with the problem of finding a dinner-jacket for a party on the Sunday night. One of the people at the hotel gave me the address of some people who would hire me a suit. This turned out to be a laundry and dry cleaners. We ran through what seemed to be the customers' clothes until we found a jacket and a separate pair of trousers which fitted me approximately. The trousers were too long even for me, so the legs were turned up, and someone lent me a tie. That left me with the problem of shoes so I took my racing shoes, which were an oil-soaked brown, had them blacked and turned up the picture of the elegant man about town.

· · · · ·

For Rouen we had used cars which were virtually the Lancia design but with modified engine and chassis, a tail tank and the side fairings removed to convert them into conventional single-seaters. For the Formula 1 race at Rheims, Ferrari sent two of these for Gendebien and I, but reverted to side fairings on the cars for Collins and Musso in the hope that the better streamlining might give a little advantage in speed.

Maserati had their usual drivers and did some practice with the 12-cylinder car, but it never went very quickly. Moss and Brooks were still not fit and Lewis-Evans provided the surprise of the practice period by taking his Vanwall round so fast that Fangio only managed to beat him by a fifth of a second for fastest lap. There were some hundreds of bottles of champagne at stake this time and these two shared them.

My car was still not going well and I was in the fourth row at the start, but I managed to work my way forward and soon got involved in a duel with Fangio which looked like developing into a repeat of our 1953 encounter.

I found I could hold Fangio if I stayed in his slipstream and I could swing out and come up alongside, but I had not sufficient power to get past. We just sat there screaming along side by side, both pressing our accelerators down to the floor; then he would grin at me and pull away again as I lost the advantage I had snatched in the slipstream. We were both trying hard, but Lewis-Evans on the Vanwall and Musso on his Ferrari were steadily drawing away from us.

The order changed for a short time when Fangio spun and I gave him a merry Victory sign as I went through, but he soon caught me and came past again; the best I could do was to hang on to his tail and prevent him getting away. Occasionally I could go ahead by a supreme effort but I could not draw away. During these encounters I was surprised to find that Fangio was going into the flat-out bend after the pits a good deal faster than I was, but coming out more slowly and he seemed to lose a lot of ground in fighting the car round the bend. With the Ferrari I found I could gain if I went in more slowly and put on full power early coming out.

This interesting study in comparative cornering was concluded when my engine started pouring forth smoke and I had to retire once again with piston failure. Collins and Gendebien had already retired with the same trouble, so only Musso was left, but his luck was in. Fangio ran out of road with brake trouble and cut his nose, leaving Musso to win ahead of Behra and Lewis-Evans.

There was a Formula 2 race at the same meeting in which Trintignant brought the new V6 Ferrari home first after a tussle with a horde of Coopers, but the race was marred by two fatal accidents in which Bill Whitehouse and Mackay Fraser were killed. Bill Whitehouse had been motor racing for years and was well known as a Formula 3 driver, but "Mac" Fraser was a young American who had made rapid progress in a short time and had shown a lot of promise in his first drive with a Formula 1 single-seater only a few days before. His crisp manner and serious approach to racing had made him a lot of friends and he seemed destined to do very well.

The loss of two popular drivers cast a gloom over the meeting and I felt that I wanted to get home, so I took off in the Gull. However, I soon found thick black clouds stretching right across the horizon and after getting involved in a thunderstorm I had to spend the night in Amiens.

The Grand Prix of Europe was held on the Aintree circuit, just out-side Liverpool, and we had Ferraris without side fairings for Collins, Musso, Trintignant and myself. I was still not happy with the handling of the long chassis car built for me and I again took over Trintignant's car as I had at Rouen and Rheims. Trintignant took the long one out and I'm afraid he did not like it either.

Stirling was fit again and took the Vanwall round in 2 min. 0.2 sec. which was the best time recorded, Behra on the Maserati and Brooks on another Vanwall being next best at 2 min. 0.4 sec. I made the best Ferrari lap in 2 min. 1.8 sec. which earned me a place in the second row alongside Fangio, an unusual position for him. Leston and Fairman were driving the B.R.M.s.

As our cars had not been doing well in the early part of the season, the Ferrari engineers decided to use some nitro-methane in the fuel for the Grand Prix of Europe, hoping that they had by now cured the piston trouble, but during practice Peter's car promptly died out in a cloud of smoke so the pistons were changed on all cars and we reverted to the old fuel. The car I was using went very well but we could not equal the performance of the Vanwalls or even of the Maseratis. The Vanwalls just left us behind on initial acceleration, and Stirling went into the lead with Behra second, while I had a struggle with Brooks for third position, which I ultimately won because his leg was still not recovered from the Le Mans injuries; I then closed up on Behra. The leading Vanwall started giving trouble, so Stirling stopped and took over Brooks's car, which dropped him back considerably, and Fangio was motoring round in eighth position with a sick engine and an ominous vibration in his transmission. I tried to take the lead from Behra and found I could catch him in the corners but he drew away on the straight and built up a lead of about 20 sec.

Moss and Lewis-Evans in the two best Vanwalls were now catching up rapidly and they were close behind me on lap 69 when the car suddenly started swinging and weaving all over the road as though a radius rod had broken or the de Dion tube had cracked. I looked down but could see nothing wrong, so took off my helmet and motored slowly round to the pits. I was just getting out of the car when Parenti spotted that one of my rear tyres was going flat and frantic activity broke out as they changed the wheel.

I was off again in a few moments, but Musso had passed me. Then I saw Behra's car in the pits, so it was now Vanwalls leading, with

Musso third and me fourth. But almost immediately I saw Lewis-Evans stationary at the roadside at Cottage Corner, and I was now third. I was gaining on Musso, but it was too late to catch him. I got acute cramp in my feet and was in agony while accelerating and braking.

This was one of those occasions when the driver does not see the whole drama and I only pieced together the story of those dramatic last laps afterwards. Behra was apparently certain of a well-earned win when his clutch disintegrated and one of the metal fragments, dropped on the track, entered one of my rear tyres. This let the two Vanwalls into the lead, but a few seconds later Lewis-Evans's engine spluttered and stopped. He whipped the bonnet off, could not see any sign of the broken throttle linkage which had caused the Vanwalls so many heartaches in the past, and then, after a quick look round, concluded that he had run out of fuel. He therefore signalled to Stirling that he was out of fuel and Stirling, taking the hint, stopped at the pits for fuel which he did not need, while Musso strove to snatch the lead. By the time Moss had got away again, still in the lead, Lewis-Evans had spotted the trouble—a control rod detached on the underside of the fuel pump.

It was a really well-earned victory and a splendid reward for all the effort and the large sums of money which Tony Vandervell has lavished on his cars. It was the turning point in Vanwall fortunes and they went on to score another fine victory at Pescara, but right to the end of the season they were still suffering mechanical troubles. In fact, none of the Grand Prix cars could be called reliable during 1957. Maserati usually managed to find a reliable mount for Fangio, but he is brilliant at finishing with cars which are below par mechanically.

## CHAPTER TWENTY-SEVEN

## BATTLING WITH FANGIO

THE NEXT round of the Grand Prix battle and one of the greatest races of the season was the German Grand Prix on the Nurburgring. I flew out for this and landed at Cologne, where I asked an R.A.F. officer if there was an aerodrome anywhere near the Ring where I could land. He said there was one about 20 miles away which was occupied by the French, and a telephone call was put through to say I was coming. I flew down there and was given a green signal to land, but the moment I taxied in I was surrounded by German airmen. It seemed the French had moved out and handed over to the new German air force and the German officers told me I must leave immediately and return to Cologne. I protested that I had just been given permission to land by telephone to Cologne and was hauled before the commanding officer. I could not understand why I was being told to leave when I had been given permission to land by telephone, but the telephone had apparantly been answered by some luckless fitter who had no right to give permission and was presumably court-martialled on my account.

As it was too late to take off again anyway, the commandant asked me how long I wanted to stay, and finally agreed to let me leave my machine with him until the Monday morning after the race. Even better, one of the officers gave me a lift over to the Ring. He had never seen a motor race, so I invited the commandant and my escort to come as my guests and when I left on the Monday I found they had become keen motor-racing enthusiasts.

This time, the Ferraris were in excellent shape. We experimented with some variations in rear spring rates and tried out two axle ratios. I preferred the higher one, but Peter chose the lower one. As a result he could always get away from me on one of the most twisty sections of the course, but I could always get past him on the straight.

The Vanwalls had never been to the Ring before, so they lacked data on the best springing and shock-absorber setting for this bumpy course and the drivers had rather a hard time finding out. Brooks in particular was still very sore from his Le Mans accident and suffered a great deal during the race.

Fangio made fastest practice lap in 9 min. 25.6 sec. and I was next with 9 min. 28.4 sec. for the tortuous 17.6 miles. With us on the front row at the start were Behra (Maserati) and Collins (Ferrari). In the second row was Schell (Maserati) between Moss and Brooks on Vanwalls. There were twenty-four starters as a Formula 2 event had been incorporated in the main one.

I was first into the first corner and very nearly broke the lap record on the standing lap. I held the lead for two laps but then Fangio came past and drew away quite quickly, partly, I think, because he was not carrying a full load of fuel and was making up time to permit a refuelling stop at half distance. He gradually built up a lead of about 20 seconds while Peter and I alternated in second and third places. Behind us were Behra, Schell, Musso and Moss.

The first part of the race was uneventful but at half distance the excitement started. I was leading Peter by a few yards and as we rushed from the narrow road onto the vast plateau of concrete between grandstand and pits, we could see the crowd standing, waving and cheering, which meant just one thing. Fangio must have stopped. But was he just ahead, or had we passed him somewhere? He was at that moment at the pit taking on fuel and new rear tyres, but at 140 m.p.h. we could not spot his car, which must have been surrounded by mechanics, officials and photographers. We only knew we must motor as fast as possible until the pit could give us the position next time round.

As we came past again, there it was; we were 45 seconds ahead of Fangio. Next time our lead was 48 seconds and I thought Fangio must be in trouble; had he lost a gear or was his engine failing? Whatever it was, victory seemed to be ours, and as we roared along the straight I motioned to Peter to come alongside and pointed behind us with thumb down to indicate that Fangio seemed to be in trouble. He nodded, put his thumb up, then pointed to me with one finger and back to himself, with two. He wanted me to win and was prepared to come second himself, which I thought was a very sporting gesture, and would save us racing against each other and perhaps breaking up both cars.

Next lap, Fangio pulled back a little time, but at that rate he obviously could not catch us. Then as we came past the pits at the end of the next lap, we had the fright of our lives. Fangio had cut our lead by 12 seconds in one lap!

No question now of sparing the cars or making private arrangements among ourselves; it was flat out all the way to stave off this new challenge. But Fangio was now driving the race of his life, pulling back about eight seconds a lap despite all that we could do. On the 20th lap he got round in the completely unheard-of time of 9 min. 17.4 sec., diving, swooping, sliding, yes—and taking off with all four wheels at some points, too, to average 91.8 m.p.h. on one of the most difficult circuits in the world. Peter and I did everything we knew to save split seconds on those countless corners—I'm told there are 176 of them, but we did not stop to count them—and all the time the World Champion was catching us up relentlessly.

At the end of that magnificent record lap he was only 100 yards behind us as we passed the stands. Coming out of the South Curve, he passed Peter, who fought back and got a few yards ahead again, only to be overwhelmed at a bend soon after the run past the back of the pits. As Peter drifted in, Fangio pulled onto the outside of the bend and went past with two wheels on the grass, showering the Ferrari with dirt and stones. It was an old trick from the hard school of long-distance inter-city racing in which Fangio served a hard apprenticeship in South America. Down the hill he went, still clipping the grass all the way, and as Peter tried vainly to hold him, a flying stone shattered his goggles.

It was now a straight fight between Fangio and I once again, and I was driving right on the limit as we rushed through the endless tree-lined curves to the Hocheichen and on to the Quiddelbacher Hohe, but just as I was going into a slow left-hand corner Fangio pulled the same trick, cut sharply inside me and forced me out onto the grass and almost into the ditch.

He looked round almost apologetically as he accelerated away and as I charged down the hill at Adenau after him I thought: "Right, now it's my turn to have a go at you!" but at that moment Fangio managed to get past Masten Gregory's blue-and-white Maserati.

It was some distance before I saw a chance to get past too and by then he had drawn away. I gained on him again on the uphill sections that followed, but on the long straight run back to the pits, the Maserati was pulling away from me. As we started the last lap he had the vital yards in hand which prevented me getting to grips on the corners, and he crossed the finishing line 3.6 seconds ahead of me. This time the race had been every bit as exciting for the drivers as for the spectators and even though Peter and I had been beaten, we enjoyed every moment of it.

Looking back, it is obvious that we two were over-confident and slowed down too soon, but the Nurburgring is such a hard circuit on car and driver that it is very tempting to take any chance of relaxing the pace slightly so as to be sure of finishing. The length of the circuit adds to the tactical problems because even at the record speeds we were maintaining a lap takes about 9½ minutes and the situation can change seriously before the pit has a chance to advise the drivers, as we found to our cost when Fangio started his final attack.

He told me afterwards that he was absolutely determined to win that race so as to make certain of the World Championship for the fifth time and on that fantastic 91.8 m.p.h. lap which put him right on our tails he did things which were risky even for the greatest driver in the world.

He said: "I did things I have never done before, and I don't ever want to drive like that again!"

Musso came in fourth to put Ferrari 2—3—4 and Moss brought the Vanwall in fifth, just beating Behra's Maserati.

. . . . .

Our next event was the Swedish sports-car Grand Prix, so Peter and his wife left their car at Cologne and flew with me in the Gull. We stayed one night in Hamburg and took off again next morning, but we had only got to about 2,000 feet when the engine cut dead. We looked at each other, rather worried, for below us were water and docks and steamers. Louise, who was sitting in the back reading a book, buried herself in that and refused to look out. Fortunately we had sufficient height to turn and I decided to try and glide back to the aerodrome. As I did so the engine began firing again on three cylinders and I picked the longest runway for the forced landing.

I had no radio and could not warn the control tower that I was in trouble; I just had a good look round for other aircraft and hoped that the control tower had seen me and would warn everyone. I landed across the wind at about 130 m.p.h., which was much too fast, and bounced along for some distance, then taxied in to the hangars where I got some mechanics to have a look at the engine. There was dirt in the fuel system and one of the main jets was blocked, so the whole installation was cleaned out and re-assembled, after which I rang the control tower for permission to do a test flight.

The controller agreed and then said: "That was a pretty hair-raising thing you did just then!"

I apologised for the bad landing, but explained that my engine had cut just previously and was only running on three cylinders. He had realised that I was in trouble and had no option about getting down as quickly as possible; even so it had shaken him somewhat, but he added: "I wasn't half as frightened as the captain of the Convair which was coming in to land on the same runway from the opposite direction."

It must have been a nasty moment, for I had not seen the Convair at all.

We took off again and flew to Malmo, where we spent a couple of days before hiring a car to drive down to Kristiansand for the Grand Prix.

Peter Collins and Phil Hill were driving one 4.1-litre Ferrari and I was driving another with Musso. There were also two of the new 3-litre V12 cars, one with normal rear axle and the other with de Dion. This model has now gone into production as the Testa Rossa and has a very light chassis developed from that of the original 4-cylinder Testa Rossa. I tried both the prototypes and liked them very much. Personally I preferred the handling of the car with the de Dion axle, although it was naturally heavier than the other.

This race is very hard on brakes so we did not do very much practice as we did not want to wear the brakes out before the race. I started the race in my car and Hill drove the other 4.1 for the first spell. Moss and Behra started in the two V8 Maseratis and the remaining Maseratis were passed around among all and sundry in the way Maserati had been adopting all the year.

I got into the lead and held it for a while until Stirling caught up and challenged me. I let him go, expecting him to draw away rapidly, but to my surprise I found that I could pass the Maserati again fairly easily on acceleration and we had a ding-dong battle until I calculated that my brakes could not possibly last the race at this pace and I slowed down. Behra then came past and soon Hill too caught me. By now the brakes were deteriorating, so I decided to drive to finish.

Bernard Cahier, the journalist and photographer who usually manages to be present with his camera when the racing incidents take place, had faithfully recorded my 1956 excursion into the cornfield and boasted that he would get some more pictures if I repeated the performance this year.

Unfortunately I did run off there quite early when the brakes started fading away and he got the picture. When I did it again later in the race I was relieved to see that there were no photographers in sight, but Cahier had got it again . . . from a helicopter.

Before handing over to Musso I noticed that the thermometer was climbing high, so I stopped, shouting: *"Acqua, acqua!"* in my best Italian and pointing to the front of the car. The mechanics checked the oil, filled up with fuel, cleaned the screen and sent Musso on his way. As he went I asked had they put in some water, but they had forgotten all about it in the rush. At this time the pit was not running smoothly; everyone was under a strain, as up to now the Ferrari team had not won a single Grand Prix race during 1957 and nerves were on edge as we moved into the last phase of the season.

Musso promptly made an excursion into the cornfield and soon afterwards a rear brake pipe went, which left us in exactly the same predicament as I had been in the same race the year before—running on front brakes only. Even so, we managed to finish fourth. One of the big Maseratis driven by both Behra and Moss won, the Hill-Collins Ferrari was second and a 3-litre Maserati which had been driven in turns by Bonnier, Scarlatti, Schell and Moss came in third. Although the Grand Prix results were disappointing, Ferrari now had a six-points lead in the sports-car World Championship, with only one more event to run, the Venezuelan race at Caracas.

. . . . .

The next event which concerned us was the Grand Prix at Pescara, but as we flew south again the situation was obscure. The race had been given World Championship status because the Dutch, Belgian and Spanish Grand Prix had been cancelled, but the committee investigating the de Portago crash in the Mille Miglia had not yet exonerated Ferrari from blame and we understood he was adhering to his decision not to race again in Italy until they did so. He had all the more reason as the Pescara circuit is a kind of miniature Nurburgring on public roads, where it is difficult to install adequate safety measures. We therefore returned to England, only to hear that Musso had been given a car to run as a "private" entry. Peter and I were annoyed as we were deprived of the chance to win points towards the World Championship and at that time I was only three points behind Musso, who was lying second. However, Ferrari made amends later by sending us to the Casablanca Grand Prix.

Musso was doing quite well in the Pescara event until his oil tank came adrift, forcing him to retire, and the event provided the second major international victory for Stirling on the Vanwall.

·      ·      ·      ·      ·

Ferrari had decided to lift his ban in the case of the Italian Grand Prix which was held on the closed private circuit at Monza and we hoped that he had at last found the extra power we needed, but the first practice runs showed that our cars were still outclassed and apparently nothing could be done about it. Maserati and Vanwall were there with full teams; Fangio led the Maserati formation supported by Behra, Schell and Scarlatti, while Vanwall had Moss, Brooks and Lewis-Evans. Our team consisted of Collins and myself, Musso and von Trips, the latter now wearing an imposing beard. There was also a big turn-out of independents, all on Maseratis.

We were using cars which were still basically Lancia in engine and chassis design, but without the side fairings between the wheels, and in view of the lack of power I suggested that on this fast circuit we might try the effect of carrying the carburetter intake forward level with the radiator air duct, as we had done years before on my Cooper-Bristol. This was done on my car and Peter's, but I cannot say we obtained any appreciable advantage from it.

The big surprise of the practice period was provided by Stuart Lewis-Evans who took his Vanwall round in 1 min. 42.4 sec. beating everyone, including Fangio and Moss. As a result, the start provided an unprecedented spectacle of three green British Vanwalls in the front row, accompanied by one red car, Fangio's six-cylinder Maserati. In the second row was Behra on a 12-cylinder Maserati, alongside, Schell with a six and Collins on the first of the Ferraris. Von Trips, Musso and I were in the third row with Ferraris, accompanied by Masten Gregory's Maserati, best of the independents, and the remaining independents, all on Maseratis, were massed behind us.

Vanwalls and Maseratis rushed away as the flag fell and during the first part of the race Moss and Behra alternated in the lead, while Fangio fought it out with Brooks and Lewis-Evans. Briefly Fangio took the lead, but could not hold the pace and the three Vanwalls, which were definitely the fastest cars in the race, grouped themselves together out in front.

Early that morning my car had been fitted with a lower axle ratio which the team manager thought would give me better acceleration in the early stages while my fuel tank was full, but I soon found that even with a full load of fuel the ratio was far too low. On the straight the engine was being over-revved badly, but there was nothing I could do about it, so I kept on, hoping it would not blow up too soon. It stood the strain remarkably well, but I found myself working hard to keep ahead of independents like Bonnier and Gregory in their privately entered Maseratis.

However, the important thing is to keep going, no matter how hopeless things appear to be. Brooks and Lewis-Evans stopped at the pits, losing a lot of time; Behra's V12 started giving trouble; Peter Collins dropped out with engine trouble; and at 60 laps I found myself running third behind Moss and Fangio. This was better than I had expected and I was hoping the engine would last out until the end, when fuel started seeping out of the louvres and spraying back over me as it had at Naples. This time it was not the pipe to the pressure gauge, which had been taken off during racing ever since the Naples incident; the main fuel pipe had fractured and it took a long time to repair it. While I was waiting I wanted to take over the von Trips car which was now running third, but with only ten laps to go, Amorotti would not call him in. We had quite a set to about it but he was adamant and by the time my car was repaired I could only finish sixth, four laps behind Stirling who had won the third victory for Vanwall in a World Championship event.

It was now demonstrated beyond question that the Vanwalls were faster than any of the cars racing against them and on the straight we simply could not compete with them. The Ferrari which we were using, derived from the Lancia design, was not particularly happy at Monza. It handled well on the Grande Curva, the fast, bumpy right-hand corner at the end of the straight past the pits, and probably took it faster than any other car, but on a long slow corner it would start understeering and the front would drift outwards. When one tried to correct this by using the throttle, the back end would whip round more than required and the corner would be taken in a series of swerves which became rather frustrating.

Once again, however, it was apparent that there was still work to be done to make the Vanwall reliable. Brooks's pit stop with a sticking throttle dropped him back so far that he only got up to seventh place again by a great effort and Lewis-Evans had to retire with a peculiar stiffening of the steering.

  .    .    .    .    .

Ferrari was not going to the *Daily Express* meeting at Silverstone, which had been postponed from its usual date earlier in the season because of the aftermath of the Suez crisis, and with the end of the season approaching the organisers were unlucky, for Maserati and Vanwall also abstained, leaving the B.R.M.s to take first three places in front of the independent Maseratis.

I drove a 3.4-litre Jaguar in the production touring car event, and won after sharing the honours for fastest lap with Archie Scott-Brown in a similar car by lapping at 84.89 m.p.h. The regulations had been tightened up since the previous year to ensure that the cars bore rather more resemblance to those you can buy and we were not permitted to use the optional disc brakes. The drum brakes were rather overloaded by this kind of motoring and during the first few laps Archie was pressing me very hard indeed, but before long his car started smoking and approaching Woodcote he suffered total brake failure. He must have been doing about 90 m.p.h., but he got second gear in, somehow. The engine hit something over 7,000 r.p.m., but fortunately stood the strain and he got the car safely to rest. I kept on, trying to conserve the brakes as far as possible, and kept ahead of Duncan Hamilton and Ivor Bueb who took the next two places, also with 3.4 Jaguars.

It is rather staggering to see the angles of roll adopted by some of the saloon cars in this type of racing, but it is very popular with the spectators and several people came up to tell me how much they had enjoyed it.

## CHAPTER TWENTY-EIGHT

## CASABLANCA

THE LAST Grand Prix of the season was at Casablanca, where Ferrari decided to try out his conception of the new Formula 1 car for the 1958 season. The Lancia engine and chassis, regarded as a brilliant feat of weight reduction when they first appeared, were now discarded as too big and heavy; in their place Ferrari produced an enlarged version of his little V-6 Formula 2 engine, mounted in the Formula 2 car.

Development work on the engines was still proceeding, so that I had a 2.2-litre, while Peter's was 2,417 c.c. and both were running on aviation petrol to obtain experience for racing under the new petrol-only rule in 1958. Although this put us at a disadvantage, the little cars went extremely well; Peter lapped the 4¾-mile circuit in 2 min. 27.2 sec. and I got round in 2 min. 27.6 sec., times which were beaten only by the three Vanwalls and two of the Maseratis.

The circuit was a new one among the sand dunes about six miles out of town, with finishing straight, pits and grandstands quite close to the sea. It was composed partly of special roads, partly of public roads and was very fast.

We were royally entertained and the day before the race we were invited to a special reception by the King of Morocco, but many of the drivers were stricken by the epidemic of Asian influenza which was then raging and were feeling quite ill. Stirling Moss was worst of all and had to be flown back to England on the morning before the race. Fangio, Peter and I were also among those affected. From the royal reception I went straight back to bed and spent the next day trying to sweat it out with the aid of a steady intake of pills.

On race day I was still feeling grim and in no condition to enjoy the colourful scene at the start when the King arrived, accompanied by a military escort with a band, to inspect the circuit and shake hands with the drivers.

When the flag dropped, Peter leapt into the lead and held it for several laps until he spun on a corner and Behra went ahead to win the race for Maserati. Fangio and I accelerated away together looking rather miserably at each other and feeling in no state to go motor racing. I came up behind Schell for a time; he was repeatedly cutting one corner, throwing up a cloud of sand which practically blinded me. I put on a spurt, got ahead and let him taste the desert sand for a change, but after a few more laps I noticed that my judgment was failing. I was leaving my braking far too late, or braking too early, and I was not controlling the car well in the corners. Just then Schell came past waving wildly and I thought at first he must be annoyed about the sand bath he had been receiving, but it seemed there was something wrong with the car. I pulled in to the pit and they found a slight oil leak from the gearbox. Gratefully I took the opportunity of retiring, went straight back to my hotel and got into bed.

Peter, after leading the race, had spun three times, and eventually damaged the car so badly that he too had to retire. However, we were delighted with the performance the cars had demonstrated with smaller engines and on straight petrol and felt our prospects in 1958 would be brighter than those of 1957. Brooks, driving the Vanwall Stirling was to have used, retired with magneto trouble, but Lewis-Evans brought the other Vanwall in second to Behra, while Trintignant finished third on one of the two B.R.M.s. Fangio, who had also been off the road, finished fourth. He and Brabham were involved in a farcical incident with the black flag during the race.

As I left the circuit I saw mechanics working on Brabham's Cooper behind the pits and they told me they were changing the gearbox so that he could get back into the race again. They made the change in a very few minutes, but as soon as the car started running again objections were raised because the repairs had not been made in front of the pits. M. Roche, the fat, dumpy and choleric Clerk of the Course from Rheims who had been hired by Casablanca for the occasion, danced about showing the black flag, but he quite forgot the regulation which says the car's number must be shown with it. Fangio, seeing the flag and perhaps having a guilty conscience about the people who had helped him to re-start after his excursion off course, stopped, but was sent on again and it was some time before Brabham was brought in.

Towards the end of the race conditions became very difficult because the setting sun was shining in the drivers' eyes on one of the trickiest parts of the circuit and unfortunately Jean Lucas left the road as a result; his Maserati hit a spectator's car, then bounced into a group of spectators and he was badly injured.

•       •       •       •       •

Still feeling far from well I flew to Lisbon where I spent a night before taking the plane for Venezuela with Peter Collins. In a few hours we were transported from the old world to one of the most fabulous parts of the new, where the riches of the oil wells have given birth to the superb modern city of Caracas. Ultra-modern architecture set among broad motorways makes the setting for a fantastically high standard of living. It seemed to me that the people are either very rich or they have nothing at all, and for those who are rich the prices are in proportion. I was told that a new house with four or five bedrooms might cost anything from sixty to a hundred-thousand pounds. The latest American cars were everywhere and homes were stuffed with the latest gadgets. But service was the big problem; if something went wrong it seemed cheaper to throw it away and buy a new one rather than try to get it mended.

Most of the European drivers were installed in one fabulously expensive hotel, while the Americans were put up in another one on the top of a mountain which could only be reached after a ten-minute trip in a funicular. On the whole we had the best of it as the Americans' hotel was usually lost in the clouds the whole time we were there.

Peter and I were met at the airport by the British Air Attaché and his wife, who looked after us wonderfully during our stay, and after checking in at our hotel we went out to inspect the circuit. It was rather a shock, for parts of it struck us as distinctly dangerous. One stretch was formed of the two tracks of a motorway, with a fly-over junction used as a means of getting from the outward stretch to the return track. The route then switched into a park, on a road varying sharply in width and coming down almost to single file at some points. There were few indications to show the drivers which way to go and it was easy to get lost, as Phil Hill found. During practice with his Ferrari he missed the turning on the motor road and went some way before he found cars coming in the other direction and realised he was no longer on the circuit.

The race was very important to us as we had to win it in order to secure the World Championship for Ferrari, but we were up against strong opposition from the V-8 Maseratis driven by Moss, Behra and Masten Gregory. We had two 4.1-litre Ferraris, one driven by Collins and Hill, the other by Musso and I; there were also two of the 3-litre V-12 cars for von Trips-Seidel and Trintignant-Gendebien. Tony Brooks had been released by David Brown to drive for Maserati, so there were four British drivers in the race.

Moss got away first at the start, with Schell, myself and von Trips behind him, but this time I was really determined to make the brakes last the distance so that I could come into the picture as the other cars wore out, for the event was going to last over 6½ hours.

Soon Masten Gregory came past me in his big 4.5 Maserati. I followed him for some distance along the motorway until we had to switch onto the fly-over and I knew Masten was going too fast to get round the corner, which was a sharp right-hander. I saw him fighting the car, which suddenly slid across the road sideways, hit the sandbags on the bridge and then, almost in slow motion, turned up on its right side, came down on the left side, bounced over onto its right side and came down upside down. I saw Masten struggling to get free as it was in mid-air, but something caught and the car fell on top of him. It all seemed to happen so slowly that I could see he was still inside the cockpit as the car turned over; I knew he would be all right, but I was very worried in case the car caught fire. By this time I had practically stopped and was very relieved indeed to learn later that Masten had kicked out the door panel and scrambled out.

I accelerated away again and was soon passed by Stirling, who had now lapped me. Behra and Peter Collins also came by, but I let them go as they were going much faster than I wanted to. I had just come off the fly-over onto the dual carriageway when I saw an enormous cloud of dust in the distance and two cars flying through the air, with the body of a driver.

When I got closer I found that it was only one car, an A.C., which had been cut completely in two. Stirling had been coming down the other side of the carriageway at about 170 m.p.h. and was just coming up to his braking point, when the A.C., driven by an American named Dressel, swung across the road in front of him. Stirling, travelling about 60 m.p.h. faster than the other car, had no hope of stopping and rammed the A.C. from behind, flinging it into the air to crash against a lamp post, which cut it in half. Stirling, with the front of the Maserati smashed in, spun on down the road sliding in all directions and by a brilliant effort brought the car to a standstill without further damage. It was one of the most amazing escapes in even Stirling's eventful career and luck was with the other driver, too, for although seriously injured, he lived and has since recovered.

It was certainly a shocking sight to watch, but I soon had my own troubles for I felt the vibration which I now recognised instantly as the sign that a tyre had thrown a tread. I managed to slow the car down without incident, and as it was nearly the end of my spell, anyway, Musso took over when the wheel was changed.

I was relaxing with a cool drink in the pits when Schell came in to refuel his V-8 Maserati. Behra, who was due to take over, was already in the cockpit when some fuel splashed onto the exhaust pipe and the car burst into flames. He leapt out like a rocket taking off, with neck and arms already scorched. Bertocchi, the chief mechanic, also got scorched as he dashed into action with the extinguisher. As soon as the flames subsided, the foam was hastily scraped off the car, but Behra was now in no condition to drive, so Stirling Moss jumped in and took it away. He was back in two laps, complaining that the car was still on fire!

As he drove round, he felt his feet and trousers growing hotter and hotter, but he thought it must be fumes from a damaged exhaust pipe. It was only when the heat started creeping round to the other side that he realised it must be something more extensive and came into the pit. By then the seat, which had been quietly smouldering, had burned through his overalls, so the extinguishers came into use again and Harry Schell climbed in to try his luck.

There were now only two Maseratis left capable of challenging the Ferraris, Schell's 4.5 and the 3-litre driven by Bonnier.

A few laps later we spotted an ominous pall of black smoke rising from the direction of the dual carriageway and both Schell and Bonnier failed to arrive.

Harry had been overhauling Bonnier on a fast right-hand curve under one of the fly-over bridges when a rear tyre on Bonnier's car, chafed through by a broken shock absorber, burst, throwing the car sideways. Schell had no chance to take avoiding action and they collided at full speed. The 3-litre with Bonnier in it was flung into a lamp post and completely wrecked, while Harry's car leapt in the air, landed on its tail, slithered spinning down the road and burst into flames. Harry luckily was uninjured, but by the time he got out of the car his clothes were well alight and he could easily have been burned to death, had it not been for a spectator who with great presence of mind rushed up and put a coat over him, smothering the flames. Even so he was painfully burned on his arms and face. This was one of those occasions when the drivers can be grateful if the spectators are not too completely isolated from the course. Bonnier also had a miraculous escape, but the disaster for Maserati was complete and the loss of so many cars may well have been a subsidiary factor influencing the directors' decision to withdraw from racing soon afterwards.

Ferraris were now certain of the race and the World Championship, provided we finished, so for the last $1\frac{3}{4}$ hours we took no chances. My brakes were deteriorating, so for a time I stayed about three-quarters of a lap behind Peter. Von Trips and Peter caught me later and we crossed the line in close order, one, two, three, with Trintignant coming in fourth soon afterwards to complete the Ferrari triumph.

We left Venezuela next day, flying back by Constellation. On the way the pitch control on one of the airscrews gave trouble, and we had to spend 24 hours in the Azores on the island of Ste Marie waiting for a replacement. The prospects looked grim as the island contained nothing but the airfield, a few houses and a single-storey hotel with camp beds and very simple furniture. But a film show was put on for us—with very old films, but perhaps no older than we get on television —and in the evening a Spanish girl came along to entertain us with songs and dances, so that we had quite a merry party.

That concluded my 1957 season, which had brought me fourth place in the World Championship and a share in winning the sports-car championship, which goes to constructors and not drivers. Before we left for Casablanca I signed with Ferrari to drive for him in Grand Prix and sports-car events during 1958, starting with the Argentine *Temporada.*

. . . . .

In concluding the story of my career so far, I would like to say how much I have enjoyed the experience of the last few years and how very grateful I am to those who made it possible.

*Farnham,*
*February, 1958.*